CW00549015

RUMNEY & ST. MELLONS

A History of two Villages

Compiled and edited by

Marjorie Neal
Sylvia Atherton
Marilyn Nurse
Allen Hambly
Sam Parker

First published August 2005

ISBN 0-95506371 - X

Cover design by Terry Evans
Typeset and printed by
Wilprint Group Limited.

Cover photographs: Nellie Hastings' niece ploughing,
Rumney Ladies' Hockey Team, Newport Road Rumney,
St. Mellons School and St. Mellons Village.

CONTENTS

FOREWORD

I feel honoured to write the foreword to this treasure of a book, born of an idea from the very successful Millennium History Exhibition, held in St. Mellons in the year 2000.

This book is the result of many hours of hard work by a small, dedicated group – members of Rumney and District Local History Society and many other contributors. I know the former also found it enjoyable, as indeed, I'm sure, the reader will.

The book gives a well-informed picture of the villages of Rumney and St. Mellons, formerly in South West Monmouthshire, over a long period. It records momentous happenings like *The Flood* in the 17th century, family histories, religious, sports and social events which were important to local inhabitants at the time. It also details the history of many local farms and estates.

There have been unbelievable changes in the area, both topographical and social, particularly since WWII. I remain ever thankful to the 'Fairy Godmother' at my christening, who donated the best gift of all – an idyllic childhood spent in St. Mellons in the 1920s.

Dilys Hughes

*The Hughes Family has lived
in Rumney, Llanrumney and
St. Mellons for generations.*

INTRODUCTION

In August 2000, at a Millennium Celebratory Exhibition held in Old St. Mellons Village Hall, of photographs, maps and memorabilia of St. Mellons, Rumney, Llanrumney, Castleton, Marshfield, Peterstone and Michaelston-y-Fedw, the germ of an idea was born, of producing a book detailing mainly local history of the villages of Rumney and St. Mellons. Rumney and District Local History Society already possessed considerable archives and local people were happy and generous enough to contribute and to lend photographs for the book.

Initially a party of ten people set to work and this group eventually formed a committee of five, namely, Marjorie Neal, Sylvia Atherton, Marilyn Nurse, Allen Hambly and Sam Parker, who became the compilers, part-contributors and editors of this book.

Information has been obtained from books, charts, maps, church records, newspapers, magazines, police records, court records, census returns, poor law accounts, archives of the Gwent and Glamorgan Record Offices, Newport and Cardiff Reference Libraries and Llanrumney, Rumney and St. Mellons Libraries.

We have enjoyed many happy hours of research, discussion and deliberation but we apologise for any items which may have been omitted from the book. We hope to include more information in a Cardiff Centenary and Jubilee History Exhibition to be held in Old St. Mellons Village Hall in August 2005.

Our thanks for the very considerable help received, go to all fellow-historians, friends and villagers who are listed in detail at the end of this book. Our sources and a list for further reading are also given, so that readers may continue to increase their knowledge of two villages which hold happy memories for us and for so many others.

Marjorie Neal, Sylvia Atherton, Marilyn Nurse, Allen Hambly and Sam Parker.

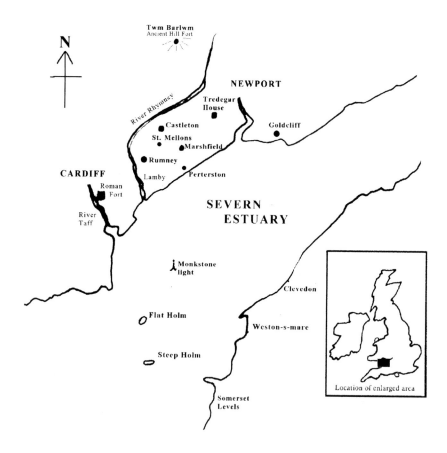

N

Twm Barlwm
Ancient Hill Fort

NEWPORT

River Rhymney

Tredegar
House

Castleton

St. Mellons

Marshfield

Goldcliff

CARDIFF

Rumney

Roman
Fort

Lamby

Perterston

River
Taff

SEVERN
ESTUARY

Monkstone
light

Clevedon

Flat Holm

Weston-s-mare

Steep Holm

Somerset
Levels

Location of enlarged area

RUMNEY AND ST. MELLONS

Names and their Origins

Since the early part of the 20th century, Rumney and St. Mellons have been engulfed by the overspill from the City of Cardiff. In earlier times they each had their own identity. Rumney and St. Mellons started as small settlements on or near the ancient overland ridgeway route across South Wales. They would later become villages, ecclesiastical parishes, and suburbs.

In 1896, Arthur Mee, journalist and amateur historian, described Rumney as 'a small place a short distance out of Cardiff - the first English village as you journey eastward along the Newport Road, being divided by a streamlet. This circumstance and the existence of the Welsh Sunday Closing Act gives Rumney an evil reputation on the 'day of rest' and has brought it into a notoriety it would not otherwise have enjoyed.'

There are many references to Rumney in the *Cardiff Records* where it is described as situated in the manor called Rompney under the lordship of Gwentllwg and possessing a handsome one-arched bridge of 1800. In Volume V (page 425) there is mention of Tredelerch (the homestead of swans), the Welsh name for the village of Rhymney or Rumney. The 'd' in Tredelerch is of philological interest, as an intrusive consonant, which appears in late Cornish, a language to which Gwentian Cornish is closely akin. In ancient times, the Rhymney River was called the Afon Elarch or Swan River. The river, moors and marshes of Rumney are thought to have been the habitat of large numbers of swans thus giving their name to the area and its river. Tredelerch was the name of a modern house on Rumney Hill, now Hillcrest Residential Home. It is also perpetuated in the new Tredelerch Park and Tredelerch Road, which linked Newport Road with New Road until 1966, when the widening of Rumney Hill resulted in closure to vehicular traffic, at its junction with Newport Road.

Rumney was formerly called Romney or Rompney and the river on which it stands is the Rhymney, which shares its name with the town at the top of the valley, but there are other variations.

1

Remni, Remne, and Rempney all appear in old documents and maps as far back as 1100. There have been various suggestions for the origin of the name. Some say Roman, others believe it derived from the Saxon word 'Rumanea' which means 'a water or watering place'. A certain John Griffiths found a river Rhymnus in the Urals, and there is said to be a Gaelic word 'Ruimne' meaning marsh. We also have the word rhyne or reen meaning a sea-marsh ditch.

All these studies suggest a connection with water, a boundary stream or marshes, which, of course, would be most appropriate, as the river used to form the boundary between Gwent and Morgannwg (Glamorgan) and Rumney includes the moors or marshes which are part of the low-lying Wentloog Level.

Swans have returned to Rumney; these are on the lake at the new Tredelerch Park.

In 1275, the area now called Llanrumney was described as 'the whole Park of Romney.' This was probably the hunting Park of the Manor of Romney. The name 'Llan' suggests that there was a church there, or possibly it was Glanrhymney, meaning on the banks of the river Rhymney.

The ancient village of St. Mellons, situated some four and a half miles to the east from the centre of Cardiff, capital city of Wales since 1955, enjoys the distinction of being the only place in Great Britain which perpetuates the memory of the first foreign missionary bishop of British extraction. Mellon, surnamed Probus, was born in Cardiola in Glamorgan in about 229 A.D. Cardiola was the Roman name for today's Caerdydd or Cardiff. Mellon was the son of notable Welsh parents who sent him, as a young man, to Rome, to accompany the taxes paid by his province. There, Mellon studied Latin, Christian truths, virtues and beliefs and was baptised by Pope Stephen I. He distinguished himself by his austerity and Christian vision and the same holy Pontiff later ordained him priest and consecrated bishop, appointing him to the See of Rouen. After 50 years of active ministry in Rouen, Mellon retired, died in 314 A.D. and was buried in the crypt of St. Gervais Church in Rouen.

The Normans, long-sworn enemies of the British race, but influenced by their own home traditions, were the first to raise a monument to the name of Mellon in Wales. The church, which they dedicated in his honour, then gave its name to the village. The name of the patron saint is now spelt St. Mellons, but until 1801 was written as St. Mellans and in Latin, the name occurs as St. Mellans or St. Melanus. Numerous variations appear in Latin, French and English. Before the Norman invasion of Wales, the village of St. Mellons bore the name of St. Lucius since it was called Llanlleurwg, later Llaneurwg or Llaneirwg in Welsh. The church is said to have been founded as early as the second century by King Lucius who introduced Christianity into Britain. Lucius or Lleurwg was the son of Coel, son of Cyllin, son of Caradawg (Caractacus), who was defeated by the Romans in A.D.51 and sent as a prisoner to Rome. The earliest reference to Lleurwg is by Bede in A.D. 180.

Rumney and St. Mellons were part of the Lordship of Gwentllwg. It is said by some that Wentloog is derived from Gwent but others disagree, saying that it is a corruption of Gwynllwg, meaning the territory or land of Gwynllyw. Gwynllyw the Warrior was the son of Glywys, lord of Glywysswg. The territory of Gwynllwg passed to him as a share of his father's kingdom. We must remember that people perhaps misheard names or pronounced them in different ways and when pen was put to paper spelt them in the way they thought that name sounded. Various spellings include: - Gunliuc, Gunlion, Gunliou, Gwentluc and Wentllooge.

St. Mellons Parish Church. Drawing by Mr. J. Vallis.

View of Wentloog Level with Steep Holm and Flat Holm in the distance.

4

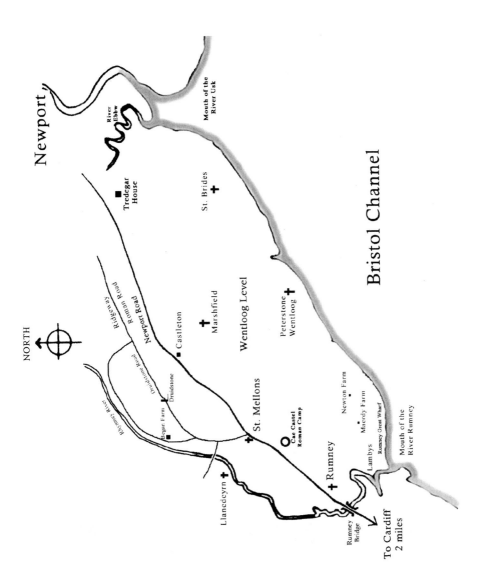

NORTH

Newport,

River
Ebbw

Mouth of the
River Usk

Tredegar
House

St. Brides

Ridgeway

Roman Road

Newport Road

Castleton

Marshfield

Wentloog Level

Peterstone
Wentloog

Bristol Channel

(Druidstone Road)

Druidstone

Bogat Farm

St. Mellons

Rhymney River

Cae Castel
Roman Camp

Newton Farm

Maerdy Farm

Rumney Great Wharf

Mouth of the
River Rumney

Lambys

Rumney

Llanedeyrn

Rumney
Bridge

To Cardiff
2 miles

5

River Rumney

Ball Farm

Rumney
Court

Ball Road

Pen-yr-heol Farm

High Croft F

Carpenters Arms
(P. H.)

Cross Inn (P. H.)

Site of Rumney
Castle

Beli Bach Cottages

Ty Mawr
Farm

St. Augustine's
Church

Rumney
Bridge

Vicarage

Whitehall
Farm

Ty Fry Farm

Rumney
Pottery

To
Cardiff

Stone
Quarry

Site of Village Cross

Brachdy Lane

PenSarn
Cottages

Rompney Castle
(P. H.)

Greenway
Farm

Wentloog Road

Downton
Farm

Oak Meadow
Cottage

Great Western Railway

Lambys

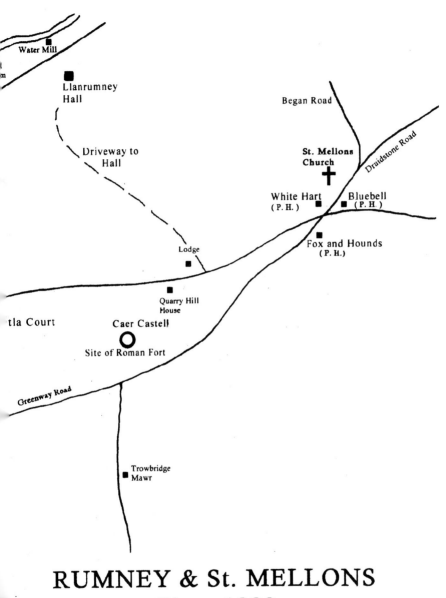

Water Mill

Llanrumney
Hall

Began Road

Driveway to
Hall

St. Mellons
Church

Druidstone Road

White Hart
(P. H.)

Bluebell
(P. H.)

Fox and Hounds
(P. H.)

Lodge

Quarry Hill
House

tla Court

Caer Castell

Site of Roman Fort

Greenway Road

Trowbridge
Mawr

RUMNEY & St. MELLONS
Circa 1890

ANCIENT HISTORY

Planet earth goes back 4,700 million years but man has lived on this planet for just a blink of an eyelid, a mere 2 million years. If you take for example 24 hours of the day to represent Earth's time, man arrived less than a minute before midnight. The world has been changing from the beginning of time and continues to do so.

What were Rumney and St. Mellons like in the past, not only in recent history, but also in prehistoric times? When did man start living in this area? How did trees, vegetation and animals differ from what we see today?

For ancient history, reference must be made to the experts who dig and look for clues and remnants of the past, such as pottery, tools made from stone or bone, cave paintings and fossilised bones and plants. For recent history, facts have been obtained from libraries, museums and record offices. Old and new books, old documents, maps and television programmes have also yielded many interesting details.

Wales, part of the British Isles, originated south of the Equator and drifted northwards passing through changing climates. Volcanoes, glaciers, deserts, tropical swamps, coral seas and dinosaurs have appeared in a constantly changing environment. Over millions of years, plants and animals have also evolved.

Drawing of ancient times. Ellis Howells, age 12 years.

8

The following article by Philip Parker outlines the local geology.
'It is difficult to believe that the rocks which underlie Rumney and St. Mellons were formed in shallow tropical seas and on coastal plains about 400 million years ago. Rocks of this age were first discovered in South Wales and geologists call this time the Silurian Period after the warlike British tribe, the Silures, who inhabited this area when the Romans arrived.'

Over most of Rumney and St. Mellons solid rock is only exposed at the surface in a few places. Perhaps the best outcrop is in Rumney Quarry where buff-coloured sandstones known as the Rumney Grit can be seen in the quarry face. These rocks were mainly quarried for repairing roads but some were used for building as can be seen in the wall of a cottage in Brachdy Road.

If you look carefully in the rocks in the quarry, you may find that some of the surfaces have ripple marks like those found on present-day beaches as evidence of their shallow water origin. A few fossil shells may be found in beds towards the top of the quarry, but Rumney's main claim to fame is that microscopic remains of some of the world's earliest plants have been recovered from these rocks.

The upper beds of the Rumney Grit are also exposed in the riverbank below the Conservative Club. Between this point and the riverbank below Rumney Hill Gardens a series of silt stones, sandstones and limestones can be seen. Some of the beds are packed with fossil shells and corals. One particular bed is a deep red-coloured rock called ironstone. This bed used to outcrop in Ty Mawr Road when it was just a track, and it was known to the residents of old Rumney as the "fossil pavement". A collection of fossils from this location can be seen in the National Museum.

The main reason that solid rocks are rarely exposed at the surface is that they are covered by stony clays and gravels formed in the last Ice Age. The ice only started to melt and retreat about 10,000 years ago, which is only yesterday in geological terms. At the end of the last glaciation period, sea level was considerably lower and the Bristol Channel was a broad, wooded valley with the River Severn flowing through it. Rivers such as the Rhymney cut deep valleys through the rocks to join the Severn because of lower sea levels.

As the ice melted, the sea gradually flooded the river valleys

9

and deposited the blue-grey clay that underlies the Wentloog Levels today. Boreholes near Maerdy Farm found some of the buried channels of the River Rhymney nearly 10 metres (30 ft aprox.) below present-day sea level.

Photograph of the quarry, foreground. Rumney Church marked with an arrow is in the background.

Taken by William Booth in 1891.

Rumney Church taken from the Quarry in 2003.

THE GREAT ICE AGE, STONE AGE AND IRON AGE

Evidence suggests that humans have lived in Wales for about 250,000 years. The Great Ice Age began 1.6 million years ago and ended 10,000 years ago. This was not a period of continuous cold and ice cover, but sometimes frequent and rapid change in the climate, with temperatures not very different from today. These periods of change were known as 'glacial' and 'interglacial'. During ancient times, early man, animals and plants adapted, developed or became extinct, according to the changes that were taking place.

The area of ice came as far south as the River Thames and South Wales, whilst the ground south of this was frozen and bare. Since there was so much water taken up in the ice, sea levels were much lower; there was dry land between Britain and France. This enabled man and animals to move north into Britain from France and the rest of Europe. Rivers such as the Rhymney and Severn would not have been tidal. Early animals included the woolly mammoth and giant deer, models of which can be seen in the National Museum of Wales in Cardiff. We can add to this list reindeer, bear, elephant, woolly rhinoceros, bison, wolf, hyaena, arctic fox, hippopotamus, and many more.

Drawings of some ancient animals that inhabited this area.

Silurian	Palaeolithic	Mesolithic	Neolithic	Bronze Age
435 million years ago	500,000 - 33,000 B.C.	8,000 - 4,250 B.C.	4,250 - 2,100 B.C.	
Plant fossils found in Rumney	Early Neanderthal handaxe found at Penylan just across the Rhymney River from 250,000 years ago	Tree stumps 6,000 - 8,000 years old on foreshore at Rhymney Great Wharf Part of the skeleton of a great-horned auroch found near Rhymney River, dated about 4,500 years The Uskmouth footprints 7,000 years ago	Neolithic prehistoric flint knife found at Began, St. Mellons	Two flint-barbed and tanged arrow-heads found at Nant Mawr, Rumney Bronze age spearhead at Rumney Great Wharf Flint scraper at St. Mellons Numerous bronze-socketed axe-heads including the St. Mellons hoard

Iron Age	43 A.D. - 400 A.D.	The Dark Ages 400 A.D. - 1066 A.D.	1066 A.D. - 2005 A.D. The Norman Conquest to present time
Undated quernstone but believed to be of this period. Found at Began, St. Mellons	Roman iron pilium at St . Mellons Numerous pieces of pottery and other items, including lumps of slag at Rumney Great Wharf	Very little information during this Period	From Norman times, records were kept and information is available

From early times the wetlands below St. Mellons which now form part of the Wentloog Level have been important to people living in this region. The landscape of the Level or Moors, as they were once known, has developed over thousands of years. At the end of the last Ice Age, as noted earlier, the Bristol Channel was a wide, wooded valley with a much smaller River Severn running through it. When the ice started to melt, sea levels rose and trees died because of the salt water. Mud flats and saltmarsh then developed.

By 4,250 BC, the rate of rise in sea level had slowed and vegetation changed once more. It went from saltmarsh to reed and sedge swamp, then trees grew again. Willow, birch and alder were superseded by a raised bog. It was inundated and once more saltmarsh developed, over which wild animals roamed. Part of the skeleton of an Auroch, a breed of wild cattle dating from 4,500 years ago, was found near the Rhymney River in 1983. In recent years, stumps of trees believed to be about 6,000 years old have been exposed again at low tide.

Drawing of an Auroch, a large animal measuring 1.8metres (6ft) at the shoulders and the ancestor of modern-day cattle. Vivian Parr.

Roots of trees believed to be 6,000 – 8,000 years old, exposed at low tide on the foreshore of Rumney Great Wharf.

Humans were more intelligent than beasts and therefore able to learn skills such as the use of stones as tools and the making of fire. They hunted and killed game and scavenged from the kills of other animals, as well as gathering edible plants. They lived in primitive dwellings made from skins and sometimes in caves.

A hand-axe of the Lower Palaeolithic period (500,000 BC - 33,000 BC) was found at Penylan, Cardiff. The hill on which St. Mellons Church was later built would have been an ideal place for early man to settle. The higher ground provided a good vantage point for sighting smaller animals, such as deer, which would be hunted using spears. Early man used fire to frighten larger animals e.g. woolly mammoth, down to the lower ground towards the rivers, trapping them in the wetlands. They were then easier to kill and provided a good supply of food for the family group.

Impression by Vivian Parr of an early settlement in St. Mellons.

As the climate improved, man was gradually changing from hunter-gatherer to farmer. Woodland was widespread, grasses and flowering herbaceous plants were growing again. Early farmers started cutting down trees with stone axes to make clearings for grasses to grow, providing grazing for their animals. While these early settlers had started to farm, they continued to hunt for the natural species of their surroundings, wild animals, fish, birds and waterfowl. Plants, berries and seeds were gathered and in their homes they made use of wood, reeds and rushes.

In the Bronze and Iron Ages, man learned how to make tools from copper, iron and bronze. He started to change and shape his environment. Late Bronze Age sites have been identified at Rumney Great Wharf and in other parts of Rumney and St. Mellons. Finds include barbed and tanged arrowheads, a bronze spearhead, a flintscraper and numerous bronze-socketed axes. The earliest man-made find for the area is a prehistoric flint knife of the Neolithic period (4,250 BC – 2,100 BC), found in Began Road, St. Mellons. The National Museum of Wales houses many examples of finds from the area.

Prehistoric finds in the area.
Left to right: -

Neolithic/Bronze Age
flint knife - Began.

Prehistoric flint scraper
- Rumney River bank.

Bronze Age flint barbed
and tanged arrowhead
- Nant-Mawr, Rumney.

Bronze Age spear
- Rumney Great Wharf.

Printed by kind permission of
The National Museum of Wales.

The hoard of Bronze Age socketed axe-heads found in St Mellons and on display at the Museum in Cardiff. Above photograph printed by kind permission of the National Museum of Wales.

Local man Sid Cruze discovered some metal objects when working on a housing development near St Mellons Hill. These proved to be Bronze Age socketed axes and are now in the collection of the National Museum in Cardiff.

Celts living in Rumney and St. Mellons probably originated in Eastern Europe. They were not a single group of people, but a number of races of close origin who spoke vaguely similar languages, namely Breton, Cornish and Welsh.

These people formed tribes and the Silures were the tribe that occupied South East Wales. The ancient Celtic tribes were considered barbaric, running around half-naked, covered in woad (blue paint) and living in very primitive conditions. They used bronze, wood, and stone for their tools, and learnt how to smelt iron to edge their ploughshares. Their houses were made with wattle walls and thatched roofs, and they grew corn, threshing it and storing it under cover in thatched barns. Whilst they used the corn to make some sort of bread and cake, from fermented honey they made mead, a sickly sweet wine. But most importantly, they made swords and axes ---- and were to make good use of them against the Romans!

Impression of a Celtic Village by Vivian Parr.

Jacqui Wood, author of **Prehistoric Cooking,** cooked a feast for television's Time Team. Below is a recipe from her book.
In pre-history the flour would have been ground by hand between two stones (a quern). Jacqui suggests that the saying 'the daily grind' refers to this laborious task.

500g. barley flour
500g. stone-ground wheat flour
1tsp. salt
250g. butter
Beer to mix

Mix the flours and salt together and rub in the butter. Add enough beer to make a soft dough and shape into small cakes. Cook on a hot stone (or griddle) until firm. This is a very light bread because of the beer and is very good with cheese.

THE ROMANS

Then came the Romans! Wales was a hostile area and caused them many problems, such as threats to the security of towns and villas in the lowland areas. Military campaigns against Welsh tribes are recorded by the historian Tacitus. These attempts to advance against the Welsh started in 47 A.D. but it was not until 74 A.D. that Julius Frontinus finally subdued the Silures and established the fortress at Caerleon.

There is very little written evidence for the period, which relates to the area of Rumney and St. Mellons. On present-day maps Roman roads are marked, but some of these roads made use of tracks that were already in existence. One such road was the ancient ridgeway route through Bassaleg, St. Mellons, Rumney and beyond to West Wales. It is interesting to note that this ancient track passes the 'Druidstone' or Guiding Stone, still standing close to Druidstone Road in St. Mellons.

Fred Hando in his book *The Pleasant Land of Gwent,* states 'This grand monolith, over 10 feet high and 7 feet wide, has been frequently described by previous writers, but none has noted that its flat face directs along the ancient trackway to Penylan and Caerleon or that it lies south of the tumulus on Twm Barlwm. Midday could thus be noted as the time when the shadow of this gigantic finger pointed towards the great hump!'

Legend has it that when the cock crows at night, Druidstone goes down to the river to bathe.

Cartoon by Vivian Parr.

20

The Druidstone near Druidstone House, St. Mellons.

The quern-stone or mill-stone found in Began Road, St.Mellons in 1921. This is held at the National Museum of Wales in Cardiff. It is a well-preserved specimen of an upper mill-stone of bee-hive shape, with a socket for a single handle. Prior to the introduction of this type of mill-stone, the corn was crushed by a stone-pounder working upon a flat slab. The bee-hive mill-stone was in use as late as circa 200 A.D., when it was superseded by the flat mill-stone which had been introduced by the Romans.

Photograph by kind permission of the National Museum of Wales

21

Apart from the Roman road, the Romans left this area with another significant legacy, the drainage system on the Wentloog Level. There are other areas of low-lying ground which border the Severn Estuary and they are known collectively as the Severn Levels. This 'historic landscape' of Wentloog is recognised as being unique in Britain and indeed in North West Europe. It lies between 2– 3 metres below the highest tides and is a flat area with the fields divided by reens (ditches).

Stephen Rippon describes the area in his book *Gwent Levels: The Evolution of a Landscape* ' The physical nature of the Levels, notably the flat relief and heavy but fertile soils, along with the process of wetland reclamation, has created a highly distinctive landscape dominated by the need to control the water system. One of the critical character-defining features of this landscape is that it has been totally hand-crafted by mankind, transforming tidally inundated saltmarsh into rich agricultural land. The whole of the Wentloog area had been enclosed by sea walls and drained at the time of the Roman occupation.' It is remarkable that this planned drainage system, originally put in place by the Romans, is still in use. Why did the Romans undertake this project?

Prior to archaeological investigations in the late 20th century many people believed that the Romans had only used the mud-flats as a route to the drier hill areas and also as a place to make pottery during the summer months. The investigations established that the Roman settlement was more extensive. Local people believed that the present line of the sea wall had originated with the Romans but this also proved to be wrong. The investigations revealed conclusive evidence that the Wentloog Level had been drained and embanked by the Romans, but this bank was further seaward than it is now. As the sea level was lower at that time, the sea wall need not have been as high or substantial. In addition, there was a legionary fortress at Caerleon and a smaller fortress at Cardiff. They would have needed large areas of land to provide food for themselves and grazing for their horses and other animals.

In the Newton area where the ground is slightly lower than that nearer the Rhymney River, the fields are regular in shape. From aerial photographs taken in the 1980s, one can see where reens on the landward side of the sea-bank are aligned with ditches on the foreshore. Archaeologists discovered that these ditches were of similar width and depth.

The sea wall runs from left to right of photograph, the dotted white lines show alignment of reens on the landward side of sea bank and ditches on the seaward side.

For an effective drainage system a Roman seabank would have been needed between the Rhymney and Ebbw Rivers continuing up the estuaries. The location of a seabank is not known, but is thought to have been 1 kilometre (just over half a mile) seaward of the present bank. The system of reens on the Wentloog Level amounted to about 320km (nearly 200miles) in length. Who carried out this work? Soldiers from Caerleon together with the local population? In *The Wentlooge Level: a Romano-British saltmarsh reclamation in South East Wales* by J.R.L. Allen and M.G. Fullford it is stated that 'D.W.A. Startin has calculated that a team of a picker and shoveller and one or two basketeers could move about 1.02 cubic metres (1.3 cubic yards) per hour. At a crude estimate, the work might have required between seven and nine million man-hours. Since we cannot guess what size of labour force might have been involved, it is impossible to calculate how long the whole operation took. It may have taken decades. The scale of the undertaking as a whole and the regularity of the ditch systems and field sizes, implies the involvement of an army.'

Impression of men working, digging ditches and building the sea defence bank by Vivian Parr.

In an in-filled sealed ditch on the foreshore, occupational debris was discovered which included Romano - British pottery from the second to mid fourth centuries, fragments of clay daub, cobbles, iron ore, coal, bones and teeth.

From these 'finds' and studies it was deduced that there had been a farming settlement there, with other activities such as working with iron and making pottery. Slag found, suggested that smelting took place. Raw materials for ironwork had to be imported, maybe from the Forest of Dean. Good access to the Severn Estuary enabled easy import of materials and export of the finished product. Farming on the seaward side of the sea defence was most likely a marginal activity. Settlement probably dates from the late second century. A pottery collection found by archaeologists has been lodged with the National Museum of Wales.

A small private collection of finds in the area is shown below. The earthenware fragment with grit incorporated into the base is thought have been used to make cream cheese. Milk would be put into the bowl and left to curdle, then the whey was poured off through the spout. The grit was useful as the curd-forming bacteria remained on its surface between cheese-makings.

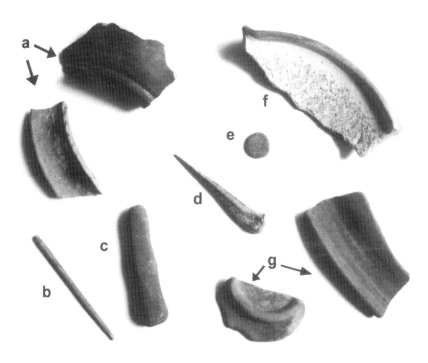

a. Greyware fragments.
b. Hairpin.
c. Small sharpening stone.
d. Chicken bone with end sharpened to make holes in leather and other materials.
e. Counter used in playing games.
f. Hard grit can be seen impregnated into the base of this bowl fragment; the pouring lip is on the left.
g. Samian ware fragments.

THE POST-ROMAN PERIOD - THE VIKINGS AND SAXONS

Little information exists on the Post-Roman period. People of the area learnt many things from the Romans yet not much progress was made during the succeeding centuries. Their lifestyle may even have regressed in some ways.

Sea defences were not maintained and sea levels rose. There were breaches to the east and west of the Wentloog area near the Rhymney and Ebbw Rivers. The ground, once again, was inundated by the sea and overflowing rivers. Due to sediment deposits, land in these two areas is higher and the reens follow natural creeks rather than the straight lines of Roman ditches between Newton and Peterstone.

The fact that Norsemen had established a settlement on the Rhymney River is proven by early names. *Lamby* in 1401, was *Langby, lang* meaning long and *by* signifying village, both early Scandinavian words. (e.g. Grimsby and Derby were founded by the Danes.) Langby or long village, was no doubt founded for trading purposes. The Vikings, (700 A.D. – 900 A.D.) had the reputation for fighting and pillaging, but later were to become early pioneers of sea-borne commerce. They are likely to have made good use of the rivers of the Bristol Channel. Their system was to build a fortification and form a trading centre, which often developed into a permanent settlement.

Below the railway bridge that leads from New Road to Tredelerch Park, the river meandered forming a hairpin bend shaped like a spearhead. This area was called *Keyscroft* in the 16th century. It probably came from the old Norse word *kesja,* a spear. On the left bank the area was called the *Luggs*. This name, used until the 19th century, probably came from the same source, denoting the lower marshy land at the foot of a slope. Downton Farm also reflects marshland; tun/ton meaning farm on marshy ground.

Rumney Great Wharf, in its early form *Warth*, is said to be derived from the Anglo-Saxon *warath* meaning seashore, or from an Old Danish word signifying untilled land. The Rhymney River as with others, in South Wales shows similar names which go back to the Viking Age.

Inhabitants of Rumney and St. Mellons have always been

26

able to look over to Steep Holm and Flat Holm. Holm is the Danish word for island. In three versions of the Anglo-Saxon Chronicle of 914 AD it is recorded that Viking raiders ' remained on the island of Steep Holm and many men had died of hunger.' A fourth version of the Chronicle records Flat Holm as the island.

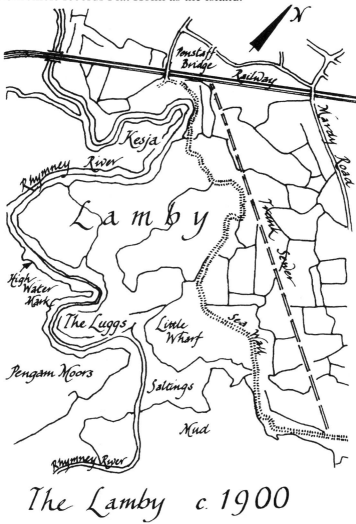

The Lamby c. 1900

Sketch Map by Allen Hambly

27

THE NORMANS AND RUMNEY CASTLE

When the Normans arrived, local inhabitants were living in thatched round houses and were leading very simple lives. Families as a whole helped in the production and preparation of food which consisted of coarse bread, meat, cheese, fish, eggs, and vegetables. Spinning, weaving and making or mending of clothes were all part of their daily lives, as well as building and repairs to dwellings and storehouses. Infant and child mortality rates were high and life expectancy was much shorter than at the present time.

A date remembered by everyone is the year 1066 – William the Conqueror and the Battle of Hastings. What links does Wales have with the Normans? In *Domesday Book,* most of the present Monmouthshire is included within the boundary of Gloucestershire and it is stated that 'the penetration of Wales by English and Normans in the 11th century had resulted in the annexation to Gloucestershire of the territory which later formed the County of Monmouthshire'. It specifies land lying between the rivers Wye and Usk and beyond. Names such as Caerleon, Chepstow, Caerwent and Penhow are mentioned. Rogerstone is the nearest place to Rumney and St. Mellons that has an entry in *Domesday Book*. It was noted that Roger of Berkely held two hides of land worth twenty shillings at Rogerstone and had six borders with one plough. A border was a smallholder who farmed wasteland, frequently woodland, that had been brought into production usually on the edge of a settlement. In 1072, Caradog ap Gruffudd, aided by Norman allies, succeeded in defeating Mareduded ap Owain in a battle on the banks of the River Rhymney. Morgannwg, now Glamorgan, was seized. The services of the Normans were secured on condition that Caradog became a vassal of the English Crown. A vassel was a person who held land from a lord in return for sworn homage.

By 1081, William the Conqueror had established an administrative centre in Cardiff and a mint was set up to serve Morgannwg, already occupied by the Normans.

Impression by Vivian Parr of the battle on the banks of the Rhymney River.

Rumney Castle was built on Rumney Hill on a site to the rear of the present day Morgan's Restaurant and Hillcrest Residential Home. The Castle mound was presumably first built on this site by the followers of Robert Fitzhamon, Earl of Gloucester, who occupied Morgannwg in the last decade of the 11th century.

The earliest documentary reference to Rumney Castle dates from the late 12th Century during the reign of Henry II. At this time Newport Castle guarded the eastern border and Rumney Castle the western border of the marcher lordship of Gwynllwg. There had been hostilities in the area and it seems the bridge over the Rhymney River had been damaged. It is recorded in the Pipe Rolls that Robert Fitzwilliam, Royal Custodian of Rumney Castle was awarded £5-4s-8d for his services, £1-11s-6d being allowed for repairs to the nearby bridge. It therefore follows that by the second half of the 12th Century, a bridge existed at this point.

Rumney Castle was described in the List of Sites of Architectural and Historic Interest as a roughly circular enclosure 60 yards in diameter. It was defended on the southeast and isolated from the rest of Rumney Hill by a ditch which was 15 feet below the edge of the enclosure. To the west the ground fell precipitously to the river whilst the ditch curved to the northwest and linked with the natural scarp above the river. This can be seen in the artist's impression below.

The type of castle at Rumney was known as a 'ringwork'. This was often constructed when some sort of defence was needed to be built quickly and cheaply – Vivian Parr.

Two separate excavations of the castle site were conducted by the Glamorgan-Gwent Archaeological Trust in 1978 and 1980/81. The first excavation was undertaken by P. Stanley and K.W.B. Lightfoot in the area behind Morgan's Restaurant. The second and much more extensive excavation was conducted by K.B.W. Lightfoot during the period 8th May 1980 to 1st December 1981, resulting in the recovery of a more complete and reliable history of the castle. Initially incorporated into the castle defences was a large timber building and possibly a palisade. A large timber gate-tower stood at the entrance, later superseded by a smaller timber structure. When defences were strengthened, the clay rampart and a small tower were constructed adjacent to the entrance. Timber buildings stood around a courtyard. The entrance was later moved and a stone tower built. In the thirteenth century the site became a manorial centre.

Unfortunately certain reports are incomplete due to a fire in 1983 at the Headquarters of the Glamorgan and Gwent Archaeological Trust. The area examined in 1978 comprised approx. 350 sq.metres of the mound and a one metre wide section across the ditch extending southeast from the edge of the mound near the south corner of the site. In 1980/81 the total area excavated on the northeast of the mound amounted to approx. 1300 sq. metres and included the entire mound summit and a limited portion of the ditch. At that time the archaeological investigation of Rumney Castle was the most extensive examination of a Norman ringwork castle in the British Isles.

In 1081, Caradog, who had taken possession of Morgannwg nine years earlier with the aid of the Normans, was himself deposed by Rhys ap Tewdur. It has been suggested that Robert Fitzhamon assumed control of an established colony after Rhys' death and used this as a base for further territorial expansion. One of those territories was Gwynllwg (Wentloog) the fertile coastal plain between the Rhymney and Usk Rivers, together with the upland commote of Machen. Gwynllwg had formed a cantref in Morgannwg with its borders largely defined by these rivers. Under Fitzhamon, this unit became a completely separate lordship. Until 1317, it was held by the Lord of Glamorgan. The former kingdom of Morgannwg came to be known as Glamorgan after its conquest by the Normans. Gwynllwg retained its own administrative centre at Newport where Fitzhamon established an important castle. By the early 12th Century it had become the demesne (land with unrestricted rights) of the chief lord. From time to time violence erupted and Welsh Princes from the hills often threatened the lowland settlements, like Rumney and St. Mellons.

The Lordship of Glamorgan and Gwynllwg passed down by inheritance and through marriage. In 1217, Gilbert de Clare inherited the Lordship. The family was to enjoy a long tenure of these lordships, ending with the partition of their estates three years after the last male in their line was killed at Bannockburn in 1314. During the 100 years that Rumney was in the possession of the de Clare family, it provided a valuable source of income.

As the Welsh controlled the upland commotes of Machen and Senghennydd there was a continuing threat to the settlements on

31

the coastal plain. This was partly overcome when, in 1267, Gilbert confiscated Senghennydd and later annexed Machen. To ensure the protection of his expanded lordship, Gilbert wasted no time in the construction of Caerphilly Castle. Llewelyn twice attacked and severely damaged it, but by the late 1270's, Caerphilly was one of the most advanced and formidable castles in the British Isles.

Rumney Castle was subsequently converted to a fortified manor house, which the archaeologists tell us was a domicile of considerable status. During a serious revolt in Wales in 1294/5 the manor house was destroyed and from then on the former castle was of little importance. Thus it sank into obscurity until the late 1970s when its history was rediscovered.

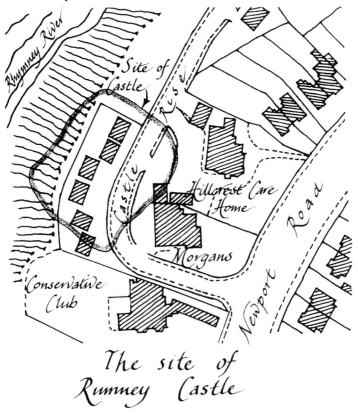

The site of
Rumney Castle

Sketch Map by Allen Hambly

32

THE LORDSHIP, MANOR AND HUNDRED

After the Norman Conquest, all land in England (this included some areas of what is now Wales near the present England/Wales border), was owned by William I. Later the Marcher Lordships became established. A feudal system already existed which defined areas of land in the late Anglo Saxon period. The Manor varied significantly in size; in feudal times it defined a territorial area but by mediaeval times it was more an economic unit, administering law, order and taxation. The *hide* and the *hundred* became units of taxation which are later found in Domesday; 100 hides equalled a hundred. Hide is defined as 'the name given to an area of land that a team of oxen could plough in a year. This was considered enough to support a family group, normally about 120 acres, which varied according to the quality of the soil and the nature of the terrain.' Rumney and St. Mellons have been influenced by both English and Welsh names and customs. The Welsh equivalent of the Hundred was the *commote,* a term used on deeds as recently as the late nineteenth century.

William I retained land for his own use, but granted a large portion to earls and barons who in turn granted it to knights (knight's fee) in return for their service to the King. There were between 5,000 and 6,000 knights' fees in England at this time. Rumney and St. Mellons came under the Lordship of Wentloog. The Lordship of Wentloog was not difficult to partition from the Norman point of view. Lands to the south, agriculturally rich and pleasant went to the Lord and his knights; lands to the north, cold and barren, wooded and steep, to the peasants. Robert Fitzhamon, mentioned in the previous chapter, evidently regarded this part of his conquest as one large demesne manor (home farm), as he only granted lands to five followers. The Welsh portion was the commote of Machen which was north of the Rhymney river. The Lord retained for his own demesne Stow, Duffryn, Pencarn, Marshfield and Rumney. His knights held the following - Bassaleg and Ebbw one knight's fee each. Coedkernew, St. Brides and St. Mellons – half a knight's fee each. At one time the Manor of Romney included Rumney and parts of Peterstone, Marshfield and St. Mellons. Details of customs in Romney Manor still exist; no information survives for St. Mellons.

A.C. Reeves in *The Custumal of Rumney Manor* states – 'Rumney was unique among the manors of the Newport lordship in the survival of a custumal which, although dating only from the sixteenth century, records longstanding customs. Other manors which formed part of the Lordship of Wentloog were Peterstone, St. Brides, St. Mellons, Marshfield, Coedkernew, Michaelston-y-Fedw, Bassaleg, Malpas, Bettws, Machen, Henllys, Risca, Bedwas, Mynyddislwyn and Bedwellty. The boundary of the Lordship of Wentloog extended from the River Severne in the south to the Brecon border in the north, with the lordships of Abergavenny, Usk and Caldicot on the eastern boundary and the county of Glamorgan to the west.'

Rumney was first organised as a marcher lordship under the name of Gwynllwg. It passed from one lord to another until 1521 when Edward, third Duke of Buckingham was executed. It then escheated (the reversion of property to the crown in the absence of legal heirs) to Henry VIII. In 1536 and 1543 with the Acts of Union, Newport ceased to be a marcher lordship.

In May 1532 King Henry VIII had given the manor in survivorship to Thomas Cromwell and his son, Gregory. Sir William Morgan wrote to Cromwell in November of that year to congratulate him on his good fortune and to mention a few traditions concerning the duty of the local residents to give suit to the shire court, which was held at Newport. He said that he would send Cromwell information on the customs of Rumney. The only document of the customs still existing is that sent by Sir William Morgan.

In this document the manor is called the Hundred of Rumney and includes land as far as Peterstone. It is stated that the lord bore the expense of three officials - a reeve, a beadle and hayward. A *reeve* was a man elected by his fellow tenants to act as intermediary with the lord of the manor and to undertake certain customary duties. A *beadle* was a town crier or crier in a law court, a minor parish official responsible for keeping order or someone who walks in front of dignitaries in a procession. A *hayward* was a manorial officer responsible for hedges and fences and for preventing cattle from straying.

There were extensive customs concerning the holding of land. Rents from tenants were due four times a year. Other rents from

34

free lands, cottages, fisheries, warths and moneywarths, together with fines and heriots were all due at Michaelmas. (Tenants paid an entry fine on acquiring a holding. A *heriot* was a payment, often the best beast, to the lord of the manor from an incoming tenant.) *Warths* were lands beyond the sea walls, which in summer provided good grazing, but according to the custumol were being eaten away year by year, by the sea.

The gates or gowts were built valve-like to allow fresh water to flow into the Bristol Channel, while preventing the sea from flooding the land at high tide. There were five stone gowts in the walls protecting Rumney. All were the responsibility of the lord, along with eight yards of wall on each side of the gowts. The remainder of the embankments were the responsibility of the lords tenants. The sea walls were of such importance that there were three closes of upland in the manor from which no heriots were collected, since the gowts were maintained for the lord.

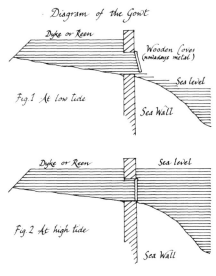

Diagram of 'The Gowt.'

There were several customs relating to the death of a tenant. Usually the whole inheritance went to the youngest son, but if there was no son, the youngest daughter inherited. When a woman who had acquired land married, the lord received as his due, the best beast the couple had.

The manor court met monthly, where matters concerning land and other judicial problems could be settled by juries of six or twelve men. Some of the freeholders of Rumney also had duties at a high court in Newport. They were obliged to take stools and cushions for the Lord's Justices, and to convey to the gallows any villains who were sentenced to death.

Other customs in the manor included:-
  i.   When a stranger died in the manor, a heriot or payment was due to the lord.
  ii.   A *woodgavel,* an annual payment of a penny, was made by the lord for each horse-load of wood delivered to his residence.
  iii. Within the manor a woman kept her father's name after marriage rather than taking that of her husband.

The plague did not seriously affect this area, consequently the work-force was still fit and able to till the land. One writer in 1384, described Rumney as flourishing, this was in contrast to other manors where the manorial system as a whole was beginning to disintegrate. During the 14th and 15th centuries the Romney (Rumney) manor developed into one of the most valuable demense holdings in the lordship of Newport, which had previously been known as Wentloog and Gwynllwg.

By the early 16th century, barns belonging to Rumney manor where dues were paid in kind, had been destroyed. Water-mills in the manor belonged to the lord, but tenants were responsible for minor repairs. The Lord did not live in Rumney and in 1610, in London, there was criticism of this because it was therefore difficult to liaise and control the manor. Before tenants of the Rumney Manor could start working the land of the lord, the ceremony of the Rod had to be performed. The Lord or his Reeve held out a rod and as a new tenant grasped it, he swore to maintain the laws and customs of the manor. At this point a share of the manor land was handed over to him and therefore, he 'grasped the rod.'

We know that Rumney Castle was used for a time as a Manorial centre but other locations have been suggested. After the demise of the castle, the centre of government moved to the Big House where Ty Mawr Farm later stood. The farm, which became the centre of government, stood at the junction of Ty Mawr Avenue and Ty Mawr Road. Some authorities believe that it was there that the farmers paid their 'dues' and delivered their grain to be stored.

The main cultivated lands lay on the Wentloog Level and there is evidence to suggest that the present-day property of Ty To Maen Farm, on Newton Road, was originally a manorial property and a collecting-centre for grain. Monasteries were often given land which was situated away from the monastery and worked by lay brothers and hired labourers. Such outlying farms were often on the productive lowlands.

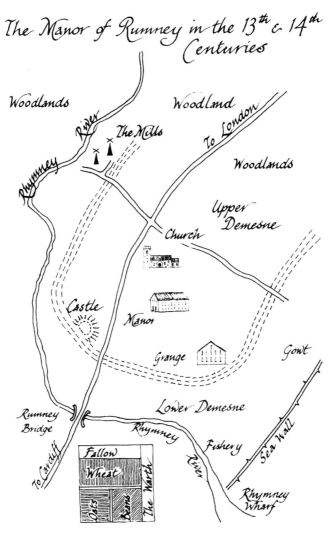

Impression by Allen Hambly of the Manor of Rumney in the 13th and 14th centuries.

THE FLOOD

As seen in records of the Manor of Rumney, great importance was placed on the maintenance of the gouts or sluice gates and the sea-defence wall. During the Post-Roman period, sea defences were neglected, but during the Mediaeval Period, improvements were made. There are times, however, when freaks of nature are beyond human control. One such example is the *Flood* of 1606 or 1607, which made a big impact on the whole of the Severn Estuary.

First, to clarify the date - the inscription on Peterstone church, records the date as 20th January 1606 whilst other accounts give 20th January 1607. This discrepancy is due to the fact that two calendars were in use at that time - the civil, ecclesiastical and legal year starting on 25th March and the 'common' year on 1st January. So at the time of the Flood many people recognised the date as 1606 with the year ending on 24th March. The confusion was not sorted out until 1752, when Britain adopted the Gregorian calendar wherein the year ended on December 31st. This took January 20th into the next year, 1607. The following account of the *Flood* printed in 1877, therefore gives the date as 1607.

The foreword in a document entitled **Recent Floods in Monmouthshire** states, 'A propos the recent floods and heavy rains, we subjoin the following interesting narrative of a great flood which took place in Monmouthshire 270 years ago and which occasioned the destruction of 26 villages. We are indebted to a contemporary for the account which he copied from a print of an extremely scarce and curious pamphlet, published by the last Mr Heath of Monmouth, the reprint being nearly now as scarce as the original'

The report states '...... *lamentable news out of Monmouthshire in Wales, Contayning the wonderfull and most fearefull accidents of the great overflowing of waters in the saide Countye, drowning infinite numbers of Cattell of all Kinds, as Sheepe, Oxen, Kine and horses, with others; together with the losse of many men, women and Children, and the subversion of xxvi Parishes in January last, 1607.......'*

It states further '..... *upon a Tuesday the sea being very tempestuouslye moved by the winds overflowed his ordinarye Banks and did drown 26 Parishes adjoining the Coast side in the aforesaid*

Countrye of Monmouthshire:the particulars whereof doe follow: all spoyld by the grievous and lamentable furie of the waters.' An area twenty-four miles long and four miles wide was affected. The water carried away ricks of hay and corn, the sea *'hath'* beaten down and scattered houses dispersing innumerable *'persones'. The damage done to cattle and goods amounted to £100,000. When the waters first burst through the bank, it had run with a swiftness so incredible as that no 'Grayehounde' could have escaped.'*

This report suggested that it would take five or six years for the ground to recover and be as serviceable as it had formerly been and that there was no probability that that part of the country would ever be inhabited again in our age as it was before the flood. However, it had been reported that this area had been the *'richest and fruitfullest place in all that countrey'* At the time that this report was written it was not known how many had drowned but suggested a figure of *'twentie hundred'* There were stories of lucky escapes such as this one:- *'a certain man and a woman having taken a tree for their succour and espynge nothing but Death before their eyes, at last among other which were arrived along in the stream they purceyved a certain article, to wit, a tube of great largenesse to come nearer and nearer unto them until it rested upon that tree werein so they were, into which as sent to them by God's Providence he and she committed themselves and were cast uppe upon the dry shore'.*

A 1607 woodcut. 'The Great Flood'

In recent years, older people living in Rumney, St. Mellons and Peterstone, have told stories which have been passed down through the generations, relating to the flood. They told how people took refuge in the Church Tower at Peterstone, of lucky escapes, such as the one related in the paragraph above. The water is supposed to have reached the bottom of St. Mellons Hill. A local farmer used to say that certain fields on his farm in St. Mellons had a feeling about them when he was there, sometimes making the hair stand up on the back of his neck. Bodies were supposed to have been washed up in this area. It is also said that a large number of bodies were buried in a communal grave near Rumney Church.

The lines on this pillar outside the Environment Agency in St.Mellons indicate the level, A.O.D. (above ordnance datum) that certain tides might reach if the Sea wall was breached. The level reached by Great Flood of 1606 is second from bottom.

In 1610, a point of Law case refers to one Henry Dunn who was attempting to prove title to his customary farm of 27 acres, including 4 acres of warffe, which had formerly belonged to John Dunn but: - *'At the great fludde & invacion of the sea in those parts the said howse of the said John Dunne was broken by force of the said sea; and at that instant the cupboards chests and coffers of the said John Dunne wherein the evidences writings and copies of the Court Rolles of his were, which concerned the premises, were caryed away by the said fludd.'*

Research undertaken by Barrie Davies, a former resident of Rumney, indicates that the howse or house mentioned is Mallocks

Hold, which he believed to be the present Newton. This is confirmed by the fact that the present owners of Middle Newton Farm purchased from the Llanrumney Estate in 1960, the same 4 acres of grazing rights on Rumney Great Wharf, which were tied to the property. These grazing rights are written into the deeds of many farms on the Moors.

Why the change of name from Mallocks Hold to Newton? Barrie Davies stated that 'the name Newton was first used for this land in 1471'. He had a strong suspicion that at some time, probably in the 14th century, a settlement at Mallock's Hold, well outside the present sea-wall, became untenable and its tenants retreated to a new settlement, the present Newton. Two names were used for this area, Mallocks Hold and later the Commote of Newton.

Middle Newton Farm circa 1910, showing the new slate roof. The late Cliff Ward, who was born at Middle Newton in February 1905, remembered his mother telling him that on the night of his birth, rats were playing in the thatch and the chamber pot froze under the bed! The house was later modernised and a new slate roof added!

Sea Defences
For centuries, people living and working on the Wentloog Level, have had to maintain some sort of sea defence. The sea defences have been strengthened and raised many times in living memory; at the present time work is being carried out on the bank from the Rumney/Peterstone boundary towards the Rhymney River. A section of the old bank remains from when the bank was straightened out in the late 1960s. This now looks rather inadequate and no defence against the present height of the tides.

A section of the mediaeval sea wall near Maerdy Farm, Rumney is now a listed ancient monument, monitored by the Glamorgan and Gwent Archaeological Trust.

In 2002, the flood of 1606/7 became the subject of a study by Dr. Simon Haslett of Bath Spa University College and Dr. Ted Bryant of the University of Wollongong, Australia. Evidence collected suggested that the flood was not just due to a major storm but to a Tsunami. Reasons such as:

i. Fine weather on the morning of the flood.
ii. The fact that the sea appears to have been driven back, before the wave struck.
iii. Reference to a hilly sea and dazzling fiery mountains with myriads of arrows.
iv. The great speed of the wave.

Haslett and Bryant undertook field work in the area and found:

i. Erosion of rock, characteristic of high velocity water flow.
ii. Deposits of layer of sand from North Devon to Gloucester and to the Gower.
iii. Stacked boulders at and above high tide limits – only easily moved by tsunami waves.
iv. An earthquake along an active fault system under the sea south of Ireland.

Interest in tsunamis has increased following the devastation caused by the Asian Tsunami, which occurred on Boxing Day 2004.

CHURCHES AND CHAPELS IN RUMNEY AND
LLANRUMNEY

St. Augustine's Parish Church.

Parish churches in particular have had a major impact on local history throughout the centuries and St. Augustine's Parish Church is no exception. From the time when the first church, constructed of wood, was built on the present site in 1108 A.D., the Roman Catholic faith was observed, until the Reformation in the fifteenth century when King Henry VIII declared himself head of the English Church. When Queen Elizabeth I succeeded Henry, she offered a 'Settlement' to former Roman Catholic priests to change over to the new Protestant faith. Bishop Kitchen, who was the Bishop of Llandaff at the time, was one of the first to accept the Queen's Bounty and was soon followed by the newly-appointed William Powell, Vicar of Rumney.

In the thirteenth century the wooden building was replaced by a stone-built one without a tower or porch. These were added in the fifteenth century. In the meantime the church was not only a place of worship but also a safe haven from the marauding Welsh, who often came down from the hills killing and stealing from the local inhabitants. On one occasion, thirteen local people were butchered in such a raid. St. Augustine's has not developed like many other churches, due to the fact that, whilst it was situated in a very prosperous manor, there was no resident lord of the manor - hence the absence of a lady chapel.

The church derived its income from tythes on all land in the parish and it was from this income that provision was made for poor relief. As a safeguard from people who might be inclined to move from parish to parish to gain benefits, a system was designed whereby anyone wishing to move out of the parish, not only had to obtain the authority of their present church, but also had to be accepted into the new parish. Any newcomer found without such authority was often whisked away at night and abandoned.

Prior to the reign of King Henry VIII, no church records were kept, or those that existed, contained minimal information and were often badly maintained and of little value. The credit for changing the situation must go to Thomas Cromwell who was the King's very unpopular minister. He ordered in 1538 that each *'Parsone, Vicare, and curate shall kepe one boke or registere wherein ye shall write the day and yere of every wedding, christening and burying made within the Parish'.* The book was to be kept in a coffer with two keys, one for the vicar and the other for the churchwarden. It would appear, however that this order was not always obeyed, because nine years later in 1547, King Edward VI decreed that a fine be imposed for failure to conform. In 1598, Queen Elizabeth paid attention to the matter when she ruled that church records should be made on parchment for their better preservation. At the same time she ruled that all entries from the previous week, should be read out at the Sunday church services. Spasmodic inspections were made in an effort to ensure the proper upkeep of all records, not only of Registers but also of Churchwardens' and Parish Overseers' account books. Despite all these efforts Rumney Church Records for the sixteenth and seventeenth centuries are missing. We can therefore only refer back to May 1774 when the Reverend James Evans made the first entry in a new register.

The period of the Napoleonic wars brought about a general laxity in moral and religious values, resulting in a high rate of illegitimacy, so it was doubly unfortunate that the Reverend Edward Richards, vicar at the time, when making an entry in the baptismal register, found himself unable to spell the word illegitimate. After a few failed attempts, he abandoned his efforts and inserted 'baseborn' instead.

The following is an extract from a Terrier (a register of all houses, lands, people etc., from which the vicar gained some benefit) dated 16th June 1795 and signed by Edward Richards, Vicar, together with the Churchwardens and parishioners' representatives. Vicarage House adjoining the churchyard, is named as belonging to the vicar. Rooms, gardens and boundaries are defined. Other fees due to the vicar are then listed.

i.   One shilling and sixpence for every barrel of cider.
ii.   There is one shilling due to be paid to him for every tenth fleece of wool.
iii.   For every cow with calf 2½d

iv.   For every barren cow without calf that is milked 2d
v.   The tenth fish to be paid and delivered to the Vicarage House if demanded.
vi.   There is due to the Vicar 2d for every pig from young or old sows to be paid at three weeks old.
vii. For every horse-colt, a penny, for every mare-colt, a halfpenny.
viii. For a man and wife there is due 4d - for every person sixteen years old 2d – servants to be paid for by their Masters or Mistresses and Children to be paid for by the owner.
ix.   One penny to be paid for the garden by the owner.
x.   For every hive of bees swarmed, fourpence.
xi.   Burying a parishioner, nothing, except he is buried in the Chancel, if then three shillings and fourpence and if within the rails, six shillings and eightpence.
xii. For Baptizing a Child that is a Parishioner nothing, for baptizing a child that is not a parishioner one shilling.
xiii. Publishing the Banns 6d every Sunday, for marrying and banns or Licence, five shillings and one shilling for entering in the book.

Although the charges are shown as just a few pence, these were very substantial amounts in those days.

In 1804, William Humphreys became Vicar and appointed William Jones as curate. He remained curate for the next forty two years. At the time of his appointment, the church building was in a rather bad state and it was due to his assiduous attention to detail, that a marked improvement in both administration and the fabric of the building was brought about. It was Curate Jones who had the clay floor of the church covered with flagstones and a new rood screen installed. Historians have a special affection for this cleric because of his habit of leaving notes in the margins of church records, giving bits of information about people for whom he had performed a ceremony. Here too, was a man ahead of his time, in that he had long recognised the necessity to provide education for children. The 1870 Education Act was still some way off at the time of his death. In his will, however, he left £100.00 for the maintenance of a school. Building of the school, on the north side of the church, commenced soon after his death and it was opened in 1856. The church continues to prosper to the present day and is currently under the guidance and guardianship of Canon David Hathaway.

An interesting memorial in the churchyard in Rumney

A sad little tale is told about this young boy whose memorial is in St. Augustine's churchyard. The boy's father, William Stokes was a master stonemason who was employed to repair the church tower in March 1849. The boy and his mother went one day to the church to take dinner to Mr Stokes. Young Arthur took the basket of food up to his father and looked out over the parapet. Suddenly he became giddy and tumbled down from the tower to the great distress of his parents.

His father carved the following memorial to him : -

Twas near this place he met his death,
And in a moment fell,
He had not time to call on God,
Or bid his friends farewell

The memorial to Arthur Stokes and his family.

His sister died in 1850 aged two and his father in 1856 aged forty. His mother, however, died in 1893, aged seventy-nine, surviving two other children who died in their forties.

In 1958, the new parish church of St. Dyfrig was opened in Llanrumney to cater for the newly-developed housing estate. About the same time St. Hilary's Church was built in Greenway Road and the new Parish of Trowbridge was formed to cater for the large housing expansion east of Wentloog Road.

St. Augustine's Church, Rumney, with the old Vicarage to the right and open countryside in foreground, circa 1920.

The Wesleyan Church, built in 1929, on the site of Paradise Gardens, Wentloog Road. The present Methodist Church now stands in front.

47

The Methodist Church

In 1789, a William Jones was ordained and settled in Llanishen, Cardiff and in 1795 he petitioned the Bishop of Llandaff to register, for the celebration of divine worship the dwelling commonly called Pen-yr-Heol and belonging to Lewis Thomas, in the Parish of Rumney.

The first Wesleyan Methodist Chapel was built on the Village Green early in the nineteenth century. It was a small square building with a fire-grate and chimney, a high pulpit and six pews. Documents refer to a second chapel in 1874, but this may have been a refurbishment of the original building.

During the 19th century, the Welsh language was in common use and the chapel at that time was a part of Cardiff Welsh Wesleyan Circuit. Preaching plans of every circuit were printed. These gave details of weekly services and preachers appointed to take each church service. This practice continues. Several old plans survive which confirm that in 1823, services were held at 4 p.m. on alternate Sundays.

By 1863, services had increased to two every Sunday at 2p.m. and 6p.m., with a service at 7p.m., on alternate Mondays. By 1890 as the use of Welsh declined, services were conducted in English and the chapel became a part of the Cardiff English Wesleyan Methodist Circuit.

In 1910 a porch and schoolroom were added to the chapel and it was these enlarged premises which were sold in 1928 to the Gospel Hall, leaving the Methodists without a building. As a temporary measure, they had to use the Rumney War Memorial Hall until, in September 1929, their new chapel was opened, sited on the eastern side of Wentloog Road adjoining Percy Thomas' Nursery Gardens.

In 1937, the 2nd Rumney Girl Guide Company was formed under their Captain, Freda Clarke. After the World War II, more space was needed for expanding youth work as the Rumney Estate developed. A temporary hut was erected at the rear of the site, which provided room for a Sunday School, Youth Club and other week-night activities. In 1947, the 22nd Cardiff Boys' Brigade Company was formed under the captaincy of George Watkins, assisted by

Allen Hambly. The Company originally met on Sundays for Bible Class and on weeknights for drill parade. The Company continues to meet, welcoming boys between the ages of six and eighteen years.

The present church fronting Wentloog Road was opened in March 1956 and the old church building was converted to a hall, the two buildings linked by a two-storey classroom block. Funding for the building of the new church came from war damage compensation, when a decision was made not to rebuild the bombed Roath Road Methodist Church at the junction of Newport Road and City Road in Cardiff. In 2003, Rumney Methodist Church celebrated 180 years of Methodism.

In 1959, a new Methodist church was built in Llanrumney at the junction of Countisbury Avenue and Washford Road. Sadly this had to close in 1984 due to insurmountable building problems.

Gilead Chapel – Methodist Church – Gospel Hall.

The Gospel Hall

Rumney Gospel Hall stands on the site of the former Gilead Wesleyan Methodist chapel on the Green. Prior to 1928, services had been held for about three years in a loft on the corner of Cae Glas Road. During the war-years numbers declined, but started to increase in 1948. A larger building was needed and the decision was made to rebuild. By dint of hard work and dedication a new, much bigger building emerged over the years. In the new millennium the Gospel Hall is now very much part of the religious life of Rumney.

The Gospel Hall situated in Ball Road Llanrumney, is now known as the Community Church.

The Baptist Chapel

In 1882, three young men from Tredegarville Baptist Church in Cardiff came to Rumney to preach the gospel. With no proper premises they were invited to use the parlour at Mr Edward Tugwell's house. Both services and Sunday School continued to be conducted there for the next eight years. Eventually they were able to purchase a piece of land adjacent to Mr Tugwell's house and a church was erected on the site by Messrs. W.E.Turner & Son. (Mr William Turner was at the time a leader in the church.) On 27th November 1889, the new church situated on the site of the present Roman Catholic Church was opened by the Rev. Alfred Tilley.

The congregation grew rapidly and it was soon found necessary to build an extension. This was officially opened in 1899. Rumney itself, was now beginning to expand and the mother church recognised the need for a full time ministry. In 1927 the Rev. J. E. Collier from Chepstow was inducted. His ministry was very successful and the congregation soon outgrew the church. The present site in Tyr-y-Sarn Road was secured at a rental of £10 a year and the first sod was cut on 9th April 1929 by Mr. James Summers Jnr. of Cardiff. J. E. North & Sons generously offered to build the church at cost price. The church was completed and opened on 23rd September 1929.

When Mr Collier retired in 1937, the debt on the building had been cleared. Mrs Bowyer, a member of the church, bought the freehold and gave it to the church in memory of her husband. This was, however, not the end of the North family's generosity as they went on to supervise the building of a hall at the rear of the church, at a cost of £1,600. In 1948, as a result of many generous donations, the hall was opened free of debt. Meanwhile, Mr J.H.North had given £240 to start an organ fund. Mr.T.J.E. Price responded with a further gift of £100. Donations soon reached the required amount and in the early 1950s. the organ was duly installed There have been eight pastors in the history of the church including its present incumbent the Rev. Stuart Ryce Davies B.D.

In 1956, the Baptists of Llanrumney began meeting together at Penybryn School, with 80 children attending Sunday School. About this time they were given £4,000 from the proceeds of the sale of an old church at Cardiff Docks. The North Brothers once again stepped in with their well-known generosity and offered to build a church. The turf cutting on a site at the bottom of Burnham Avenue took place on the 13th December 1957. Siloam Baptist church opened its doors on 21st May 1958 with about 300 people present. The first Deaconess was Eileen Gane. Boys' and Girls' Brigade Companies were soon established, as was a Sisterhood. At the present time the church is not only a place of worship, but also a centre for various community activities.

The Baptist Chapel in Wentloog Road which was later the Roman Catholic Church. The house to the right of the picture is the present home of the priest and the former home of Edward Tugwell where the first Baptist services were held in Rumney.

51

The Roman Catholic Church

From the time of the Reformation until 1929, the Roman Catholic Church did not have a place of worship in Rumney, except for a period in the nineteenth century, when the Heywood family at Witla Court invited local people to use their private chapel. Subsequently they had to travel into Cardiff. In 1929, the Baptist chapel in Wentloog Road became available and was purchased by the Roman Catholic Church for the sum of £400. In 1931 after alterations, the chapel was consecrated. In 1938, the adjacent Maerdy House became available and was bought for conversion into a presbytery for a parish priest. Father John Mahoney was the first Parish Priest of a very large Parish which incorporated Peterstone Wentloog, St. Brides Wentloog, St. Mellons, Cefn Mably, Castleton and Marshfield, as far as the Ebbw Bridge at Newport.

In 1947, due to the influx of residents in newly-developing Rumney, the church could not accommodate the increased congregation and worshippers were bussed into Cardiff at 10.30am each Sunday. The bus became known as the Vatican Express. Father William Morris became priest in 1954 and in 1957 was responsible for the building of St. Cadoc's Church on the new Llanrumney Estate. In 1958, he started the building project of the present Church of the Blessed Sacrament in Wentloog Road which was officially opened by Archbishop McGrath in March 1960. The first person to serve Mass in the new church was Roger Brabyn whose parents were the first couple to be married in the old church. Canon Morris was also responsible for the building of the Parish Hall on the site of the former church (old Baptist chapel). His enterprise did not stop there, because new development was taking place at Trowbridge, so his endeavours turned to providing a school and church to serve the area. By late 1975, he had completed his task and St. John Lloyd Church and School were established.

The Church of the Blessed Sacrament holds what is believed to be a unique record, in that four of its organists have been exceptionally young. The first was Leisha Hayter, just nine and a half years old, followed by Carmel Hugglestone and then Geraldine Affley. Carmel Davies nee Hugglestone, spent some time away from Rumney after her marriage, during which time a young man, John

52

Cope took over. He was the eldest of the quartet at just under twelve years of age. On her return Carmel once again became the sole organist and is still there, making her tenure about fifty years. Another record worth noting is the service of June Cody who was housekeeper to Canon Morris for some thirty-six years.

Time for a chat at the stile. (pre lych-gate days.)

The very stylish wedding of Miss Cubitt, Rumney House in 1914.
Harry Pacey, coachman to the Cubitts in shiny topper.

CHURCH AND CHAPELS IN ST. MELLONS

St. Mellons Parish Church

The ancient parish church of St. Mellons has a dignity and an atmosphere which is all its own. The settlement or village of St. Mellons grew around the early Christian foundation. According to Professor Edward Augustus Freeman, the famous historian and authority on Church architecture, who lived at nearby Llanrumney Hall, the large size of St. Mellons church is a reflection of the principle of our ancestors, that the larger the church, the greater the glory to God.

St.Mellons Church on the hill overlooking the village.

The church is set upon a hill, visible from a great deal of the surrounding area and its strong square embattled tower commands excellent views. At one time an illuminated cross on the tower served as a landmark for shipping in the Bristol Channel. The present church building, dating from approx. 1360 A.D. and described as a building of the *Decorated* style with the exception of the porch, must have had a predecessor of even greater size. During restoration work on the font, its steps were found to be part of a massive Norman pier - evidence of the Normans at St. Mellons. Mr. A. H. Williams, former headmaster of St. Mellons School, stated that it was also likely that there was an even earlier wattle and daub church on the site. Professor Freeman had no doubt that St. Mellons certainly possessed a church in the 12th century.

The church has been considerably modified, particularly during the late Perpendicular period in the 15th century. Its main entrance was formerly at the base of the tower but this was changed into a window and the main entry blocked. The south porch entrance then took its place. There is a splendid well-preserved cradle-roof dating from 1400 A.D. and it is large for a Welsh church, being approximately 105 feet long. It has a long broad Nave, a short narrow Chancel and attached to the Chancel is a North Chapel, formerly the cemetery of the Morgan family of Llanrumney Hall and now known as the Llanrumney Chapel. In the south, forming a transept, is a Lady Chapel. The Lady Chapel has two arches opening into the Nave and one into the Chancel. The Chancel and Llanrumney Chapel are entered from the Nave by two arches of different size, side by side and divided by a pillar. This arrangement is unique and in the words of Professor Freeman 'of singular effect'.

There are signs of a large Rood loft - a Roman Catholic feature - stretching across the two arches at the east of the Nave. The little stone staircase in the wall near the present pulpit would have given access to this Rood loft. This was obviously an added feature after the original wall was built, for there are signs of the wall having been widened and an arch having been filled in.

Between the Chancel and the Llanrumney Chapel to the north, there is a large squint which would have enabled worshippers to see the priest at the time of the elevation of the Host during the Communion Service. It is important to remember that at one time, St. Mellons Church would have belonged to the Church of Rome and services were sung in Latin. In the early 20th century it was part of the Church of England, in the Diocese of Llandaff, in the Province of Canterbury. Nowadays, it belongs to the Church in Wales, in the Diocese of Monmouth, in the Province of Wales.

A statement from Archaeologica Cambrensis, dated 1857, notes that the walls at that time were white-washed. The solid open pews were also painted white at one time and did not fill the church. A photograph taken at the turn of the century and reproduced in a

1992 church magazine, shows the church with a Tabernacle on the altar before the Rood screen was erected by Matthew Cope in memory of his wife. The church, at that time, was lit by oil lamps which were mounted half-way along the pews.

Electric lighting was not installed until 1953 in the time of Vicar Gower-Rees, when work was also done on cleaning and treating with wood preservative, the whole of the roof timbers to prevent further ravages by the wood-boring beetle. Decayed roof timbers were renewed, as were decayed stone mullions in the east window. At the same time plastered portions between the roof timbers were lime-washed and exterior faces of main walls were re-pointed.

Interior of St. Mellons Parish Church – 1906.

There is a belfry and bell-chamber in which hang six bells, five of which were originally cast in 1713. The six bells were re-cast in 1913 in the time of the Rev. Stephen Jackson and bear the original inscriptions. Fund-raising is in progress in the new Millenium to enable restoration work to be undertaken on the bells and bell-frame. In recent years, thanks to fund-raising by parishioners and to a Heritage Grant, much restoration work has been completed on the roof, porch and exterior walls, but the pipe-organ, dating from 1907, although still in place under one of the arches opening into the Nave from the Lady Chapel, has sadly been superseded by an electronic instrument. Parishioners must have been very pleased in 1954, when a faculty was granted for the installation of a new gas-fired low pressure central heating system in the church. Much of the same system is still in use today.

Windows in St. Mellons Church vary in construction, some dating from the 14th century, whilst others are no older than those in the neighbouring parish churches of Rumney and Llanedeyrn, dating from the reign of Richard II. The church has many fine stained-glass windows, among them the beautiful east window given in 1937 by Sir William Cope K.S., of Quarry Hill in memory of his parents. Previously in 1917, a stained-glass window was placed in the Llanrumney Chapel in memory of Mr. G. C. Williams J.P. of Llanrumney Hall, who was churchwarden for many years. In 1920, another stained-glass window was given as an offering of thanks for the safe return from World War I of Captains R. C. and W. H. Wilson.

St. Mellons Church Registers date back to the year 1722 and until 1812, they are on parchment. Church Records are now preserved in the archives of the Gwent Record Office. Interestingly, the list of incumbents of St. Mellons Church compiled from the Llandaff Diocesan Records deposited in the National Library of Wales, gives much earlier details of the succession of Vicars than those listed on the notice board hanging in church. There are several discrepancies, for the notice-board includes curates who may have had responsibility for the church when there was no incumbent. The early details are as follows: -

Incumbents of St.Mellons.

William Jones. Jan. 1540/41
William Thomas July 1582
Robert Williams.* Feb. 1612
Griffith Thomas. June 1669
Thomas Harris. July 1736
Howell Thomas. Dec. 1788

David Lewys. Feb. 1554/45
Robert Williams. April 1607
Henry Williams. Dec. 1665
Thomas Lingen Apr. 1716
William Edwards. Apr.1740/43
William Berkin Meakham. Mar. 1798

John Sunderland. Mar, 1799　　　　　William Williams. Jan. 1807
Thomas Price. Mar. 1808　　　　　　　Edward Jenkins. June 1846
John Williams Evans. Nov. 1864　　　 Theophilus Rees. Nov. 1893
Stephen Jackson. May 1908

St. Mellons Church notice-board lists the following additions:
John Evans. Curate 1760　　　　　　　Edward Bevan. Curate. 1840
Erasmus Parry. Curate. 1845.　　　　　J. Philip Jones. Curate. 1907

More recent incumbents are then listed:
Connop L. Price. 1927.　　　　　　　　T. Parry Price. 1949
C.R. Gower Rees. 1952.　　　　　　　　W.D. Llewellyn. 1977
David Kellen. 1988.

At the entrance to Church Lane, there is a simple carved Lych-Gate of dignified beauty, with inscriptions in both Welsh and English. In the lower part of the churchyard, there is the stump of an old stone Cross. Legend has it that the top was hidden in the church-yard, at the time Oliver Cromwell's Roundheads were nearby at Cefn Mably. Near the Porch entrance to the church, stands the Hemingway Memorial in the shape of a severed column. The column represents Life and the fact that Death might cut short that Life at any time. The Lych-gate, Stone Cross and the Hemingway Memorial are all listed as being of architectural and historic interest, as indeed is St. Mellons church.

St Mellons Baptist Church.

In 1794, at a time of General Reform, Revolution and possible French Invasion, about ten poor, largely uneducated worshippers met in an upper rented room of St. Mellons Workhouse. They declared themselves to be 'A Congregation of Protestant Dissenters called Particular or Calvinistic Baptists.' The story had begun in 1642, when King Charles raised his standard at Nottingham. Civil War followed and that event also began a chain of events which contributed to the beginning of Baptist witness at St. Mellons.

In 1649, at Ilston-on-the-Gower, the first Baptist Church on Welsh ground had come into being with John Miles, Puritan 'lecturer' or preacher and 'approver' or magistrate for Llanelli, appointed as its pastor by the Cromwellian Government of

58

1642-1660. William Pritchard of Blaenau, a disciple of John Miles was granted a licence to preach under the 1672 Act of Indulgence, at his own house in Llantilio Pertholy near Abergavenny and later a church was established at Llanwenarth. From the Llanwenarth Church, preaching stations were set up in Monmouthshire.

In 1713, believers were baptised at nearby Castleton and it is thought that some of those were, in fact, St Mellons people. For the next 43 years believers from Castleton and St. Mellons then worshipped in the kitchens of local farmhouses with Castleton and St. Mellons enjoying close family and community links. In 1756, all the Llanwenarth members, including those of Castleton and St. Mellons, were formed into a church which met at Cefn, Tydu, known today as Bethesda, Rogerstone.

The first proof of believers meeting in St. Mellons is in the Caersalem Church Book of 1854. 1t states 'Preaching began here in 1794 in a dwelling-house for the poor of the parish.' This workhouse was used until 1830 when the first chapel was built. The original small Caersalem Chapel was built in what is now the chapel graveyard and the congregation numbered 22.

Castleton believers had already formed into a church independently of Rogerstone and in 1841, the congregation at St. Mellons was also formed into a separate church called Caersalem. Mr. Owen Jones, minister of the church at Llanidloes became the first minister of a truly independent Caersalem in the spring of 1842 with a low agreed salary of 'one shilling a day and all his beer.' Owen Jones' preaching drew large numbers and a gallery was added to the chapel. Unfortunately, Owen Jones had on 'over fondness' for strong drink and within a short time he left for Pembrokeshire.

Caersalem joined the County Association of churches in 1842 and three ministers served in the next 28 years. Mr. David Evans was ordained, stayed for 9 years and in 1854, Rev. William Williams settled at St. Mellons. When he left in 1858, membership stood at 78, with a Sunday School of 60 and 10 teachers. During this time of Revival, many people were converted and Baptist communicants had risen, by 1871 membership at Caersalem was more than 100.

Then followed a time of language transition and theological uncertainty. English was replacing Welsh in the County as the everyday language of the people but Welsh was still in use in church services. Caersalem was without a pastor, the pulpit being largely supplied by students from the Pontypool Baptist College. Surprisingly, the church actually added to its membership. In addition, a membership of 17 was transferred to Rumney where a church was formed in 1890 under the auspices of the church in Tredegarville, Cardiff. It was during this time too, that a step in faith was taken to erect a new chapel, Caersalem Newydd. The chapel was built in 1884, the site having been a free gift of Richard Allen Esq. who lived in nearby 'Ty-To Maen.' The building was to cost £1,516 excluding the cost of haulage of material, namely stone from local quarries and sand from the river at Pandy Farm. Just as happens today, the estimate was exceeded, for the chapel, duly erected and ready for worship cost £2,000.

Caersalem Baptist Chapel Tyr Winch Road St. Mellons.

The Opening Service was held in May 1884 and the pastors were Rev. Dr. John Rhys Morgan (Lleurwg) of Llanelly and the Rev. Dr. Thomas Davies of Haverfordwest College. Both had been born and brought up in St. Mellons, receiving their early religious experience and instruction in the old chapel. During the early 20th century, there followed a period of far- reaching social and political changes. The church reached its peak, both spiritually and numerically, but then followed a decline in the life of the church. In 1934, the Golden Jubilee of the present chapel was celebrated and with it the induction of the church's eleventh pastor, the Rev. W. H. Jones whose pastorate was to last nearly 25 years. No records survive of the next 15 years but were resumed when the newly-appointed Church Secretary Mr. W. George Cox returned from active service in World War II. In August 1958, Pastor Jones retired at the age of 84 years.

Mr. Russell Williams of the South Wales Bible College, Barry, was invited to the pastorate of Caersalem following a period of student pastorate. After completing theological training, Mr Williams became pastor in September 1966. Membership of the church then stood at 35 but by 1971 had risen to 72. There were also 100 in attendance at Sunday School with church members providing a shuttle with their cars to bring the children in from the surrounding estate. A problem of too few committed Sunday School teachers was resolved with witnesses of conversions and baptisms. In March 1971, Caersalem seceded from the Baptist Union. In May 1980, when the new Baptist Assembly came into being, Caersalem became one of its founder members. In the early 1990s, Caersalem affiliated to the A.E.C.W. (Associating Evangelical Churches of Wales), strengthening its long association with the Evangelical Movement of Wales.

St Mellons had changed from a semi-rural village to a large East Cardiff urban spread with many thousands of inhabitants and Caersalem soon recognised a need for outreach and expansion on the new estate. Initially there were tensions between old and new communities, but recognising the inevitability of change, these have now eased.

Rev. Russell Williams retired from the pastorate in July 1999, after 33 years service. The church is greatly indebted to him for his ministry and he and his family are regarded with much affection not only by church members, but by all the community of St. Mellons. Rev. Andrew Christofides, who began his ministry on September 11th 2000, now leads Caersalem in the 21st century.

Wesleyan Methodism

John Wesley visited Cardiff on April 9th 1740 and again on Thursday October 1st 1741, having made a brief visit to Newport in 1739 where he preached 'to the most insensible ill-behaved people' he had met in Wales. In response to a request from Howell Harris, Wesley returned to Wales a few weeks later, when he visited two or three places in Glamorgan, and then returned to Newport. Although there is no mention of Rumney or St. Mellons in his journal, Wesley must have used the old turnpike road and paid a toll to cross the river at Rumney when coming to Cardiff after preaching at Newport.

The 1846 Tithe Map records that as well as the Parish Church there were two chapels: - the Baptist chapel opposite the entrance to the Parish church and the Calvinistic Methodist chapel. The Religious Census of Wales of 1851, shows that apart from the Parish Church, there were three chapels in St. Mellons Parish (population 637) :

    i.   Bethania – Calvinistic Methodist. Erected 1820. Average morning attendance 120. Afternoon, scholars 90. Evening 170.

    ii.   Soar Independent. Erected 1837. Seating 122 and standing 50. Average attendance 100.

    iii.   Caersalem Baptist. Erected 1830. Seating 229 and standing 100. Average attendance a.m.150, p.m. 200.

Was there ever a Wesleyan Methodist Chapel in St. Mellons?

The only document that gives a clue is the Wesleyan Methodist Preaching Plan for the Cardiff English Circuit for July/Oct 1852. This plan shows the circuit divided into two sections with nine preaching places in the Cardiff area (including the Wesleyan Day School in Working Street) and five preaching places in the Pontypridd area. St. Mellons appears ninth on the list with a Sunday service at 3 p.m. and an evening meeting on alternate Mondays at 7 p.m. In the absence of a Wesleyan Chapel, it is likely that services were held in private houses or by arrangement, in either the Calvinistic Methodist Chapel House or the Independent Chapel.

Calvinistic Methodism in St. Mellons.

In May 1920, the Centenary and Jubilee of Bethania Presbyterian Church of Wales, Calvinistic Methodists, were held at St. Mellons. The Presbyterian Church in Wales (Calvinistic Methodists) was the result of a series of revivals which began in Wales in about 1735. The Calvinistic Methodist cause therefore goes back to the 18th century when Rev. Daniel Rowland, Llangeitho and Rev. Howell Harris of Trevecca awakened Welsh people to the moral, social and religious darkness in which they lived.

In 1776, Edward Coslett moved from Machen to Castleton to follow his trade as a country blacksmith. Whilst at Machen, he had been converted under the ministry of William Edwards of Groeswen, a Methodist preacher who won fame as the builder of the famous one-arched bridge over the River Taff at Pontypridd. Coslett started religious services in his own house over the smithy and these services attracted Miss Blanche Evans of Peny-pil Farm St. Mellons, together with others of Methodist leanings. Miss Blanche Evans had been persuaded to join the Revivalists by the Methodist vicar of Llangan, the Rev. David Jones. Both Coslett and Miss Evans were members of the church at Llangan and attended monthly Communion Service, Coslett on foot, Miss Evans on her palfrey. (lady's saddle-horse)

In 1779, Sunday School started in the cottage of John Morgan of Tyn-y-ffynon and its founder was Shon Bowen of Tyn y Parc. Mr. A. H. Williams, former St. Mellons Village School Headmaster, stated in his notebooks that Methodist services were also held in a cottage in Bethania Row. This was the first real home of the Methodist cause at St. Mellons and when they erected their first chapel, they remained at that place. The first Methodist Chapel was not built in St. Mellons until 1820, ten years after the death of Rev. David Jones. Land for the chapel was given by Mr. Thomas Lloyd of Brynhyfryd, St. Mellons and there were many local donations. It was erected on the western side of the present churchyard with its front facing the Moors and its back on the main lower road to Cardiff at that time. Chapel House is all that remains of it. The chapel accommodated 30 worshippers. The leader in the Calvinistic Movement was the first minister Rev. Henry Jones, a tenant of Miss Blanche Evans.

In 1823, new Deacons were elected. Young men were called to take the place of their fathers, having been nurtured in the cause. Workers came from Rumney, St. Mellons and the Moors. In 1828, members of the Methodist connexion used to walk 16 miles to Cowbridge to take Communion. They started out at 2 or 3 a.m. and returned the same day. Pilgrims walked but were accompanied by a wagon which picked up the weary.

The chapel was reconstructed in 1841. Miss Blanche Evans did much for the church, for poor preachers, the poor of the parish and for the cause at St. Mellons. When she died, she was buried in the graveyard of the church she loved. In 1869, the present chapel was built to seat 500 persons and was opened in May 1870, at a total cost of £2,200.The builder reduced this amount by £500 after members undertook haulage towards the building and the old church materials were used in the walling. Clerics or preachers were poorly paid. One preacher, Rev. David Evans, was given a sovereign instead of a shilling for preaching two sermons. Daniel Evans, the treasurer, ran after the preacher, catching up with him on Rumney Hill where the sovereign was duly returned and the shilling substituted. On another occasion, 3/6 was paid to a cleric for his day's work.

During the years 1830 to 1850, there was healthy rivalry between the Baptist and Methodist Sunday Schools. It appears that many students attended both, for that of the Baptists was held in the morning and that of the Methodists in the afternoon. Some families had members of both churches and it was said that girls were often attracted to the Baptist cause by the glamour of open baptism in the River Rhymney. The Rev. David James, who definitely added fame to the honoured name of Llaneurwg in Methodism, was sent, with his two older brothers to the Baptist Sunday School, where he was taught by Rev. J. R. Morgan. (Lleurwg) David James later became a shining light in the Welsh Methodist pulpit and a great asset to the church at St. Mellons. In spite of a poor early education he made himself one of the most potent influences in the religious life of his day. He is also famous for starting a day school at St. Mellons about the middle of the 19th century. The church was also proud of its two other young lads who became preachers. Edmund Edmunds and his brother, Abraham, also held honourable places in the history of the church.

In 1882, an American organ was purchased for the chapel at a cost of £27-11s-0d. In 1884 and 1886 ministers left the neighbourhood but membership did not decline. In 1888, it was decided to conduct services entirely in English, mainly for the sake of the young of the church who had lost the capacity to converse in their native tongue. In the early part of the 20th century, however, at times morning services were still held in Welsh.

During the early 1900s, three new pastors came and went, outstanding debt on the building was reduced and new heating apparatus was installed in the chapel after laudable fund-raising.

Methodist Chapel, St. Mellons.

By 1920, when its centenary was celebrated, the chapel was known as Bethania Presbyterian Church in Wales. After the Revivals in Wales, when the Methodists opened their chapels, Presbyterians would find a form of service with which they were fairly familiar. Regular worship continued through the 20th century and many residents of today still talk of the joy of singing and worshipping, of attending Sunday School and of being married at Bethania. Unfortunately, due to a general decline in church attendance in the

1970s the church was closed and the building sold. Bethania Chapel was then bought for use as an Independent Presbyterian place of worship. At the present time services are held in the building and it is a meeting place for young people and for evangelism.

The Welsh Independent Chapel erected between 1837 and 1840 in the centre of the village, was a single storey structure with a slate-hipped roof. There were three tall round-headed arches with shorter round-headed windows to the front of the building. At the rear there was a small burial ground. Use of the building as a place of worship had ceased by the end of the nineteenth century. During the 20th century the building had several uses including a sports and social club, an educational centre and a meeting hall for the Women's Institute. In the 1970s the building was acquired by the Jehovah Witnesses and was known as Kingdom Hall. In the 21st Century it is once again a place of worship.

OPERATION OF THE POOR LAW

It is well known that the Tudors made the mediaeval parish, already organized on a religious basis, into an instrument for Poor Relief, since a system of control could be offered through its church-wardens.

    Rating had earlier been based on voluntary contributions, but an Act of Parliament introduced in 1572, made it compulsory and ordered that Overseers of the Poor and other parochial officers be appointed. To ensure that this procedure was respected and to safeguard the system, Tudor Justices of the Peace were empowered to assess the rates if parish officials failed to carry out their duties and supervise expenditure. Later Acts of Parliament in the seventeenth and eighteenth centuries expanded the duties of parish officials and Justices of the Peace, whilst introducing innovations whenever Government thought fit. These new regulations enabled the Justices to hear appeals from the poor, if the parish had refused relief. Justices could also intervene to appoint competent overseers or other officials. At the same time, the regulations gave them power over parish officials and empowered them to levy a general rate through the Vestries.

There were two kinds of Vestries, open and closed. Open Vestries were attended by a fairly large number of principal parishioners, who were ratepayers. It was from this group that the Overseer of the Poor and the Surveyor of Highways were appointed. Unlike the Vestry Clerk, they were unpaid. Closed Vestries were made up of men who were usually life members. An Overseer's main concern was, of course, the needs of the poor, but records of disbursements show that he was called upon occasionally to carry out other duties, such as accompanying unmarried mothers to register their children, compiling militia lists and the destruction of vermin.

In 1662, an Act of Parliament gave the Overseer certain rights over all persons who inhabited dwellings worth ten pounds a year or less. Anyone in this category was likely to become a charge on the Poor Rates and could be moved back to his or her place of birth. This applied mainly to the old, infirm, infants and labourers likely to become poor. Payments were made for Outdoor Relief to the aged, to widows overburdened with children, to wives whose husbands were ill or in prison and to help the poor with their rents. Relief was also given in kind, by way of clothes, coal, shoes and medical attention. There was an obligation to board children and to issue certificates to labourers seeking work elsewhere. Such certificates were issued because of an agreement between parishes, that if a man became chargeable on the Poor Rates, he would be returned to his own parish. Foot passes to sailors were another charge on the parish and there were regular disbursements in the accounts for this charge, since Rumney and St. Mellons were on the route between two ports. A 1714 Act of Parliament, which protected sailors from being classed as vagabonds, read as follows:-

'All persons shall be deemed as rogues and vagabonds except soldiers, mariners and seafaring men licensed by some testimonial or writing under the hands and seal of a Justice of the Peace setting down the time and place of his or their landing and the place to which they have to pass.'

Disbursements were many, so it was essential that proper accounts were kept. In 1743 an order was made to compel Overseers to keep Poor Law accounts. Failure to do so became punishable by a further order in 1792. King Edward VI classified the poor as follows:-

i.   Poor by impotency, meaning, children, the aged and the diseased.
ii.   Poor by casualty, namely the discharged soldier, the decayed householder and those in ill-health.
iii. The thriftless, vagabonds and the idle.

Rumney Poor Law

In Rumney, Vestries held to discuss matters concerning the Poor Law in the early nineteenth century, took place at one of two locations, Pen- yr-Heol, or the Pear Tree Inn (Rompney Castle). In addition to the Poor Law, the parish had to raise a rate to meet the yearly charge of nine pounds on the Rhymney River Bridge and a further Highways Rate plus the Level Rate applicable to the low-lying areas. The total rate bill for the year April 1825 to March 1826, amounted to approx. £340. It became necessary to control expenditure covering hospitality at Vestry meetings. Disbursements for six years from 1825 in the Overseers accounts illustrate aspects of parish relief. The most prominent group in the accounts are the aged poor. Most of these people lived in village cottages and received rent allowances. At that time, there was only one Poor House, which was owned by the church, although almshouses were later provided on the village green.

A further category of the designated poor was (iv) the sick labourer. The Overseer was authorised to give relief to some of these to augment wages. If the poor labourer had a family, the parish could make allowances for his children, or could board out some of his children. John Mathews, a labourer, is shown in the Surveyor of Highways accounts, as earning one shilling a day, so it is not surprising that he needed to seek assistance. In 1826, he was removed from his home in Beili Bach, at a cost of five shillings. He was then allowed five shillings relief, eight shillings and sixpence for coal, four shillings for a shirt and nine shillings further relief. His daughter was given an allowance of seven shillings and sixpence. An outstanding example of relief was that given to Isaac Richards, an agricultural labourer at Downton Farm who married in 1800. At least four children were born between the years 1808 and 1822. During the period 1825 to 1831, he was given eighteen pounds for rent in addition to free coal. In 1825, he was also given subsistence for twelve weeks at two shillings a week. In 1826, a further period of subsistence was allowed and he obtained small sums to purchase clothes etc. In 1838 Isaac sought parish assistance, finding it impossible to live on 1/- a day for five and a half days' work.

Rumney poor houses in Brachdy Road where the Library now stands.

The boarding-out system originally designed for the ailing and infirm, later favoured children and was a relief to poor parishioners, both from a space and subsistence point of view. Such a case was that of Edmund Edmunds, a shoemaker, who, although a craftsman, also suffered from a chronic condition and sought relief to pay his rent. The parish also paid Mary Evans one pound nineteen shillings to nurse the child of Edmund Edmunds for about three months. This support continued for a further two years.

An entry in the Overseers accounts for the second quarter of 1825 describes a payment made to Merthyr Tydfil for the suspension of an order of removal and relief to Thomas Llewellin and his family of Merthyr. Ann Llewellin, his wife, received three shillings a week relief and Thomas himself was handsomely treated. A statement attached to the Parish accounts stated that Thomas Llewellin went to work in Merthyr by certificate on September 1st 1825 and promised to pay eight shillings a week to support his family. Provided that the eight shillings was paid regularly, the parish was prepared to give assistance to his wife and children. Ann Llewellin received in excess of five pounds, also a bed-gown and flannel for petticoats for six months. This dropped to three shillings a week, due to the failure of her husband to make his promised payment. After September, no more payments were recorded. Ann had died in the poorhouse and an account was rendered as follows:-

i.	To coffin for Ann Llewellin £1-10s-0d
ii.	To digging grave and the passing Bell 2/6
iii.	To shifts and caps 3/-
iv.	To half pound of soap 4½d
v.	To beer at burial and bottle of ale at laying out corpse 3/-

The children remained the responsibility of the parish, but it is thought that prior to their mother's death, they had been boarded out due to her ill-health. There was no further reference to the children. Their father, however, was arrested and a further record in the accounts in early 1826, details that three shillings was paid to apprehend Thomas Llewellin, plus half a crown for the cost of the journey.

Subsistence for boys was always smaller than that for girls, since boys could earn money for killing vermin. All manner of birds and animals were in the vermin category, a John Thomas was paid 1s-4d for killing hedgehocks, (hedgehog). Mary Collins for killing a fitchock, (polecat) 8d, Daniel Edmunds and Ada Rees for two polecats 1s-4d and the son of William Rees for killing 4 hedgehocks 1s-4d Edward Evans earned 1s-0d for two moles and Isaac Timothy received 4s-0d for killing sixteen dozen birds. There were other ways in which the poor could supplement their income. Mary Harry, a needlewoman, who lived in the Poorhouse, was often called upon by the Overseer to make garments for the poor. The parish also paid her to make bedding and shrouds.

Poor relief paid for medical attention. The overseer would occasionally call upon a doctor from Cardiff to minister to the sick. Swearing of illegitimate children was compulsory by law, which meant that a woman pregnant with a bastard child, had to declare the matter and name the father. If the man named was unable to provide securities, he was sent to gaol for a month. The system was sometimes abused and a single promiscuous woman, unscrupulous enough to blame any man able to pay for her child, would readily victimise a quite innocent man. Rumney had its share of promiscuous women, such as Ann Richard, Leah Thomas, and Mary John, who appear in the Overseer's accounts on frequent occasions.

The treatment of vagrants was quite inhumane. Starving families and the sick were pushed from parish to parish, as quickly as possible, in order to save charges on the parish. The parish had a duty to provide sustenance for twenty-four hours and to convey them for one mile out of the parish.

Poor Law in St. Mellons

St. Mellons Vestry Meetings were held alternately in the White Hart and Bluebell Inns until 1854, when the Poor House was purchased for two shillings and six pence for use as a school. When the Rate was set, it had to be announced in church on the Sunday after the Rate had been allowed by the Justices. This was followed by a celebration with much drinking and feasting. The St. Mellons Poor Accounts for the period March-July 1805, have the following entries which indicate that there was certainly celebration when the rates were set that year :-

i.   Paid   - David William for ale at a parish meeting 15/6
ii. Paid   - Thos. Edmund for ale at 2 Vestrys 14/-

Outdoor relief had to be paid by the Overseer to the aged, to labourers and to women with many children. Women whose husbands were in prison or ill, had to be helped, rents had to be paid for the poor and relief given such as coal, clothes, shoes and medical attention. Often the full expenses of a funeral were accounted for out of the Poor Rate.

In St. Mellons, the building known to many residents as the old village school on the Ton and now sadly destroyed by fire, was erected as a Poor House between the years 1629 and 1631.

St.Mellons Poor Accounts:-
March-July 1805: -
Margt Richard 2 sacks coal 2/2
Keeping her for 13 weeks 19/6
Dr. Brewer for curing Thos. Harry. £3-3-0d

29th October 1813 - 21st January 1814
David Rosser £3-16s-0d - 13 weeks' keep.
Paid for burying his wife £2-12s-2d
Paid to move household goods of David Rosser from Malpas 2/-
Paid for washing David Rosser's bed and shirt 1/-
Paid for filling his bed with chaff 1/-
Paid for pair of bed cords for ditto 2/-
Paid for setting up bedstead for ditto 6/-
2 journeys to Malpas concerning David Rosser 6/-
Paid for candles 2d; writing paper and a letter concerning Illegitimate - 10d
2nd Apr. 1824 - 2nd July 1824.
Abednego Gabriel 13 weeks £2-5-6
Pair of shoes and stockings for ditto 11/6
Wm. Rowland's son
2½yds and 6 yds of flannel, thread, cloth and making 7/-
Pair of stockings 1/6
2 ½ yards of Duck for a smock 3s-6½d.
Thread 4d. Making smock 1/-, 1½ yards of fustian 3/9d
Thread, buttons & making 1/5
Thos. Phillip half-year house rent £1-10-0
Mary Rowland 1 yr house rent £2.
Keeping Ann Morgan 5 weeks £1-3-0, Midwife 5/-
Keeping her son 12 weeks £1-10-0
Pair of quarter boots for Issac Morgan 7/6
Pair of shoes for Lewis Harry 10/-
Parish Records St. Mellons
Labourers hired for Highway Repairs *1828-29 and 1835-36.*
24th Oct. 1828 Abraham Edmunds, blacksmith, for mending parish tools. 7/7
14th Oct. 1829.
Stones and Hauling.
William Matthews for a cart, 3 horses and a man for 3 days hauling stones to the road. £1-14-0

24th Oct. 1829.

Lewis Harry 6 days 7/-

(Note - the rate of pay in 1829 for a hard day's work was 1s-2d and the same rate of pay still applied in 1835. Pay rises were few or none.)

With the consent of the Churchwardens and Vestry, children had to be boarded, labourers seeking work elsewhere had to be given certificates and there was a responsibility for the upkeep of the Poor House. Overseers had been compelled by the Order of 1743-44 to keep Poor Accounts. Failure to do so was made punishable in 1792. The Poor Law Amendment Act in 1834, established a Board of Guardians in each parish who authorised the building of Workhouses. Thus the needs of the poor, sick and aged within the parish of St. Mellons, were, to some extent, gradually met.

The old school on the Ton in St. Mellons. This building was originally used as a Poor House.

73

Friendly Societies.

Conditions changed with the formation of the Friendly Societies in the latter part of the nineteenth century. By paying as little as a penny a week people were helped to obtain benefits in time of need. Some poor people were unable to afford even that amount. As far back as 1823, a group of well-meaning men including two from Rumney and one from St. Mellons appeared at Monmouthshire Assizes at Usk, seeking authority to promote a Friendly Society in the villages. The following is a part of the transcript of their application:

To the Worshipful his Majesty's Justices of the Peace for the County of Monmouth in their General Quarter Sessions of the Peace assembled.
The Humble Memorial and Petition of William Morgan of the Parish of Rumney in the County of Monmouth Gentleman Thomas Morgan of the same Parish and County Carpenter Thomas Jenkins of the Parish of St. Mellons in the same County Yeoman George Stephens of the said Parish of Rumney in the said County Innholder John Morgan of the Town of Cardiff in the County of Glamorgan Gentleman Evan Thomas of the Parish of Rumney in the said County of Monmouth Gentleman and others.
Sheweth that your Memorialists are desirous of forming themselves into a friendly Society to provide for the maintenance and assistance of the Members thereof their wives and children in sickness infancy old age and widowhood under the authority and subject to the provisions of a Certain Act of Parliament made and passed in the fifty-ninth year of the reign of His late Majesty King George the Third Entitled "An Act for the further Protection and Encouragement of Friendly Societies and for preventing Frauds and Abuses therein." And we propose that The Reverend William Jones Rector of Rumney The Reverend David Davies Vicar of Marshfield and William Morgan of Rumney aforesaid Gentleman All Substantial Freeholders and severally assessed to the Relief of the Poor upon a Sum not less than Fifty pounds and whose hands are hereunto subscribed and set by the Trustees of such Society and that the said Society be governed by the Rules Orders and Regulations.....................

Poor Law legislation can be traced back to the time of Queen Elizabeth I and poor relief over the country in the nineteenth century was very unsatisfactory and unjust. Within 16,000 parishes, many grouped themselves together and set up workhouses. No doubt the

Parish Councils were only too happy when they lost their responsibility for the poor as this work was transferred to elected Boards of Guardians. In 1836 the County of Glamorgan was divided into 5 Poor Law Unions: Bridgend and Cowbridge, Cardiff, Merthyr Tydfil, Neath and Swansea. The Cardiff Poor Law Union consisted of 45 parishes including the parishes of Rumney and St. Mellons.

The following are extracts from the accounts of the Cardiff Board of Guardians.

Half year ending 25th March 1853.

Parish of Rumney   Thomas Baker - Guardian

Mery Charles aged 79 years requesting relief for old age 3/- per week 26 weeks - £3-18-0

Edward Edmunds aged 63 years   Old age Illness 2/6 per week 26 weeks - £3-5-0

John Rees aged 13 years Orphan - 26 weeks @ 4/- plus clothing - £6-11-0

William Richards aged 55 years   weekly relief to asylum   £4-16-0

Thomas Evans' wife and 5 children 6/- shillings weekly.

Man's illness   26 weeks £7-16-0

13 Outdoor paupers listed   Total cost   £45-17-0

....

Parish of St. Mellons

32 persons listed (a few residents away from St. Mellons).

Martha Phillips (Cardiff) Aged 63 years   3/- a week.

26 weeks @ 3/7¾ - £4-1-7¾

Total expenditure   £125-2-1¾

....

Half year ending March 1854

Parish of Rumney   Thomas Baker   -   Guardian

2 Indoor paupers chargeable to the parish ---

-Mary Rees and Esther Rees   £97-13-0¼

8 Outdoor paupers chargeable to the parish -   £35-14-6

6 Outdoor paupers chargeable to the common fund -   £9-18-6

Total account   £143-6-0¼

....

75

Parish of St.Mellons   Thomas Richards - Guardian
Total of 33 Outdoor Paupers chargeable to the parish   £130-7-3
                    Total account   £288-10-6½
....

Left - The White Hart Inn. Centre – The Blue Bell Inn - the original venues for Vestry meetings.

      David Lloyd George, who was Prime Minister at the end of the 1914-1918 War, introduced a major step in the treatment of the poor, by bringing forward his Old Age Pensions and Insurance Bill. Under the *Poor Law Act of 1934*, the old rural poorhouses were to disappear, with poor and sometimes homeless people put into Union Workhouses. They were usually grim, prison-like establishments, nick-named the 'grubbers' by the frightened people of Rumney. It was a sad day when they were turned out of their rural home and refuges, then taken down Rumney Hill, through Cardiff to Canton to the new workhouse, the City Lodge later St. David's Hospital.

      During WWII, Lord William Beveridge, a Liberal, designed a new National Health and Social Security Plan, which was enacted by the 1945 Labour Government and came into being in 1948.

LAW AND ORDER

The County of Monmouthshire came into existence in 1536 and comprised the Marcher lordships of Newport, Abergavenny, Monmouth, Chepstow, Caerleon and Usk. The second Act of Union in 1543 established the Court of Great Session, a distinct Welsh system of courts, until its abolition in 1830. As Monmouthshire was not included in the system, the notion arose that it had ceased to be part of Wales and legislation passed between 1536 and 1900 assumed that Monmouthshire was not part of Wales.

From 17th century documents, inhabitants of the area appear to have been rather troublesome and disorderly. One states – 'the inhabitants of the Hundred of Wentlooge in which the lordship of Rempney lies are very disorderly persons' – 'the said inhabitants had committed divers misdemeanours and affrays upon sheriffs in that Hundred.' Disputes usually centred around property rights and the payment of debts, rents, etc. Friction was intensified by the absence of the large landowners and the reluctance of their tenants to accept the authority of stewards and other officials.

The following are extracts from Quarter Sessions records and newspaper reports.

Court of Quarter Sessions   1752   Rumney

Mrs. Mary Nicholls of Cae Main, Glamorgan presented by William Matthews, Petty Constable for not repairing the highway leading from Pen yr Heol to the dwelling house of Thomas Richards.

Hon. William Morgan of Tredegar and William Richards of Cardiff for a defective highway leading from the Church House to a spring or well of water called the Church Well.

1754

Thomas Morgan of Rhiwbina for a defective pool on the road leading from Rumney to Peterstone.

1765

John Roberts for scandalizing William Stephens of his good name and reputation.

1771

John Rimron for an assault on Thomas Lewis.

From a random search of the records it is evident that in the early 18th century, petty crime such as theft and disturbances caused by drunkenness were the two principal misdemeanours. Today imprisonment is the usual punishment for convicted criminals, this was not so in the past. Most criminal offences were punishable by death or by a fine and or whipping. There were some 220 offences for which the death penalty could be imposed.

The following details are recorded in the Criminal Registers deposited at the Public Record Office, Kew.

Persons resident in Monmouthshire between 1805 and 1816

1805	William Ablact	Horse stealing	death	reprieved
1807	George Parry	Sheep stealing	death	
1807	Thomas Parry	Sheep stealing	death	
1808	William Beaven	House breaking + larceny	death	
1808	William Watkins	Burglary	death	
1810	William Knott	Horse stealing	death	
1810	John Morgan	Horse stealing	death	
1811	John Morgan	Horse stealing	death	
1812	William Edwards	Shooting with intent	death	
1813	George Williams	Sheep stealing	death	reprieved
1814	James Roberts	Sheep stealing	death	reprieved
1814	James Abraham	Sheep stealing	death	reprieved
1814	Joseph Harris	Burglary	death	reprieved
1814	John Jones	Burglary	death	
1815	Thomas Parry	Sheep stealing	death	reprieved
1816	John Thomas	Horse stealing	death	reprieved
1816	Charles Williams	Burglary	death	
1816	John Williams	House breaking	death	reprieved

1820 - At a General adjourned Quarter Session of the Peace held at the Magistrates Room in the Gaol in Monmouth this 4th day of May 1820, before James Jones Esq. and James Barnard Davies, clerks to the Justices of the Peace for the said County. It is ordered that insolvent debtors including Daniel Griffiths of Rumney Manor, confined in the said Gaol, be certified as entitled to their discharge.

Calendar of Indictments. 1828 (Easter) St. Mellons

William Roberts, labourer, convicted of riding in a wagon and not having any person to lead or ride the horse.　　Fined 5/-

1831 (Midsummer) Rumney

Patrick Lucy, labourer, presented for stealing one coat valued at 1/-, one blanket valued at 1/-, the goods and chattels of John Griffiths on 11th May 1839.

John Matthews was fined the sum of one guinea for using a fishing net in that part of the River Rhymney within the Parish of Rumney without the consent of John Hodder Moggridge Esquire, the owner thereof. Howard Rimron was also fined the sum of one guinea. Transportation was adopted as an humane alternative to the death penalty. Seven years before Waterloo, Sir Samuel Romilly M.P. seeking to improve the penal code, persuaded the House of Commons to accept the penalty of transportation for life instead of hanging as a punishment for pickpockets. Convicts were held in prison but there was much overcrowding. This led to the use of old ships (prison hulks) moored in coastal waters. In 1770 Australia was established as a British Colony and penal settlement. This was a solution to the crisis of overcrowding. Transportation which had begun in 1717, initially to America, ceased in 1776 at the time of the American Revolution. It is estimated that between 1787 and 1868 over 160,000 people were transported to Australia. Terrible conditions were endured and many died on the six months long journey. On arrival in this new land of opportunity, male convicts were put to work clearing the bush to create farms, in order to provide for the growing need for food. Factories were set up and female convicts were sent to work in them.

To determine whether any convicts came from Rumney and St. Mellons, it is necessary to know details of place of conviction, name of ship and date of its sailing. In the records of women transported to New South Wales Australia between 1788 and 1828, Margaret Griffiths of St. Mellons was deported for seven years and sailed for Australia from Portsmouth. There were 110 female convicts on board the 'Northampton' and after a journey of 169 days they disembarked in New South Wales.

Margaret Griffiths had been convicted at the Glamorgan Court of Sessions in early 1814. She was charged with a series of offences in which she allegedly obtained goods under false pretences. The method she used was to go into a shop pretending that she was the wife of a man of some respectability and to obtain goods saying that her husband would settle the account later. The court record gives details of her visits to shops in Cardiff on one day; Margaret Griffiths charged upon the oath of Alice Jones, the wife of Thomas Jones, of the town of Cardiff, draper, with having on the third day of March instant obtained from the said Alice Jones, by the said Margaret Griffiths, representing herself to be the wife of Evan David, of the Little Mill at Ely and by other false pretences, goods as follows, the property of the said Thomas Jones; that is to say:

- Seven yards of dowlais at 2/- per yard
- Five and a half yards of black bombazett at 2/4 per yard
- Three and a quarter yards of green beaver at 14/- per yard
- One yard of brown Holland at 1/6 per yard
- A quantity of sewing silks at 2/-
- A quantity of thread at 2½
- Three muslin handkerchiefs at 2/4 each
- One dozen large bone moulds at 3d per dozen
- One dozen of the same sort at 2d
- One pair of leather gloves at 2/6
- One pair of muslin gloves at 1/6
- Two earthen jugs at 1/- each
- One large oval dish at 1/-
- Two small dishes at 8d each
- Three pennyworth of twist

She was also charged upon the oath of John Davies Bird, of the town of Cardiff, bookseller, with having on the third day of March instant, obtained from him by falsely and deceitfully representing herself to be the wife of David Roberts of Rumney, in the county of Monmouth and by other false pretences, the goods, as follows:-

- One pair of worsted and leather men's braces at 2/6
- One yard of black silk at 8/6
- One leather thread lace at 1/- per yard
- one yard of thread lace at 6/6 per yard
- A quantity of sewing silk, an iron bodkin at 3d
- one ivory small tooth comb
- One iron and horn penknife at 6d
- Two black worsted stay laces at 2d
- A quantity of brass pins, wire and thread buttons at 10d

Margaret Griffiths was further charged on the oath of Henry Partridge, of the town of Cardiff, Ironmonger, with having on the third day of March instant, obtained from him by falsely and deceitfully representing herself to be the wife of Morgan Williams of Dynas Powis, and by other false pretences the following goods, the property of his father, Samuel Partridge, Ironmonger, that is to say:-

- One tea tray at 10/6
- One tin Japan tea caddy at 4/6
- One brass and iron toaster at 5/-

The defendant was found guilty on all charges and sentenced. Margaret Griffiths left Great Britain 1st January 1815 and arrived in Australia on 18th June 1815. She married and remained in Australia.

A St. Mellons man at Monmouth Assizes, was sentenced to death for sheep-stealing. This sentence was commuted to transportation but he did not survive the journey. Transportation was supposedly abolished in 1857 but in fact did not cease until 1868.

Newspaper Reports

Extract from the *Cardiff Times 12th Feb 1859*

Shocking Death

'Mr George Emerson, a farm Bailiff to Colonel Tynte, of Cefn Mably was found dead on the road. He had been to Cardiff on Friday and on the way back to Cefn Mably, he stopped at the Carpenters Arms. After drinking he went to bed. On Saturday at noon he left in a phaeton, being unable to ride his horse. At 2 p.m. he entered the Unicorn, Llanedarn where he remained till 7 o'clock drinking and sleeping. When he left on horseback to go home was the last time he was seen alive. He was found at noon on Sunday on his back on the road and it appeared that he had fallen from his horse in a fit as there were no external signs of violence. He was a man of intemperate habits. The body was taken to the Unicorn, where an inquest was held on Monday. An open verdict was returned.'

Extract from the *Monmouthshire Merlin 1860*

Another Prize Fight near Cardiff.

'The disgusting and brutal exhibitions called "prize fights" are becoming frequent into this locality. On Monday last, two men named Charles Collins and James Fitzgerald, aspirants to fistic fame, fought on the Rumney Moors, just beyond the boundaries of Glamorganshire, in the presence of large numbers of persons. The battle lasted two hours and 25 minutes, during which time the combatants had 115 rounds! The notorious "Jack Matthews" acted as referee, and so determined was each man not to give in to the other, that in the end the referee was at length bound to separate them. A more butchering spectacle has seldom been witnessed, as Collins has already been apprehended by the Monmouthshire Constabulary and will appear before the County Magistrates at Newport, tomorrow (Saturday) and a warrant has been issued against James. Several of the "respectables" who were present, have or so we believe, been summoned. We trust the magistrates will inflict the full penalty, and thus evince their determination to put down these disgraceful proceedings.'

Extract from *Monmouthshire Merlin & South Wales Advertiser May 26th 1860* - Man killed in public house. 'The inquest on the death of Philip Hedges aged 38. William Rowlands, landlord of the Star Inn St. Mellons was on Saturday last brought before the County magistrates at Newport Petty Sessions charged with the manslaughter of Hedges and was remanded on bail till the following Saturday. Rowlands and the deceased were drinking at the Blue Bell Inn St. Mellons. The deceased who appears to have been of a very quarrelsome disposition, struck Rowlands, who is reputed to be a quiet and inoffensive man several times in the face, and at length Rowlands rose from his seat and struck him a blow in the face which knocked him against the fire-grate, and caused his death a few minutes afterwards. The jury viewed the body and the following evidence was given. Evan Thomas, the late landlord of the Blue Bell Inn, deposed that on Friday, William Rowlands and the deceased were drinking in his house at about five o'clock in the evening. The deceased kept annoying William Rowlands by slapping his face and drawing his hat over his eyes. Rowlands told him to sit down, when the deceased struck him several times in the face and refused to be seated. Rowlands got off his chair and struck the deceased in his face with his fist. The deceased fell against the grate in the fireplace. The witness immediately picked him up and placed him in a chair. The witness then laid him on the ground, he breathed about four times and then died.

The coroner summed up – it had been proved that death was caused by violence. They would have the room cleared to consider their verdict, which he thought should be one of manslaughter. The question of justifiable homicide was raised with the coroner who explained the difference between that and manslaughter. Two members of the Jury observed that they could not agree to a verdict of manslaughter. The coroner: "Well, gentlemen, I shall leave you to consult again. In my opinion there is no doubt whatsoever of it being a case of manslaughter." The room was again cleared and ultimately they returned a verdict of manslaughter against William Rowlands. He was subsequently admitted to bail under the new Act.'

The South Wales Echo   Early February 1901
The Echo gave much space to reports on the trial at Monmouth Assizes of Morris Evans, a labourer, aged 29 years, charged with the murder of Hannah Williams on Saturday, 10th November 1900: - 'She was an old woman between the age of 70 and 80 years and was of active habits. She lived at a place called Mullen Cottage, St.Mellons, with her niece. Mrs Williams was known to have money and her niece had the habit of leaving her Aunt alone in the house when she visited Cardiff Market. Sometime in the afternoon about 3 or 4 p.m. she was found lying in the house, the victim of a most murderous outrage. There were no less than three fractures in her skull. Some things were missing from the house, but not her money which she kept partly upstairs done up in a bundle of rags and partly in a packet underneath her clothes.'

Tuesday, 19th February 1901   It was reported as follows: -
'Morris Evans charged with the wilful murder of Mrs Williams of St. Mellons. The case was heard at the Monmouth Assizes where accommodation, which had been previously booked for those professionally engaged and for visitors, was being taxed to its fullest extent. Applications for tickets of admission to the court during the murder trial have been received from every part of Glamorgan and Monmouthshire. There was much speculation as to the Defence and Prosecuting Counsel .... Morris Evans was being held in Usk Prison......'

Thursday, 21st February 1901
Two full columns of this issue dealt at length with the trial and the subsequent euphoria. The following is a summary.
'Evans is indicted for the murder on 10th November 1900. Evans' home had been visited and his wife and mother-in-law were seen. Certain clothes were taken away. A razor was found in a hedge some time after the event. The analyst could not confirm that the stains on

the clothes were of human blood - could have been animal blood - possibly from a rabbit.

The summing –up

The murder was committed by someone who knew about the circumstances at Mullen Cottage. The prisoner had not given a very convincing account of his whereabouts on the day of the murder.

At 6.40p.m., Mr Lawrence, Prosecuting Counsel, addressed the Court and at 7.00p.m., the Defence Council stated that suspicion was not sufficient grounds for a conviction. Bloodstains on the clothes could have come from a man killing a rabbit by knocking it against a tree whilst poaching. The Judge, in his summing-up, advised the jury that if they had any reasonable doubt, they should give the prisoner the benefit of it.

The jury, having retired at 8.40p.m., returned a verdict of Not Guilty, so the prisoner was discharged. The Judge said that he was not happy with the way in which proofs of evidence had been circulated and afterwards had words with the Chief Constable. After the discharge, Morris Evans left the Town hall in the company of two friendly warders from the Usk Gaol with the intention of slipping quietly into the King's Head opposite but a huge crowd had assembled round the door and they cheered loudly when Evans appeared. He eventually managed to get into the King's Head where he was interviewed by the press. He said that he had been treated well at the Gaol - "....they have been congratulating me all round and I must express my heartfelt thanks to the South Wales Daily News and Echo for the justice and fair play which I have received............ tomorrow I shall go down to Newport and then on to St. Mellons and spend an few days with my wife and family at Cefn Mably Cottages........"

This crime was the talk of St. Mellons, as was reported in the Echo on 27th February and they persuaded Evans to make public his statement which was not given at the trial. He was a labourer living at Cefn Mably Cottages. He had come from Shropshire 8 years ago and married 5 years ago. He had two children. "On the day (Saturday) I left home at 6.30 a.m. I went along the road to Rudry and when I came to within 200 yards of Pantwyn Colliery I turned off and went up Rudry Mountain and set two traps. I caught two rabbits and killed them by hitting them against a tree. I started home when the Waterloo

Tin Works hooter blew at half past one and I reached home at twenty to three."

Signed, Morris Evans.

Finally Evans said that he had been offered work at a local place of amusement but intimated that he was going to leave the district immediately to take work elsewhere.'

Fingerprinting was introduced in 1901 and the first conviction based on fingerprint evidence came the following year. This was too late to be of assistance in the above-mentioned case.

Crime and Punishment in the 19th century

Were our forebears any less well-behaved than we are today? Old newspapers report that there was a great deal of crime in past centuries and that courts were kept very busy. Today murders are committed every day and very little notice is taken, unless the details are particularly gruesome or more than one victim is involved. Punishment has changed and the death penalty has been abolished. In the 19th century, less serious crimes could result in the death penalty and life sentence actually meant imprisonment for life.

A considerable archive exists in Record Offices and libraries giving accounts of court proceedings, but the difficulty for the researcher is to find reference to the persons concerned, as actual places of residence of the accused are not provided. It might be expected that villages such as Rumney and St. Mellons were peaceful places and that there was little work for the local policeman. There was an extremely small force compared with that of today, usually comprising one constable, who was responsible for a large rural area.

In the reign of Henry VIII, the Acts of Union had replaced the traditional laws of Wales with a new legal system. Magistrates, called Justices of the Peace, were appointed and made responsible for upholding the law. Once a year the people of every parish chose one of their community to be their Parish Constable. His duties included arresting suspected criminals and serving warrants.

" Now then young feller: what are you loitering about here for?

Oh! If you please Sir, I m only waiting for the young gal, vot I pays my attention to

A contemporary cartoon following the establishment of the Metropolitan Police Act of 1829.

In the early 19th century, many parts of the country began to employ their own paid force and in 1829, the first professional police force, the Metropolitan Police, was founded in London by the then Home Secretary, Robert Peel. Incidentally his descendant, also Robert Peel, started the fruit farm and farm shop at Berry Hill Farm, Coedkernew in 1980. By 1835 the government had set up a system of selected borough councils with authority to administer their own police forces. The Glamorganshire Constabulary was established in 1841, when the first Chief Constable employed 34 constables. Cardiff City Police Force was established when Cardiff became a city in 1905.

The Constabulary Account for Monmouthshire in 1873 stated that the salary of the Chief Constable was £400 and the pay for his Force of 4 Superintendents, 3 Inspectors, 18 Sergeants, and 98 Constables amounted to £7,632-17s-0d.

Police work in Victorian times.
Following is an extract from *A History of Police in England and Wales, 900 to 1966* by T H Critchley

In the 1850s, men were paraded before going out to patrol their beats. The Sergeant would read over the instructions for the day or night for the benefit of any who were unable to read themselves. Men took notebooks with them and occasionally carried lists of known criminals. An early force instruction read, 'Constables will proceed to their respective "meets" or "places of conference" by the nearest Turnpike Road, or if there be none, by the nearest highway, but not diverge through lanes or fields. They will wait at the "meet" half an hour, and state in their diaries the time of arrival of the other constables, the duration of the conference and the subject on which conferred.'

No meal breaks were allowed in the early days of policing and a man's ingenuity was constantly taxed by the need to find privacy, where he could eat a snack to sustain himself over the 6 or 7 hours of each shift. In one force, men were granted the 'privilege' of eating a snack in public conveniences, but the more athletic would shin up gaslights in the street to warm a can of tea on the gas- jet.

Calendar of Prisoners in the House of Correction at Usk, Monmouthshire, for trial at the Sessions to be held at the Town Hall in Usk on Monday, 1ˢᵗ January, 1838.

No. 8. Charles Hobbs, aged 42. Committed November 14th 1837, by James Coles, clerk, charged by the oath of Margaret Pearce and others with having, on the 12th day of November instant, in the Parish of St. Mellons, feloniously stolen, taken and carried away, one goose of the value of five shillings, property of the said Margaret Pearce.
....

Convict — William Williams
Aged 48 years born at
Peterstone, Monmouthshire.
Occupation-Labourer. Married.
Convicted -Monmouth Assizes
4th Aug.1870
Offence: unlawfully cutting and
wounding on the head with
intent of doing grievous bodily
harm.
Sentence: 12 calendar months
hard labour. Served at Usk
Prisoner No. 31.

The Census of 1831 had shown that a million families were engaged in agriculture, but the majority were barely able to exist on a wage of 2/6d a day, which was the minimum demanded in 1830. It is not surprising, therefore, that there was much petty crime.

The censuses of 1871 to 1901 indicated that there was a constable in St. Mellons between those years but that there were no resident policemen in Rumney. The usual mode of transport for a constable was the bicycle.

'No rabbit stew tonight, Dad's off to the lock-up!'

Monmouthshire Police
Police Constables in St. Mellons

1871 John Carey, aged 39, born Bisley, Gloucestershire. Married with a daughter of 6, resident 'at the village'.

1881 William Cornway, aged 27, born Rhymney, Mon., living in St. Mellons village (no exact address) with wife and daughter aged 3. (incidentally listed as a scholar)

1891 John Hale, aged 43, born Somerset, living in the Police Station in the village (no exact address) with wife and six children.

1901 Two Police Constables.
John Morris - Constable in charge. Aged 30, born Herefordshire. Married with wife and two small sons, resident in the Police Station. This is listed between two residences in Church Lane. Locals however have stated that the police station was in Llandaff Square, St. Mellons, prior to the building of the Police Station in Newport Road, St. Mellons.
Walter Cooke, aged 30, single, also born in Hereford, entered as a Police Constable, boarding in the Police Station.

This illustration shows that some policemen were more mobile in the early 20th century.

89

Rumney Police Station, 766, Newport Road, Rumney.

Prior to WWII, there was a constable of the Monmouthshire Police Force in Rumney. In 1938 when Rumney became a part of the city, a constable of the Cardiff City Police Force was installed. This person was Sgt. Williams, whose youngest son, David, confirms that his father was appointed directly as a result of a referendum, in which the people of Rumney voted to be administered by Cardiff instead of Newport. Sgt. Williams, is still remembered today by many of the older residents of Rumney. He resided at Rumney Police Station, 766 Newport Road, a semi-detached house. The 'office' was what ordinarily would have been the front room of the house. There was no police cell there and any person arrested by the local policeman, had to be kept in the office. They were collected by car and taken to Clifton Street Police Station in Roath.

Rumney Police Station 1950s.

St. Mellons Police Station 1970s.

Sergeant Williams.

Sergeant Johns.

90

CENSUS ENUMERATION COMPARISON 1851 and 1901

Census 1891

Old Lady — What's this?
Enumerator — The new census
for you .
Old Lady — Dear me, my senses
are all right; I don t want any new
ones !!

In the early 19th century, life in South Wales was simple, as it was in most of the British Isles. Life in Rumney and St. Mellons has changed from being agricultural and mainly self-supporting, to the urbanised existence today. A limited census of population taken in 1801 and thereafter every 10 years gives the following information:-

Year	1801	1811	1821	1831	1841	1851
St. Mellons	451	515	551	564	613	655
Rumney	235	237	255	264	305	308

From this chart it is evident that the population of St. Mellons was much higher than that of Rumney - in 1851, more than double. In 1801 and 1811, the census recorded only the number of males and females, a little more detail was added in 1821. In Rumney, there were 45 houses inhabited by 60 families. There was one house under construction and two were uninhabitable. Of the 255 inhabitants, 123 were males, 132 were females including children. Agriculture was the main occupation, employing 38 persons, 9 were in trade, and 13 in other occupations. This census, on a single sheet of paper, gave details for 'Rumney in the county of Monmouthshire and the Hundred of Wentloog. The Account was taken according to Act of Parliament by Lewis Thomas, Churchwarden and Overseer of the said Parish.'

Nothing similar has survived for St. Mellons. The only census records found for the first half of the 19th century were in large fragile ledgers. These gave total populations for all districts in the whole of England, Scotland and Wales. In 1841, more questions were asked of the inhabitants. Houses were vaguely identified. Names of all the occupiers and their occupations were listed. The entry for each property started with the Head of the Household.

The 1851 census required additional information: relationship to the head of the household, age and place of birth. The population in St. Mellons continued to exceed that of Rumney throughout the 19th century, but by 1901 the difference had diminished with a population in Rumney of 581 – as against 637 in St. Mellons.

Occupations in the two villages were very similar in 1851. Most men worked on the land as farmers, agricultural labourers, hay-cutters or hay merchants, wheelwrights or hauliers. St. Mellons had eight cordwainers or cobblers as they were later called, whereas Rumney had only two, probably because of the smaller population. Both villages had two blacksmiths, a tiler and plasterer, a highway labourer and a vicar. St. Mellons, in addition, had a Calvinistic Methodist Minister and two Independent ministers as well as a schoolmaster. Rumney boasted three potters, a fisherman and two railway labourers, due, no doubt, to its proximity to the river and the railway line. St. Mellons had more specialised trades such as carpenters, tailors (six of these), a saddler, two thatchers, a cooper, a horse jockey, and two beer-house keepers. Rumney had one stonemason and two victuallers who combined their occupation with farming. Incidentally, one of these was a woman. She was the only woman farmer in Rumney. St. Mellons had four women farmers.

There were four dressmakers in St. Mellons and three in Rumney, one of whom was thirteen years old. St. Mellons had two women grocers, a governess, thirty-two house servants, some of whom were ten, eleven and thirteen years old. There were three ladies of independent means. Other women were described as wives or daughters, but one, obviously a forerunner of the Feminist Movement, described herself as 'concerned with the domestic business of the house'. There were ten paupers in St. Mellons and only two in Rumney, again the difference in the population could account for this disparity. One Rumney lady was described as a 'pauper charwoman.' Living with her family, aged ninety-six years, she was the oldest inhabitant recorded on either census.

Picking peas at Ford's market garden, Earlswood Farm, Greenway Road.

St. Mellons Parish Church
Marriages Register 1837-1900.
It is interesting to note the occupations shown in the register. Couples tended to marry in their early twenties but some were still minors and needed parental permission to marry. St. Mellons residents were farmers, thatchers, cordwinders, carpenters, blacksmiths, yeomen, weavers, flannel-makers, tilers, joiners, cattle-dealers, shoemakers, farm-labourers and millers in the 1840s and 1850s. Brides were invariably farmers' daughters, dressmakers or servant-maids. Since many women died in childbirth and life expectancy for men was also lower, there are numerous examples of the re-marriages of widows and widowers. There are also many examples of an X in the register instead of a signature, for many country-people were unable to read or write.

In later years, in the 1880s and 1890s, there are fewer Xs in the St. Mellons Register of Marriages and occupations seem to be less directly related to the countryside, e.g. boatswain, surgeon, coachman, groom, ship-owner, builder, merchant, iron-founder, plasterer, innkeeper, collier, ostler, tailor, basket-maker, engine-driver, tea-merchant, solicitor and sawyer.

St. Mellons has changed greatly over the past two centuries but the parish registers continue to mirror life in the village and to throw light on political and social changes in the area.

The census returns note that in 1901 St. Mellons had a postman, a post-office worker, telephonist and telephone attendant who were all women. Generally occupations were still traditional, but residing in the village there were also a driver of an electric engine, an estate agent, stockbroker, two dental mechanics, law student and a registrar of births and deaths. St. Mellons had two police constables. Neither Rumney nor St. Mellons had a doctor. The Allen family at Ty To Maen, the head of which was a grain merchant, employed a housekeeper, cook, first, second and third housemaids and a nurse. Llanrumney Hall had a butler, coachman, cook and kitchen maid. The Cope family of Quarry Hill, the head of which was a colliery proprietor, had a domestic worker, cook, parlour maid and housemaid. At Vaindre Hall, John Henry Patrick Brain aged 5 years and his sister Helen Mary Brain aged one year had been left in the charge of a housemaid, parlour maid, nurse, lady's maid, cook, and kitchen maid. Where were the parents? Perhaps on a Grand European tour?

The Rumney 1851 census states, that one woman was ninety-six years old, one man was over 80 and three men and four women over seventy. In St. Mellons, five men and two women were over eighty, six men and seven women were over seventy. In 1901, one man in St. Mellons was ninety, four men and three women over eighty, four men and ten women over seventy. With the population now almost equal, Rumney had two men over eighty, four men and five women over seventy.

Ages of schoolchildren and employees very much reflect the social circumstances of the day. One child of four was recorded as a scholar, whereas some children of five were recorded and others not. A number of nine to thirteen year olds were working mostly as agricultural labourers or house servants. In 1851 a young man of seventeen was recorded as a scholar, whilst in 1901, a fifteen year old girl was described as a schoolmistress.

Census returns indicate that by 1901, the range of occupations had substantially increased, especially in Rumney. This was due to its close proximity to the growing town of Cardiff. The number of farmers had increased slightly, but the number of agricultural labourers had decreased significantly. Emphasis was on food production for the town and for big houses. There were nine market gardens, one with a superintendent manager, a cucumber grower, plus fifteen domestic gardeners and their labourers. A number of jobs were associated with the docks, working with coal and directly with ships. The 'plum' jobs seemed to be in engineering. Rumney had two big houses. The Galloway family employed a governess, cook, parlour-maid, and housemaid. The Cubitts at Rumney House boasted a cook, housemaid, kitchen-maid, nursemaid, governess and butler. Rumney also had a schoolmaster, schoolmistress, assistant schoolmistress and a sub-postmistress

Some marriages took place at an early age judging by the ages of the children in relation to those of their parents. Other couples did not marry until their forties. The number of nephews and nieces living with families suggests that they had been orphaned. A fifty-three year old widower had children of 19, 17, 16, 14, 12 and 10 years of age. Not difficult to see why he was a widower!

Also of interest, is the number of lodgers or logers shown in the 1851 census. By 1901, they were referred to as boarders. In those days few people expected to own a house. At the time of both 1851 and 1901 census enumerations there were large numbers of visitors in both villages. In 1851 although there were visitors and lodgers in the two villages, most were born locally. Many Rumney people were born in St. Mellons, fewer St. Mellons residents had been born in Rumney, others in Llanedyrn. More Rumney people came from Glamorgan than Monmouthshire, whereas in St. Mellons, those who originated from the two counties were evenly divided – 91 from Glamorgan, 90 from Monmouthshire. Cardiff did not figure largely as a place of origin, but present-day suburbs were listed separately as independent villages e.g. Lisvane, Llandaff, Llanishen, Whitchurch and Roath. Apart from four other Welsh counties listed as places of birth, English counties (mainly adjoining Wales or on the opposite side of the Bristol Channel) accounted for only 20 residents of Rumney. St. Mellons had even fewer residents whose origins were in

England, but the areas they came from were more widely dispersed, including one man from York. There were 5 people listed as British subjects and a number named only the county of birth.

By 1901 things had changed dramatically. Although Rumney was still the birthplace of the largest number of its inhabitants, there were very few from St. Mellons and the surrounding villages. Many Rumney inhabitants were from Cardiff, small numbers from twenty-four English counties, six from Ireland, (mainly gardeners) a butler from Switzerland, two housemaids from France and the United States and four of unknown origin, two of whom thought they had been born in Wales.

Most St. Mellons residents were born in the village. An increased number were of Cardiff origin with a few from surrounding villages, and seven other Welsh counties. Other residents came from twenty-six English counties ranging from Cornwall to Northumbria, and Westmorland to Middlesex. Five people came from Ireland (a gardener and his wife, a cattleman, a hospital nurse, and an agricultural labourer.) Further residents included a coachman from Scotland, the Australian-born wife of a grain merchant, two children of a gentleman (i.e. of independent means) who had been born in California, a housemaid born in Berlin and a domestic gardener from the West Indies. By 1901 with travel becoming easier, some people were prepared to journey further afield to find work.

Most people in Rumney and St. Mellons originally spoke Welsh. In the 1891 census, Rumney had 16 monoglot Welsh speakers and 120 bilingual inhabitants out of a population of 540. There was one German speaker, one French speaker and an imbecile who was not listed as speaking either Welsh or English. Babies and very young children were, of course, not included in the total. St. Mellons had 41 monoglot Welsh speakers and 208 bilingual residents out of a population of 650. By 1901 numbers of Welsh speakers had decreased. Rumney now had 25 monoglot Welsh speakers, with 77 bilingual inhabitants in a population of 581. St. Mellons had only 1 monoglot Welsh speaker and 153 bilingual residents in a population of 637.

The 1851 census had a column asking whether the resident was blind or deaf-and-dumb. From 1861 onwards the categories of

96

lunatic, imbecile, idiot or feeble-minded were also included. In Rumney in 1851, one deaf woman was listed, in 1881 an unfortunate family had a deaf daughter and an imbecile son, who was, however, shown as a scholar. There was one other imbecile and a deaf woman who was 74. In 1901 two epileptics were indicated (presumably to distinguish them from imbeciles), with one imbecile, one deaf-and-dumb man, and one blind woman. There were no entries in the lunatic column.

In 1851 St. Mellons had a deaf-and-dumb man, an eighty-two year old male pauper who was deaf and in 1861 a seventy-three year old woman who was blind. In 1881 a seventy-eight year old woman was listed as deaf and a younger man as blind. The 1891 census listed an eighty-two year old man as an imbecile and a younger man as partly blind. The age of some of the deaf and blind possibly accounted for their condition.

Surnames from 1851 and 1901 Census Returns:

1851 – Top ten	Rumney	St Mellons Surnames
	1 Edmunds	Edmunds
	2 Richards	Jones
	3 Morgan	Lewis
	4 Thomas	Roberts
	5 Lewis	David
	6 Rees	Llewellyn
	7 Williams	Morgan
	8 Timothy	Richards
	9 Davies	Evans
	10 Evans	Williams
1901 – Top ten Surnames	1 Williams	Thomas
	2 Giles	Jones
	3 Davies	Williams
	4 Evans	Lewis
	5 Richards	Roberts
	6 Scrivens	Davies
	7 Gerrish	David
	8 Rowland	Hughes
	9 Bradshaw	Hill
	10 James	Morgan

Six new names in Rumney in 1901, Giles, Scrivens, Gerrish, Bradshaw, Rowland and James, reflect the influx of large families coming to Cardiff to look for work. It is interesting that although the surnames were predominately Welsh, the Christian names were mainly English with a smattering of Biblical ones.

Woman milking in late 19th century at Greenway Farm, Rumney.

In **1901** the population of Rumney was **581,** St. Mellons **637**- total **1,218.**

1st April 1938 - Rumney administered by Cardiff.
9[th]April 1951 - Part of St. Mellons administered by Cardiff.
5th April 1974- Remainder of St. Mellons administered by Cardiff.

In **1951** census, Rumney was included with other wards of Cardiff East, therefore, no accurate figure is available. St. Mellons, when the 1951 census was held in March, was still within the Magor and St. Mellons District boundary and the number of people on the census return was 901, Pontprennau was mainly fields, with few residents. These were included in the district of Llanedyrn.

For administrative purposes. boundaries changed again by the time of the **2001** census. Population of Old St. Mellons including Pontprennau - **8,037**
Rumney – **8,964**   Llanrumney – **11,226**   Trowbridge – **14,801**
1901 Rumney, St. Mellons and Pontprennau total residents - **1,218**
2001 Rumney, St. Mellons and Pontprennau total residents - **43,028**

WORK, TRADES AND PROFESSIONS

As seen in the census and church records of former times, people in Rumney and St. Mellons were principally employed in agriculture and associated trades, such as hay-cutters, hay-merchants, wheelwrights, hauliers, blacksmiths, etc. Man had started farming to provide food for the family group. Fish formed a big part of the diet of early man and through Roman, Mediaeval and later periods. The abundance of fish in the rivers was fully exploited. Farmers and fishermen very gradually moved on to a more commercial level, but their work was still a way of life.

Small boats left the Rhymney River to fish in the Bristol Channel. There are records showing one John Dunn as a fisherman in 1610. Other records have shown more fishermen with that surname, the trade passing from one generation to another. In the early 20th century Jimmy Dunn is remembered by some older residents of Rumney. He had a cottage in Wentloog Road opposite the Grove. Here, fish were prepared and shrimps boiled ready for sale. Not only was a boat used for fishing, hang- nets were put out on willow stakes in the mud near low tide mark. Willow stakes were used as they would bend with the flow of water. For shrimps a different type of funnel or cone-shaped net was used. Salmon baskets were also used. To collect the fish from the nets and baskets, men had a long difficult walk across the mud at low tide, sometimes pushing a sledge.

John Rowlands, followed by his son Ivor, fished in this way. Ivor Rowlands was the last fisherman in Rumney to catch shrimps. They were prepared ready for sale by his sisters Gwenny and Edie at their home, Pwll Mawr Cottage at the bottom of Wentloog Road. Ivor retired from fishing in the late 1950s. There are now only two fishermen who have nets out on the muddy foreshore, Will Hughes and Ken Bater, known as 'Spud'. Fishing is now enjoyed as a pastime and many local anglers still fish from the lynches, sea bank and Rhymney River.

Men who worked for Jimmy Dunn, early 1900s.

Will. Hughes and Luisa Neal
gathering the fish 2004.

Ken Bater's son with a
selection of the day's catch 2004.

Will. Hughes and Ken (Spud) Bater complain that fish numbers have
decreased in recent years and that members of the younger generation are
not interested in this method of fishing.

Farming

At the time of the manorial system, land was owned by only a few people. Manorial records show that in the 1400s, the Manor of Rumney was large and valuable. Accounts record that a high proportion of the overall income of the manor was provided by taxes. In 1401, a guide to the income listed :-

Rent from freeholders and copyholders	--	£132-19s-8d
The farme of demesne lands	--	£101-12s-6d
Casual profits	--	£ 58- 1s-6d
Taxation	--	£244-8s-10d

Taxation was a burden even in those long bygone days, with rules and regulations, fines, tythes and other dues. As in most manors, the tenants were obliged to grind their corn at the lord's mills, the fine for not doing so was 10 shillings. These mills were on long leases and the cost of repairs had to be borne by the farmer/tenant. Eventually the cost of repairs exceeded the profit. By the end of the 15th century, only Rempnesmylle, (Rumney's mill) survived. This was leased to John Lloyd Kemys at £2-13s-4d. From the manorial records, it is evident that the economy was deteriorating from around 1400. Income from the farms, land and mills was decreasing.

The Rumney demesne (home farm) had previously been let for 20d an acre, but in 1400 it was fetching only 16d per acre on a 10 year lease. In 1447/8 it was leased to 24 tenants, most of whom had less than 10 acres. The rent by then had dropped to 12d and this did not change significantly over the next 50 years. This resulted in the granting of longer leases and leases for life. Most of the beneficiaries were families who later became prominent officers of the lordship, particularly the Kemys family. William Kemys had 12 acres in Rumney and other members of the Kemys family held land in and around the area.

A system of crop rotation was established by the 14th century. Wheat, oats and beans were grown, followed by pasture. Changing the crops grown, helped to prevent a build-up of insect and fungal pests; it also added nutrients to the soil. Legumes, such as beans, increased the level of nitrates in the soil. Beans were grown on a significant scale, which was unusual. The Provost's account gives the division on the demesne acreage, for the year 1316, as follows: -

Wheat - 20½ acres.   Beans - 34 acres
Oats   - 39 acres   Fallow - 26 acres
Pasture - 48 acres

With plant selection and development, production has improved over the centuries. In 1316, 6 quarters 3 bushels of wheat seed was planted and 19 quarters 1 bushel was harvested. This was called wheat to the third grain – three times as much grain harvested as was sown. Today, we can expect a yield of three and three quarter tons of wheat to one and a half cwt of seed sown. Using the terms of those far-off days, this is wheat to the fiftieth grain, the yield being fifty times greater than the seed sown.

Farming continued, gradually changing and improving. A map, dated 1800, names the tenants of Romney Manor. Surnames that we still recognise today are mentioned e.g. Tynte, Tredegar, Morgan and Wood. Ownership of the land passed to a greater number of people. The shape and size of the fields is interesting; those on the Wentloog Level remaining much the same until the 1970s. Then due to the amalgamation of small farms, herds of beef cattle and dairy cows increased in size as did flocks of sheep. Larger machines were used, small fields were joined together and gateways made wider. During the nineteenth century, as machinery was introduced instead of manual labour, it became difficult to cultivate arable crops on this low-lying ground, so the levels were once again used as pasture-land.

In the 1880s, Monmouthshire County Council already had a **Department of Agriculture Dairy Schools Horticulture and Aboriculture.** It was this department that organized courses on cheese making. One such course was held at Greenmoor Farm, (now Greenmoor Nurseries) in St. Brides Wentloog. Farmers' daughters from Rumney and St. Mellons, e.g. Gladys Scrivens from Pwll Mawr Farm in Rumney, spent a week there learning how to make butter and cheese. They were taught how important it was that the dairy should be dry and well-ventilated, with a hard floor and no crevices where milk, whey and impure water could collect. This was very important as milk could acquire a taint from any impurities or smells.

They were also taught that all utensils should be thoroughly cleaned with pure water. The pastures where the cows grazed had to be free from strong herbs such as garlic, because again the milk could carry the taint from any strong-flavoured herbage.

Caerphilly cheese is reputed to have been made on the Wentloog Moors, but it takes its name from the market where it was sold. It was enjoyed by the iron and coal industry workers, especially the miners, who found it tasty and convenient to take down the pit. This cheese was produced on small farms, some with only 2 or 3 cows, others with up to 10. These farms were between the River Ebbw and the River Ely. The area had the climatic conditions, combined with a suitable herbage and the formation of soil which gave the cheese its distinct flavour. It was described as being easy to digest, with a thin wrinkled rind, moist, rich and palatable.

The original cheese press used for the cheese-making courses at Greenmoor Farm, St. Brides.

Changes in agriculture, as with other trades and industries increased at the end of the nineteenth century. The growing population of Cardiff needed more fresh produce and agriculture in Rumney and St. Mellons developed to meet that need. Milk, meat, fish, eggs, fruit and vegetables were produced and sold locally and in Cardiff. Further changes took place during the 20th century. Individual producers and suppliers made door-to-door deliveries. Bread, meat, fruit, vegetables, coal and of course milk, arrived on a daily basis. Milk is one of the few products that is still delivered today, though many people now prefer to use the supermarkets.

In earlier times, people had gone to farms with their jugs to collect milk. As the population grew, farmers started to deliver milk to customers. At first they took the milk in churns and ladled it into jugs which the customer brought to the milk float. Then a big change came with the introduction of the milk bottle. The early ones had a wide neck with a cardboard stopper. Stuart Scrivens recalled that in the old days, there were no milk bottles or milk lorries, but lovely milk floats decorated with artistic scrolls and bearing the name of the farm or dairy. They were often highly varnished and always spotlessly clean. Milk floats bore their shining milk churns across the common from Rumney and St. Mellons, delivering milk to all parts of Cardiff. It was like a chariot race as each one tried to outflank the other.

Most of the names painted on milk floats are still remembered; dairymen such as Reg Richards, Hadden Jeffries, Eddie Horrell, Harry Horrell, Harry Vincent, Jack James, Jack Davies, Reg Addis and Cyril Thomas. Farmers who also had milk rounds included:- The Davids-Cummins Farm, Llewellyn Jones-Ty Coch, Rhys Edwards-Bridge Farm, Rhys Richards the Maerdy, Bill John Richards the Downton, Huxham of Whitehall, later of Ty Fry, Fred Miles- Hendre Farm, Handford- Seabank Farm, Sammy King- Oak Meadow Farm and Scrivens- Pwll Mawr Farm. On the Moors almost every farm as far as Peterstone had milk rounds:- Cliff, Albert and Jim Ward – Newlands Farm, Edgar Scrivens – Shire Newton Farm and in Peterstone, Wynford Prosser – Sluice Farm, Alf Eddins – Sluice House Farm and Gordon Preece – Ton-y-Pil Farm.

Fred Miles with milk float.

104

The Milk Marketing Board was formed in 1933. From that date farmers sold their milk to the M.M.B. and the Board then sold it to the dairymen. More and more controls were introduced, such as cleanliness in the production and treatment of milk and the health of cows. Pasteurisation of milk became compulsory and cows were tested for tuberculosis.

The War Agriculutural Executive Committee, or the 'War Ag'

During the two World Wars, it was necessary to produce as much food as possible at home. To help farmers increase production, County 'War Ag' Committees were set up to supervise their local area. They were really the local arm of national government, based, in this area, at Castleton. They oversaw the ploughing of land and the achievement of production targets. During WWII, large acreages of meadow and permanent pasture were ploughed up and sown with oats, wheat or barley. Due to poor summer weather, it was sometimes impossible to ripen crops. Mangolds and swedes were grown as cattle feed. Wartime saw the introduction of artificial fertilisers, though these, of course, were rationed. Farmers were frequently in dispute with 'the man from the War Ag'. If the committee felt that the land was not being farmed correctly, they had statutory powers to commandeer the farm and evict the farmer with little, or more often, no compensation. Nationally some 15,000 farms were seized in this way, often with the farmer and his family never regaining the land after the war.

Understandably, members of the 'War Ag' were not always popular with local farmers, but their role was vital in stimulating the increase in home production. Between 1939 and 1942, the production of food at home increased by 70%. The policy of endeavouring to make the country self-sufficient, continued long after the war ended. Before the war only farmyard manure, lime and basic slag were used; later more fertilizer was available and this increased crop yields. Grassland was reseeded and fertilized; the breeding of dairy cows was improved, thereby increasing milk production. Subsidies were introduced to aid the objective of self-sufficiency and keep home- produced food prices down. Farmers did this successfully for forty years until the food surpluses of the 1980s.

In 1948, ten farmers and dairymen had joined together to form *The Farmers and Dairymen,* which had a dairy on Rumney Common. *Horrell's* in Wentloog Road also purchased milk from local farms. Gradually, over the next ten to twenty years, farmers gave up their milk rounds and bigger dairies took over.

The Demise of Farming in Rumney and St. Mellons

After WWII, more houses were needed and in later years, housing development replaced farms in Rumney, Llanrumney and St.Mellons. The size of remaining farms increased substantially; small farms amalgamated with bigger ones. In 1951, on the Wentloog Moors, between Rumney and St. Brides, there were an estimated 700 cows owned by 38 dairy farmers. By 1985, the number of cows had increased slightly, but the number of producers was down to 10. This period was the most productive time in agriculture for the Wentloog Levels; but it was not to last. By 1994, the number of cows remained the same but there were now only six producers.

John Scrivens with his first heifer, a Shorthorn; this was a dual-purpose breed, widely kept in the early 20th century, for milk and beef production.

A modern friesian dairy heifer bred by John Scrivens' great-grandson and one of the last farm animals kept at Middle Newton Farm.

Since the mid-1990s, the farming scene has continued to change. At the present time there are only three milk producers - all in St. Brides. A large pig production unit, at Newton Willows Farm, built up by Chris and Sheila Neal and their family, did not restart after the 500 sows and their progeny, a total of 4,500 pigs, were slaughtered as a precaution, at the time of the foot and mouth outbreak in 2001. Middle Newton Farm, from 1960, incorporated Shire Newton, Pen Pill, Lower Newton, Maerdy and Ty To Maen Farms and by 1992 John and Marjorie Neal and their family were milking nearly 300 cows, with more than 300 young stock and beef animals. Milk production ceased in 1998 and the last beef cattle were sold in December 2003. Farming has now finished completely in Rumney. The 'agricultural' land remaining is utilised for growing turf and for the recycling of soil.

Tyla Farm is the last working farm in St. Mellons. As a result of boundary changes, it now lies within the area controlled by Newport City Council. Many things have affected farming. Food surpluses, commercial and housing developments and uncertainties in the future of agriculture have all played their part.

David Wilde of Tyla Farm checking the ewes and lambs.

Market Gardening
With the growth of Cardiff and the increase of population, market gardens were established in both Rumney and St. Mellons. A 1911

107

sale catalogue records their size in this advertisement. The sale was advertised thus – *Valuable Freehold and Copyhold Lands (now used as a Market Garden) and Orchard Land. To be sold in two lots at The Mart, 5 High St. Cardiff.* This was land on the east side of Wentloog Road being sold by a Mrs Case who had occupied the property for thirty years.

Lot 1, known as Paradise Gardens, eight acres of copyhold land, almost half of which is covered in greenhouses - including 10 Tomato Houses, 9 Cucumber Houses, 11 Greenhouses, 3 Double Greenhouses and a Fern House. At the entrance to the Gardens, there is an office with National Telephone Installation, Store room, Implement Shed, Packing room, Sorting Warehouse, Store rooms etc. There is a well with a plentiful and never-failing supply of good water, which is pumped into tanks from where it gravitates to all parts of the property. Cardiff Corporation Water is also laid on.

Lot 2, Eight acres 3 rods 31 perches of Freehold & Copyhold Orchard Lands adjoining Lot 1, only 2 rods 24 perches is copyhold, the remainder being freehold. The land is used as orchards, planted with choice apples, pears and gooseberries. The principal apples are Cox's Orange Pippin and Worcester Permain. The pear trees are mainly Beorre Clerques and Duchess.

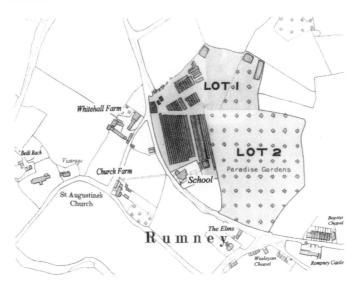

Map from 1911 sale catalogue for Paradise Gardens.

108

The property was purchased by G. W. Drake. He remained there until 1922 and traded from a stall in Cardiff Market. Percy Thomas, who had a well-established greengrocery shop in Albany Road, acquired Paradise Gardens in the 1920s. He remained there for more than thirty years, the gardens closing in the late 1950s. In the later years of his occupancy, the gardens specialised in flowers which were sold mainly from their retail outlet in Albany Road. Eventually the gardens were replaced by housing development.

There were other orchards; a visitor recalls seeing apple blossom in the spring as he walked up Rumney Hill. Noteworthy names of market gardeners for two or more generations were Shute, Bolt and Tugwell of Rumney and Hastings, Ford and Jones-Ty Coch of St. Mellons.

Reg. Ford started his market garden in 1936, in Began Road St. Mellons. Throughout WWII, Land Army girls comprised a large part of the workforce. At the age of 14 years, Gordon Tanner started work there when he left school in 1945. He recalls that a wide variety of vegetables was grown; cabbages, beans, potatoes, celery and many more. The gardens were irrigated with water from the Rhymney River. During busy periods, such as potato picking, prisoners were brought out from Cardiff prison to add to the workforce. Gordon sometimes drove a tractor for cultivating the ground and at other times a lorry. Lorries were used for various purposes; to deliver the vegetables into Cardiff Fruit and Vegetable Market, which at that time was in Custom House Street, or to collect seed potatoes from as far away as Kent. Women from the new housing estates were given lifts by lorry into work.

During the 1970s, there was a great interest in 'Pick Your Own' and families spent many happy summer days picking strawberries and raspberries at Ford's market garden. The family tradition of horticulture continues in the new Millennium with Rob Urquhart, grandson of Reg. who sells plants, tubs and flower baskets. Van Heynigen Tomato Nurseries and Colin Evans' market garden, also on Began Road, were flourishing horticulturists in the 1970s. Due to boundary changes, they are no longer within the St. Mellons area. Uskley Nurseries on Newport Road is the site of the present Blooms' Garden Centre

The Brith Mawr Apple

In 2001, St. Mellons Women's Institute entered a competition run by the W.I. County Federation for a handbook entitled 'All About Apples.' Muriel Beck and Jane Baker took on the task of compiling the handbook and enlisted the help of other members to research local apples for a section on local apple-growing. Yvonne Rees unearthed a number of sources including the fact that there was an old tree of Brith Mawr in a Newport Road, Old St. Mellons garden. The tree has always been known to the family as Brith Mawr and is estimated to be about 150 years old.

Members of the W.I. from old farming families remembered having trees of Brith Mawr – each farm would have had a tree for domestic use, as the apples are both cookers and eaters.

It was not until a connection had been made with M.A.N. (the Marches Apple Network) that the significance of this find was realised. M.A.N., a voluntary organisation but with considerable expertise in identification of apple varieties, had found only one reference to Brith Mawr, which was the *Royal Horticultural Society's Varieties in Cultivation 1934.* It was recorded there as having been sent from South Wales, among the apples exhibited at the Fruit Conference 1934 and was meagrely described as a 'conical size 3 striped red'.

M.A.N. was so interested that graftwood taken from the tree was requested. In January 2002, pieces of twigs were sent to Paul Davis of Dolau-hirion Fruit Nursery, Capel Isaac, Llandeilo, who grafted them on to root stocks. In October 2003, one of these was replanted in the Old St. Mellons garden.

The problem M.A.N. had, was to verify that the St. Mellons tree was in fact a Brith Mawr. In spite of extensive research and many false trails, no other tree could be found in the area with which to compare the fruit. During the research, contact was made with Joe Broome who used to run the Fair Oak Nursery in Bassaleg. The nursery had been in the family for several generations growing many varieties of apple commercially. In their 1920s catalogue, seventy-two varieties were listed. The Brith Mawr was not grown for sale but there were some trees on nursery land, so Joe Broome knew what the fruit was like. In 2003 there were good examples of fruit on the old tree and three were taken to Joe for him to verify if they were Brith

110

Mawr. Two were not typical, but the third and largest he confirmed was definitely a Brith Mawr apple, adding that the fruit he was holding was ridged – a feature remembered as being typical of the variety. The three apples were sent to M.A.N. for them to make a detailed record for future identification and also add to the growing number of old Welsh varieties saved from extinction.

Pottery

As with fishing and farming, the history of pottery is rooted in ancient times. In a previous chapter numerous finds of Roman and Mediaeval pottery are listed. The name of Giles has been synonymous with pottery in Rumney from the second half of the 19th century until the present time.

Richard Giles left his home in Penhow, Monmouthshire to find work in Coventry. It was there that his son, also Richard, was born in 1853. This family, an example of many at this time, often moved on to improve their lives. For a while they live in Brosely, Shropshire, in 1855 they were in Bridgend and by 1861 they had settled in Rumney. The 1851 census notes that on the front lawn of the present Rumney Pottery stood the River Bridge Toll House. The proprietor lived in the Toll House and there were two further dwellings, one occupied by a haulier and his family and the other by a potter and his family. This last family included a 14-year-old son and two lodgers who were all potters.

From 1860 the Giles family worked, leased and since 1951, owned Rumney Pottery. Robert Giles recalled that in the early days, clay was obtained from clay pits on Rumney Common. Later it was delivered by Mr Wadsworth using a horse and cart from his stables on Newport Road opposite Colchester Avenue. Deliveries were made every two to three weeks and blocks had to be placed under the wheels of the cart as it came down from Newport Road. The road into the pottery was steep and with the weight of the clay, both horse and cart could have ended up in the house. This clay was raw and straight from the pits. It was then mixed in a variety of ways and a lovely rich brown pottery was the end result.

There is a large and unusual pot kiln inside the pottery. The chimney of the kiln was partially demolished by the last land mine that dropped in Rumney during WWII. The kiln was not used during

111

the War, as the flames could be seen from the chimney and this contravened the blackout regulations. Instead, a smaller kiln, built in the old stables, was used during the War. The stables had formerly housed up to six horses, which were used to deliver the pottery within a radius of twenty miles. Horses were also used as a source of power in the pottery. The area where they worked, can still be identified by slats built into the floor and a curved wall with notches cut out of the main beams, which allowed the horses to pass underneath.

When steam-power replaced horsepower, the engine was situated outside the pottery and a shaft passed through a hole in the wall. Oil was used later, followed by electricity.

The Giles family digging clay on Rumney Common. Rhymney River bridge and the pottery can be seen in the background.

There is documentary evidence of a pottery at Pwll Mawr. (Big Pool) This is in the area where Rumney Welding and Construction Co. and Thayer's ice-cream factory are located at the bottom of Wentloog Road.

A ninety-nine year lease dated 17th July 1847 describes land for a proposed pottery, twenty pounds per annum to be paid twice yearly on 2nd February and 2nd August. William David leased to Elias John of Rumney, a potter, two parcels of grazing land estimated to be four acres three roods and thirty-nine perches. One field was to the south of the railway line, the other north of it. Elias John was given authority to dig, work and take the clay of the said premises to make bricks, tiles and potters ware. He was also given permission to erect and set up all such sheds and conveniences needed for the making of the items listed.

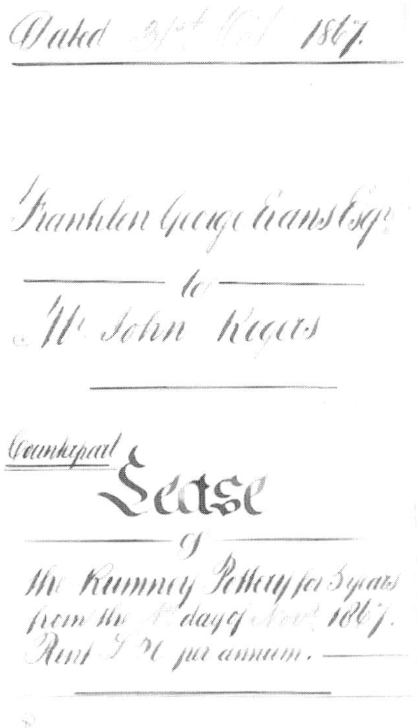

Dated ... 1867.

Franklen George Evans Esq

to

Mr John Rogers

A five-year lease, dated 31st Oct. 1867 between Franklen George Evans and John Rogers for Rumney Pottery at a rent of £20 per annum.

Counterpart Lease

of

The Rumney Pottery for 5 years
from the ... day of ... 1867.
Rent £20 per annum. —

113

In April 1867, the lease was terminated and in October of that year, a new five-year lease was granted to John Rogers for Rumney Pottery. As in the previous lease, the ground is identified together with the pottery and works, sheds, mills, erections, buildings, machinery and premises standing thereon.

Another twenty-one year lease dated 7th December 1872 shows the same area of land including buildings, sheds and other erections, used as a pottery. On a mortgage dated June 1873, some buildings remained but others had been converted into four dwellings; these four cottages on the 1881 census were called Pottery Row. The end cottage together with the buildings and the two fields were later known as Pwll Mawr Farm from about 1910 until the 1950s. When John Scrivens retired from farming, Rumney Welding Co. occupied the buildings. Thayer's Ice-cream Co. later purchased the four cottages in Pottery Row and the ground behind them. The cottages were demolished when the Ice-cream factory was extended.

Inns, Beer-houses and Public Houses

The brewing of beer goes back to prehistoric times. The most common drink in the Mediaeval Period was ale made from barley, water and yeast. It was cloudy, full of carbohydrates and proteins, making it a good source of nutrition for nobleman and peasant alike. In the 15th century hops were introduced, giving a bitterness to the ale. Hops were thought to have preservative qualities. The drink with hops was called beer and without hops was called ale. Over the following centuries beers were developed; bitters, stouts, milds, porters, all enhanced with a variety of flavours. Monasteries had breweries for the use of monks and passing travellers. Later, hostels were built close by for shelter and these assumed the characters of inns. In Rumney and St. Mellons in the 19th century, inns or pubs were often also farms, e.g. the Pear Tree and the Carpenters Arms. Occupiers of some private houses or cottages made and sold beer from their front rooms. Inns have always been controlled by the laws of the land regulating the quality of the beer, price and taxation.

Everyday types of employment during the 19th and early 20th centuries, included agricultural labourer, hay-cutter, wheelwright, blacksmith and farrier. Newly-built large houses of that time were owned by professional and self-employed people, a tea merchant, ironfounder and shipowner to name a few. These people employed others to serve them, caring for their homes, gardens, horses and carriages.

Ploughing at Nellie Hastings' market garden in St. Mellons.

Harold Gosling delivering bread, 1930.

SCHOOLS IN RUMNEY AND ST. MELLONS

Until the mid-nineteenth century, schooling was only for the rich and was provided mainly by private tutors. Church records indicate that many ordinary people could neither read nor write. Parents recognised the need for education but were unable to pay for tuition. The church, mindful of its responsibilities towards the young, encouraged attendance at Sunday school, where basic literacy was taught and children learnt how to sign their names. As stated earlier, William Jones, curate at Rumney for some 42 years died in 1846 and in his will left £100 for the maintenance of a school. Building of the school on the north side of the church commenced soon after his death and it was opened in 1856, catering for pupils, day and evening. As a result of the 1870 Education Act, a much larger school was opened in Wentloog Road.

Prior to 1870, elementary education had been provided by two leading voluntary bodies - the National Society, and the British and Foreign School Society. The State recognized this work and the government channelled public money for education through these voluntary bodies. Individual employers played a significant part in the education of the children of their employees. In 1853, there were 14 British schools in South Wales plus a number of privately-sponsored works schools. By 1860, in the four South Wales counties of Monmouth, Glamorgan, Brecon and Carmarthen there were 85 British schools educating boys, girls, and infants. From a report of inspected schools there were 17,705 pupils in National Society Schools, 17,230 in British and Foreign School Society Schools and 16,081 in Schools of the Works' School System.

The passing of the 1870 Education Act, meant that the State became more interventionist and encouraged voluntary action, assisted by local authorities. By 1874, over 5,000 new schools had been founded in Britain. The Act also enabled women to vote and stand for election to School Boards. England and Wales were divided into about 2,500 school districts and School Boards were elected by the ratepayers in each district. The School Boards were empowered to examine the provision of elementary education in their district, which up to that time had been provided by voluntary societies. If there were not enough school places they could build and maintain schools out of the rates. School Boards could make their own by-laws and waive fees and they were given powers to enforce attendance of most children below the age of thirteen years.

During the nineteenth century, in addition to voluntary schools, there were many small private schools. These were often held in private houses, though there are few records of their existence. It is possible that some existed in both Rumney and St. Mellons.

The old Rumney School in Wentloog Road, where the Nursery School was situated until recently. It was demolished after the new two-storey Junior and Infants' school was built just before WWII.

The Rumney School Board May 1890

An extract from the Western Mail reads as follows, 'The exceedingly strange proceedings which have taken place from time to time at the meetings of the Rumney School Board are well-known to the public and on a recent Tuesday evening, another characteristic gathering took place. Mr. Lascelles Carr was in the chair.

When the Chairman read the minutes of the preceding meeting, in which it was recorded that certain matters had been carried by the casting vote of the Chairman, the Vicar (Mr. Morgan) enquired how many casting votes the Chairman possessed, that gentleman replying, "As many as were necessary to conduct the business of the Board and as many as the law allowed." This answer brought from Mr. Morgan an expression of regret that the Board could not conduct its affairs more harmoniously and observed that Mr. Carr was always giving casting votes in his own favour. "Yes, I can't vote in favour of a better man, so far as I know," rejoined the Chairman, Mr. Morgan retorting, "I hope you don't think you're the best man in Rumney."

Complaints have been received concerning children being sent on personal errands by the headmaster, which he claimed were untrue. Mr Morgan asked, "Which of the children do you send for beer." The Vicar then proceeded to make charges of drunkenness against the schoolmaster. The Chairman remarked that Mr Morgan's conduct was undignified and improper. "You should bring times, dates, places etc. if you wish to make charges." The Chairman said "Mr Vicar, you are making a foul attack on a defenceless man – I will not submit to it!"

The Chairman - "If the schoolmaster is wisely advised, he will take you before your equals and will make you prove these charges." Mr. Badcock, who once or twice essayed to speak, now exclaimed, "You have opened your mouth and put your foot in it tonight, Mr.Vicar." The scene concluded with the observation from the Chairman, "Don't you reduce yourself to the level of the Vicar, Mr. Badcock."…….'

A further meeting was called in July 1890 to discuss the improvement of attendance. Mr. Rowlands (Attendance Officer), having reported on a number of absentees and irregular attenders, it was suggested that the Attendance Officer prepare a census of all children under 14 in the village. It had been taken previously but not kept up to date. Learning by children first attending school at 6 or 7 years, when they should have commenced at 5 years, was adversely affected. It was also decided to resort to the practice of giving prizes for regular attendance and certificates for passing examinations.

Opening of a New School

Cardiff and Suburban News October 8th 1932 reported that a new Senior Mixed Council School was formally opened at Rumney on Wednesday last, by the Monmouthshire Education Committee. Alderman William Dunn declared the school open and Councillor James Payne, Chairman of the Committee presided. The school has places for 230 scholars.

Rumney Elementary School

Selected Entries from the Headmaster's Diary 1934/6.
1934
April 11th

I propose adding a new form to be known as 1B as soon as the exam for new entrance is completed.
I have decided to arrange the forms: -

i.	3A	Mr Hicks B.Sc.
ii.	3B	Mrs. E. M. Shepherd
iii.	2A	Miss E. Protheroe
iv.	2B	Mr. W. Stevens
v.	1A	Miss I. Charles
vi.	1B	Head Teacher (temporary)

June 1st 1934 Letter from the Director of Education informing me that three pupils – Nancy Toozer, Florence Hann and Donald Normansell cannot be allowed to leave school until the end of school term.

October 23rd A boy, Stanley Sayce, cut his head in the manual room with a chisel whilst sharpening a pencil in Mr. Bevan's absence.
Signed-Mr. H.F. Barnden
The school is closed for the wedding of the Duke of Kent.

1935
March 20th 27 pupils sitting the entrance examination at Bassaleg. They have all received their attendance mark.

March 29th A boy, Joseph Simms, hurt his shoulder in the playing-field today. I sent him home for his mother's attention, as it might be serious.
Signed-Mr Hicks.

June 19th Thunderstorm–chimney of the Ladies' staffroom struck by lightning. Had to forgo playtime.
Dismiss 3.45p.m.

June 29th The travelling school clinic is here for dental fillings.
Signed-Mr Stevens Mr Barnden

July 15th Schools closed - mark of respect for the funeral of the Director of Education.
Signed-Miss Protheroe

Teachers at Rumney Junior and Infants' School in the 1930s; some of them were still there in the 1940s.
Back row: l-r Miss M. Collier, Mr. Sully, Mr. Furzy, Miss O. Jones and Miss T. Shepstone.
Front row: l-r Miss Sully, Miss E. Morgan, Mr. Jones, (Headmaster) Miss Draisey, Miss M. Shapland, Miss Williams.

School memories of Ada Wyatt, nee Young, born 1912.

'We walked to school in the morning taking our lunch with us. The journey took us along Ball Road and down Wentloog Road past Case's Gardens where a bell rang at 8.30am to signal the works' breakfast. If we heard the 9a.m. return to work bell, we knew we were late for school.

The old school was built in a rectangular shape, with the entrance gates in front and the paths to the doors in the shape of a "V". The schoolhouse was next door and the playground at the back. The boys' cloakroom was made into a woodwork room. Mr. Bevan was the woodwork master. He was a good teacher -- a wonderful man.

My classroom was a large room with a curtain down the centre. There was Standard one and Standard two in there. Further along were the infants' classes and then the doors leading out to the playground. Next to that was the headmaster's office -- then the doors leading out to the boys' playground. There was a folding partition between Standards three and four and Standards five and six. – Mr. Barnden had those two classes. Mr. Mathewson, the headmaster didn't take a class, but used to come in to test us, when we had examinations. He was very strict and he used the cane.

One lovely day we were sitting out on the grass after lunch, Mr. Mathewson suggested that we went for a walk. So right, we went for a walk. Coming back we were late for school weren't we? Meeting us at the gate Mr. Barnden asked, "Why are you late? Go and line up!" Out came Mr. Mathewson. (Dai Matt we used to call him) "Why are you late?" he demanded. I said to him, "You told us to go for a walk, Sir and we went!" He just said, "Go to your classes!" He could be all right, you know.

A friend of mine, Doris James and I collected the registers and counted how many children were in school and put it on the notice board. To do this we had to go into his office in playtime. One day we did this and then went into his room. "I wonder where Dai is?" we said to each other. As we shut the door, there he was, writing out the music on the music-sheet on the back of the door -- so he'd been there all the time! Phew!!!'

121

School memories of Stuart Scrivens, born *1913*

Stuart Scrivens recalls that the old school was on the site of the present nursery school in Wentloog Road. 'I would be walking up the village road at maybe ten to nine in the morning, the bell would be ringing and the children would be coming from the village, from Blacksmith's Lane, now known as Ball Road and from the Moors. The Wards came from Newlands, the James family from Lower Newton and though they had so far to walk, they were never late. There were no platform-soles or high heels then, nor Wellington boots either, but little hob-nailed boots. Many in the parish could not afford an overcoat and the children would often come wet through and be dried out around the old coke-stove in the infants' room. There were no school meals in those days, so we sat around the stove eating our bread and jam sandwiches and drinking cups of water.

The infants' teacher was Ethel Pacey, whose father was chauffeur to the Cubitts, a good and generous gentry family. The headmaster was Mr. Mathewson, a big Irishman going on 14 stone and the best part of 6 ft tall. There was wonderful discipline in the school, such as is not known today. Mr. Mathewson would punish you with his great stick which he called his iron rod, or eye-ron as his Irish pronunciation made it. There was more than the three R's to be learnt in what was then an agricultural area. You had to learn to dig a garden adjacent to the school. A pair of boys, thirteen or fourteen years of age were allocated a plot of ground to dig, plant and look after properly, so that when you left school you would be quite capable of digging your own garden The old Master would always lecture us about digging holes to bury compost, not compost heaps as we have today. I recall one time when we wanted to get our own back on the schoolmaster. We had previously dug a hole in the clay which had filled up with rainwater, so for a bit of a joke, we covered the hole up with old bean sticks and green-stuff from last season's beans. Unfortunately, when the schoolmaster came in, he stepped on the poles and fell in up to his waist in red water. When he got out he locked the gate, grabbed a bean stick and chased us round the garden, hitting out left and right, not with a little stick but with a thick bean stick, leaving an indelible memory of my school days. Another unforgettable school day recollection is of the morning Mr

122

Barndon was taking us in Standard 7 and Mr Mathewson came in and said, "Right Mr Barndon, I'll take this class this morning." He was as usual carrying his stick. Mr Mathewson would sit on the desk, with his three-foot stick, pressing it across his knees, and if you dared move as much as a finger, he'd tap you across the knuckles. He was like a viper striking with that stick. The lesson that morning and those of us in that class have never forgotten, was the introduction of cocoa to England. At the end he said he would question us the following morning. The following morning came, and we knew that he meant what he said and we wondered who was to have a few cuts across the hand with the stick. I remember passing one answer down the aisle to a pal, a Spaniard by the name of Cortez (pronounced by us Corteez), but my message was misunderstood and the lad gave the answer to the master "cold tea." Of course, he was not a good-tempered man at the best of times, but this he thought was done with deliberation and everyone in the class had two cuts. I challenged him to ask me the question, but, "I don't doubt you know the answer, Scrivens," he said, "and you can tell me, but you'll still get two cuts, I've already caned half the class and it wouldn't be fair not to cane you too." That was the discipline of those days and although we didn't like it, I don't honestly think it did us any harm.'

School memories of Gwyn Rees, born *1939*

'I left the Senior Council school at 15. I remember Mr Mathewson was the headmaster when my aunt was going to school -- he used to run the school plays. The only headmaster I remember was when I was in the senior school -- I'd be about 13 or 14 and the headmaster then was a Mr. Davies, a short chap, about five-feet tall. I remember him because of an incident at school. Three boys were caught smoking – John Paradise, Walter Hayman and another boy. Mr. Davies had them in the woodwork class with all of us and he said to John Paradise who was about six foot two inches tall, "Hold your hand out shoulder height!" So John did that. Mr. Davies took one look at him -- and wondered what he had let himself in for. But he had to continue and there he was almost jumping up and down as he delivered the punishment. He gave him six and he gave Walter six and he gave the other fellow six of the best. Walter came home and

123

he had weals across his hands. His mother went to the school and saw the master who admitted that he had caned Walter. He said that he'd been smoking and he disapproved of the boys smoking. The upshot of that was that Walter was transferred from Rumney to a school in Cardiff. It was funny as he was seen doing it and we all had to try and keep straight faces.'

The above photograph shows Ellis Baker in his wheelchair centre front. Ellis, perfectly healthy until the age of 5 years, suffered from a dreadful progressive illness which made him a chronic invalid. His classmates were always sympathetic and kind, going out of their way to make his days happier. On rambles they carried his Merlin chair over rough ground and lifted it and him over stiles. His particular best friend was Bernard Mathewson.

Ellis made good progress in learning, in spite of his physical infirmity and reading was his passion. Following a family move to Cwmcarn, Ellis caught a cold, which developed into pleurisy and pneumonia. He died in 1923, at the young age of 16 years.

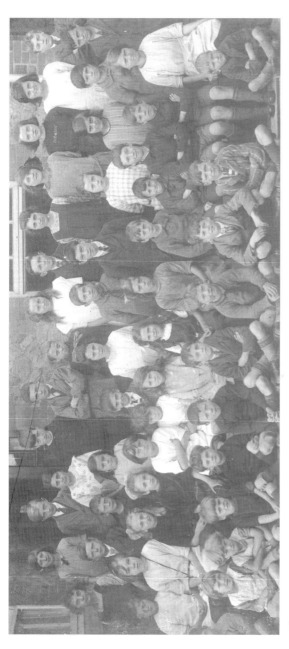

Circa 1920.
Back row: l-r Dilys Redwood, ?, Ivy Bartlett, ?, ?, Billy James, Dorothy James, Rees Thomas, Doreen Thomas, Violet Bartlett, Beaty Carpenter, Mary Tugwell, George Bradshaw.
3rd row: l-r ?, Alfie Powell, ?, Mary Lucas, Gordon Sullivan, Mary Sullivan, Lawrence Francis, Ernie Francis, Edna Powell, Bernice Tugwell, Melvin Marsh, Eric Marsh.
2nd row: l-r ?, Gladys Roberts, Betty Marshall, Olive Marshall, Peggy Dando, ?, ?, ?, Lilian Cutter,?, ?, Cecil Waite, Basil Waite, ?
Front: ?, Bobbie Mathewson, Queenie Emmanuel, Joseph Emmanuel, ?, -Lowder, Leslie Bradshaw, ?, Teddy Edwards, ?, ?, ?

125

Directed by the Headmaster, Mr Mathewson, pupils of Rumney Council School performed several operettas during the early 1920s.

Foreground: Alfie Powell and Ewart Richards. Others include Edna Powell, Bernice Tugwell, Winnie and Beryl Richards, Winnie Adams - the early 1920's

Back row: Kathleen Pearce, Pat Bennett, ?, ?, Thelma Gosling, Dorothy Jones, ?, Margaret Wyatt, -Hulbert.

3rd row: -Brown, - Price, Shirley Berrow, Olive Haines, Lilian Toozer, Phyllis Morgan, Thelma Carter, Betty Chamberlain, Enid Mabbs, Barbara Speak.

2nd row: June Brooker, Josephine Lyle, Valerie Vincent, Rosemary Kestall, Audrey Jones, Margaret Thomas, Jean Dainton, Beryl Bruton, Rona Waters, Iris Morse.

Front row: Joan Ashmore, Wenna Richards, Cynthia Long, - Evans, Edna Hulbert, Joan Hoare, ?

Back row: ?, ?, ?, Jamie Summers, David Davies, Rosalie -, ?

4th row: ?, Jean Watkins, Elsie Ford, ?, Avril Rees, Bernice (Girlie) Horrell, Elsie Bridges, ?, Nesta Thomas.

3rd row: ?, Rhona Walters, Shirley -, -Hall, Olive Webb, ?, Derek Thorne, Mary Trapnell, Pat Lang, Valerie Morris, ?, Bobby Medford, Edith Wright.

2nd row: ?, Simon -, Thelma Greenslade, ?, John North, Sidney Bowes, ?, Ivor Pengelly, Bunny Rees, ?, Margaret Higgins.

Front row: Christopher -, ?, Olga Maitland, ?, Doreen Rees, ?, ?, Graham Williams, Phyllis Penny.

Back row: l-r Iris Ford, Anne Massey, Thelma Greenslade, Stephanie Jones, Emily Dixon, Margaret Higgins, Edna Hulbert, ?
3rd row: Twin—Lewis, ?, ?, Graham Evans, Graham Chadwick, Idris Evans, Alec Connelly, ?, Reg Crabtree,
2nd row: Leslie Perriam, Colin Simon, Josephine Lyles, Audrey Jones, -Waters, ?, ?, ?, - Withers.
Seated: Twin-Lewis, Derek Thorne, Gordon Day, Chris Jones, Trevor Jones, ?,?,?

130

Back row: l-r John Banks, John Day, ?, Vernon Barber, Clifford Watts, Kenneth Bateman, Peter Rolfe ,?, Roger Powell, John Tunnicliff, ?,?,?,?,?, Miss Singer.
Seated: Anne Steele, Margaret Saunders, Marjorie Scrivens, Betty Radmore, Gillian Rorke, Valerie Scott, Pamela Merrett, Ann Pickering, Janet Williams, Diane Whitehead, Sylvia Sutton.
Kneeling: ?, Marcia Rees, ?, ?

131

St. Mellons School

The village school building was reputedly built in 1629-31 as a Poor House and was later adapted to form a school. It was opened in 1864 as a National School and was enlarged in 1886 to hold 140 children - average attendance 101. The school logbooks which are deposited in the Gwent Record Office, date from 1888 with one volume missing for the years 1910-1917.

The Headmaster in 1901 was John Porter, assisted by Misses E. Parish and E. Soderland, the latter, a sixteen year-old pupil teacher. In the 1930's, pupils had the opportunity of sitting the Annual County Entrance Examination, which was held in May each year, for admission to Secondary Schools. As St. Mellons and Rumney lay within the County of Monmouthshire, pupils who were successful in this exam, which was known as the Scholarship Examination, went to the school in Rhiwderin and from 1935, to the new County Secondary School in Forge Lane, Bassaleg. St. Mellons continued to cater for children of all ages until 1958 when the children of secondary school age transferred to the new Graig Secondary School in Bassaleg. St. Mellons was then a Primary school, Juniors and Infants only, with four teachers.

As the number of village children had increased, pre-fabricated buildings were erected in the 1950's to accommodate the Infants. The school in Church Lane had to close in 1980 when the additional buildings were vandalised. The original school building however continued to be used by the Scout Group and other village organisations. In June 1989, vandals set fire to the roof of the old school building itself, which was a Grade II listed building. The St. Mellons Church in Wales Primary School then moved to Dunster Road, Llanrumney and is currently under the leadership of Mrs. Rosemary James, Headteacher.

Extracts from Log Books of the St. Mellons Non-Provided School. (After 1st April 1906, the school became the St. Mellons Monmouthshire Church of England School.)

1872

Oct. 2nd   School closed for feast day....... Headmaster.

Oct 3rd   I visited the school and found it shut; the schoolmaster was in the White Hart, insolent and drunk...... John Evans.

Oct. 4th Children in school – schoolmaster in White Hart again. I at once dismissed him…….John Evans.

1896

Oct. 20th Holiday for competitions in connection with St. Mellons & District Farmers Association; it takes place today and forms the attraction of the year in this agricultural district.

Oct 27th Attendance this week irregular largely due to the children being kept home lifting and gathering potatoes.

1901

Jan. 17th Girls to have tests in needlework and knitting. The teacher comments the following week - Ada Hill worked her gusset wonderfully well.

July 31st School year now ends July 31st instead of February.

Sept. 22nd Dr Shiach called at the school at the request of Mrs Cope to examine cases of ringworm. Two boys were found to be scalp cases another on the face. They were recommended to stay home and the ringworm treated with tincture of iodine.

Oct. 21st Three children off with scarlet fever, a boy living next door to a case was not allowed to attend school.

Nov. 5th Water supply available to the school for the first time. It is explained to the children that the water must be paid for and therefore there must be no waste. The use of the taps supplying the lavatories and offices are explained to the boys and girls separately.

Nov. 29th The taps in the lavatories have all leaked through faulty construction and have been remedied without the aid of the plumber.

1906 – Average attendance for year 108.1 pupils.

March 1st The school was granted a half-day holiday by the County Education Committee in honour of St. David's Day. The last half hour of the morning was spent singing National Welsh songs in a lesson on 'True Patriotism.' (Love of Country and Honour)

March 30th Eliz. Williams reported that she was leaving this afternoon to go 'into service.' This girl was the cleverest scholar in the school and her conduct was at all times a pattern for the other scholars.

May 2nd Early closure. Attended sale of work and entertainment organised by Mrs. Cope in the grounds of Quarry Hill.

May 31st Complaints about the cleanliness of 4 children ----

June 30th Anniversary of the Battle of Waterloo – a special lesson.

July 14th Left school early to attend public meeting and tea arranged in honour of the new Baptist minister.

Welsh and Temperance teaching will be introduced after the holidays. Unfortunately none of the staff are capable of speaking Welsh. A difficulty will therefore arise.

Aug. 13th School re-opened, 106 children present. Remodelling of Welsh teaching – not this year to be taken in Standard Three and only three times a week instead of five, as at first proposed.

Aug. 15th A large card containing facts relating to the 'Abuse of Alcohol' issued by the director was received and placed in a prominent position in the schoolroom.

Sept. 7th Mr Pryce Jones the itinerant lecturer in Temperance for the County visited the school in the afternoon and delivered a lecture on Temperance to the children.

Sept. 27th This morning a girl was found to have told a number of untruths. For this fault she had been reprimanded. In the interests of the girl on this occasion, it was thought necessary to inflict slight corporal punishment – one stroke on the hand. This is the first occasion that corporal punishment has been resorted to in the case of a girl for over a year.

Oct. 10th Owing to heavy rain it was impossible to take drill this morning. Mental arithmetic was substituted.

Oct. 12th Several of the children are suffering from severe colds and some are away through chest infections.

Oct.16th Notification from the Director that the committee recommended that Welsh instruction in this school be not taken at present. When a fresh assistant is required in the school one will be appointed who is competent to teach Welsh and then the Welsh language will at once be taken.

Oct. 26th Owing to the percentage of attendance for September being over 90% (it was 96.3%) the children were granted a half-day holiday this afternoon.

Nov. 2nd The number of children paying the penny per week school fee is gradually becoming smaller. Several parents have sent to say that they will not pay in future, considering evidently that the fee should be abolished – a view shared by the local managers but not by the County Committee. The parents who now pay, have been informed that the payment is quite voluntary.

Nov. 16th It has been arranged that the children into dinner each day shall be in the charge of the assistants and head teacher in turn.

Nov. 21st Instead of the weekly temperance lesson the head teacher gave a lesson on the harm smoking does to boys.

Nov. 30th Miss Parish and Miss Griffiths complained that on their way to and from school they were insulted by a woman named Mrs. L…. who shouted after them several insulting remarks, apparently due to the fact that her grandson was kept in from play as a punishment for inattention at work. The parents of the boy, Clem……. were seen by the local head teacher. They apologised for the conduct of the grandmother explaining that the woman was under the influence of drink.

Dec. 20th School ceased at 4pm for the Christmas Holidays – a fortnight. Re-assemble January 7th 1907. Florence Parish this afternoon left to take up a situation in Cardiff. She gives her reason that the salary here of two shillings a week is far too small.

1907

Jan. 9th Head teacher late, suffering from acute blood poisoning. Scratched while removing a cord from new window in the classroom. Later underwent an operation.

Jan. 22nd Snow fell this morning and in consequence only eighty-seven children were present.

Apr. 15th Jane Jones is away owing to scarlet fever, she was in school this day last week.

Apr. 18th Dolne Stickler is away on the plea that she had some spots on her. The attention of the attendance officer has been drawn to the fact that she is really acting as nurse-maid to a neighbour.

May 27th School re-opened after Whitson Holidays. Attendance poor due to sickness. Jane Jones, a boy whose surname was Budd and two brothers by the name of Sargent are away owing to their brothers suffering from scarlet fever. A few children have been kept home it appears owing to parents having a fear their children may contract the fever through attending school.

June 13th Thirty-two children actually ill with measles. At noon a telegram was received from the Medical Officer ordering that the school be at once closed. It was specified that the school should not be re-opened until July 1st.

Aug. 19th School re-opened after total closure of nine weeks – five weeks through infections and four weeks for summer holiday.

Sept. 4th A letter was received this morning from the Director (J.W.Hall Esq.) instructing the head teacher to close the school tomorrow, Thursday, on the occasion of the St Mellons Methodist Sunday School excursion to Barry. The outing would have caused the absence of over 50% of the children.

Oct. 7th Scarlet fever again! Only one case confirmed so far but wild rumours and panic.

Oct. 14th Surprise visit by Director, "There is a nice air about the school and the Master is doing well."

Oct. 25th The stove in the main room is out of order and the head teacher has asked a Cardiff firm to repair it. The stove has not been started in the schoolroom yet but since October 14th the classroom fire has been lit. A supply of coal was delivered to-day. Mrs Thomas sent a message that unless Mansel Thomas was allowed to leave the room when he wanted to, she would send her children to Rumney School.

Oct. 30th A workman called to examine the stove but found that he had not brought the necessary materials to repair it.

Punishments

Early 20th century discipline was much more strict than it is to-day. Some of the reasons for corporal punishment were:

   i.   Rudeness to a teacher after a caution.

   ii.   Repeated truancy.

   iii. Continued inattention to work.

   iv.   Entering the girls' lavatory during the dinner hour when a number of girls were there and used bad language.

   v.   Throwing stones at someone.

   vi.   Loitering on the way to school.

23 punishments were carried out in 1910.

     Further reasons and number of strokes-

Talking during lessons	1-to the hand.
Idleness	2-to the hand.
Impertinence to the teacher	4-to the hand and 3- to the back.
Continued annoyance	2-to the hand and 3-to the back.
Copying	1- to the hand.
Smoking on the Ton, (2nd offence, tobacco destroyed)	1- to the hand.
Following Hunt and truancy	3 - to the hand.
Bullying	2- to the hand.
Disobedience and Insolence	6-to the body.

1946
Mar. 1ˢᵗ Special lessons were given on St. David and a concert was given by the children, all the items being Welsh. These were pianoforte, choruses, solos and recitations, there being twenty-six items in all. Drawings and paintings of the Welsh Emblems – daffodil, leek, dragon, harp and Prince of Wales feathers – decorated the classroom walls. School closed at 12-15pm.

Mar. 13ᵗʰ The travelling-van visited the school this afternoon when the dentist extracted the teeth of twenty-two children.

Mar. 15ᵗʰ Received a letter from Mr. G. M. Ace stating that his daughter Betty will be confined to her bed for a few days as a result of her having teeth extracted. They had to take her to Cardiff Royal Infirmary at 1a.m. as their private doctor could not stop the bleeding and she thinks a blood transfusion may be necessary. Notified the Medical Officer.

Apr. 3ʳᵈ Mrs. D. Lea Banner, Organiser and Lecturer of the King Edward V11 Welsh National Memorial Association visited the school in the afternoon and gave a lecture on 'The Prevention, Treatment and Abolition of Tuberculosis.'

Apr. 28ᵗʰ School re-opened this morning after the Easter Holiday. Mr Jones, the temperance lecturer, visited the school this morning and talked to thirty-five of the older scholars.

May 6ᵗʰ School closed for Labour Day.

May 16ᵗʰ Glenys Watkins from Class 2 fell down going to the girls' back premises with a cup in her hand and cut her hand badly in two places. This was dressed by members of Staff. Mrs Watkins was sent for and Mr Ball kindly consented to take the girl and her mother to the Nurse in Castleton, who is the little girl's Aunty, for her to dress the cuts.

May 24ᵗʰ Empire Day message read to the school in Assembly. A talk on the Empire was given to the children. Average attendance for the week 81.8%.

June 27ᵗʰ School closed for Religious Instruction Examination. 84 children present for the examination – registers not marked.

July 19ᵗʰ This afternoon I am attending the funeral of Lord Cope of St. Mellons, one of the Managers of the school and an old pupil. The Top Class of the school are also attending and helping in the choir.

Sept. 3ʳᵈ School opened after the Summer Holidays at 9.15 a.m.

There were 76 children present out of 80 on the books. Circular No. 14 received re: Form 7A and the abolishing of the 'Good Attendance' Half Holiday. Received the Circular No. 119 Re: Milk in Schools Scheme. Notified by Director that a holiday is granted on Wednesday Sept. 4th on the occasion of the St. Mellons Agricultural Show.

Dec. 20th The school closed at 4 p.m. for the Christmas Holidays. The children then had their Christmas party in the main classroom which was beautifully decorated with paper decorations, holly and coloured lights. After tea, a presentation of a clock was made by Squire C. C. Williams Esq. on behalf of the Managers, Staff and the Scholars to Mrs. A. Lloyd who was retiring after many years service at the school. The Vicar and the Headmaster also wished her well in her retirement. After tea the children were entertained by Mr. C. Page, ventriloquist and conjuror. The children sang carols to the parents who had been invited. The children were given bags containing two apples, two oranges, bars of chocolate, chocolate biscuits and a packet of Smith's crisps.

1947

Jan. 8th Miss M. Davy took charge of class 2 this morning. The school opened at 9.15am when there were 75 children present out of 80.

Jan. 28th The attendance has been poor for the last two days, sixty children being present. Today there are forty-three children present out of eighty on the books. This is due entirely to the bitter wintry weather and the heavy falls of snow.

Jan. 30th Telephoned County Hall and obtained permission to close school at 9.45am owing to the heavy fall of snow.

Jan. 31st – Feb. 12th The Headmaster records poor attendance and the bad weather conditions affecting the children from the outlying districts especially.

Feb. 13th Circular received from County Hall stating that all schools were closed until Monday 17th Feb. owing to the severity of the weather.

Feb. 17th Telephoned County Hall and received instructions to close until Wednesday, owing to frozen lavatories.

Feb. 19th School re-opened at 9.15am although there were bursts in the pipes and consequently no water in school. The caretaker flushes the lavatories with buckets of water from the house. The attendance is still very poor, 51 children being present.

Mar. 10th No school was held on the 5th, 6th and 7th owing to the worst snowstorms in living memory. The conditions are still very bad this morning, the melting snow causing great pools of water all around the school making it practically impossible to get into school without having wet feet. The few children who arrived were therefore sent home, a number of these having wet feet.

Mar. 14th Circular No.3 to Head Teacher received this morning dealing with the following: Raising the School-leaving Age, Infectious Diseases, Handicapped Pupils and Registration of Handicapped Pupils.

May 12th Circular received regarding employment of children in Agriculture. Decided to give permission for children 13 years of age and over to be employed.

Oct. 7th Letter received from County Hall stating that the Committee has resolved that tenders for the demolition of the air-raid shelter be invited.

1948

Feb. 18th The top-class boys spent the afternoon up the garden digging their plots. Some time was spent choosing the seeds from the seed list. The order for seeds and manure was sent to the Three Salmons Seed Store Usk. The allowance for seeds granted by the Education Authority was £3-0-0.

Mar. 1st Mr. D. E. Jones, Lecturer in Temperance, visited the school and gave a lecture on temperance to thirty of the senior children. After the morning break a concert was held. The programme was made up of Welsh songs sung by the children, solos, pianoforte solos and recitations. The school closed at 12.15 p.m. for the usual St. David's Day holiday.

Sept. 8th **Report by H. M. Inspectors** on St. Mellons Church of England School, Monmouthshire, inspected on 13th May 1948. Mixed and Infants Department.

The building contains three well-lit and adequately-heated classrooms, one of which accommodates two classes. The surface of the playground is in a very bad condition. Part of it is still occupied by an air-raid shelter and space for physical training is thereby very restricted. A nearby field is available for organized games. It is understood that arrangements are being made to convey mid-day meals to the school.

There are 79 children on the roll organized in four classes. The school is staffed by the headmaster who, is in charge of the top class and three young women teachers, all of whom are qualified. The schemes of work are well conceived and are carefully co-ordinated throughout. The need for toys and sense-training apparatus for the first group is fully realised and the equipment is gradually being supplemented. Much care has been taken in the choice of suitable material for class reading and the standard reached by the children is high. Class libraries are being formed.

The time and care devoted to Speech Training is well justified. Very pleasing choral-speaking was heard and delightful story-telling. Speech-making is another interesting feature of the work. Carefully-prepared five minute speeches were remarkably well delivered by children aged eight to ten years. Considerable ability in written expression has also been developed and there were some outstandingly good examples of Composition on a wide range of topics.

1949

May 30th The following children were successful in qualifying for admission to a Grammar School on the results of the County Grading Examination: Clive Choulds, David Connolly, Gillian Gerrish, Alan Morgan, Beth Morgan, Lionel Pretty, Georgina Price, Graham Rees and Arthur Thomas.

1950

Nov. 14th During the dinner interval the Tredegar Farmers Foxhounds went through the village after a fox. W. Lewis, Chas. Prosser, A. Monk and Willie Edwards followed them and did not return for the afternoon. The four were punished on attending assembly next day.

1951

Jan. 18th Fires not lit by caretaker – no coal, children given milk then dismissed. County Hall informed.

Nov. 11th Had occasion to cane 10 boys for immoral offences which took place near the playground.

1953

May 22nd Miss Muriel Davies and members of St. Mellons

140

Coronation Committee presented five-shilling pieces and Coronation Souvenirs to all the children. School closed at 4 p.m. for Whitsun Holidays and Coronation celebrations.

1954

Oct. 15th Head teacher absent from 2:10 p.m. until 3:30 p.m. attending the funeral of Colonel Emerson Davies, who was for several years a manager of this school.

1955

June 10th Grading Examination Results received today. Of the thirteen children who sat the following were successful: Glyn Davey, Elizabeth Kendall, Catherine Rocyn-Jones, Paul Walkey and Peter Rees.

June 15th Dr. Cox visited school – examined 6 year old maladjusted child.

Oct. 24th Commenced National Foundation Testing with 7yrs + children.

1958

September The school changed from an all-age school to Juniors and Infants only. Pupils of Secondary age were transferred to the Graig Secondary School in Bassaleg.

1962

Oct. 26th The school was granted a day's holiday on the occasion of the visit of the Queen to Newport.

1963

Jan. 7th School re-opened. Due to heavy snowfall only 42 children in this morning. The boys' toilets were frozen. 58 children attended in the afternoon.

Oct. 10th The Bic pen has been introduced into use in the school today – as an experiment.

1966

Dec. 8th Mrs Thomas the Canteen Assistant, returned to her duties.

The Parish Council, led by their Chairman Mrs. Edna Potter and accompanied by Miss Muriel Davies attended school this morning. A short ceremony took place during which the Council presented to the school a plaque to commemorate the service of Miss Muriel Davies to the district and village of St. Mellons. The plaque with her name was hung on the wall in the Main Hall. In addition there will be an annual Muriel Davies Nature Award donated by the Parish Council to a boy or girl who shows a keen interest and love for the countryside and the world of nature as a whole, the Staff to be the judges. On behalf of the school, Alun Thomas and Sandra Davies proposed a vote of thanks and Karen King presented Miss Davies with a bouquet of flowers. The school was closed in the afternoon to commemorate this important and proud day in its history.

1969
June 24th Notified by Miss Davies, Headmistress of Michaelstone-y-Vedw School, that her school would definitely close at the end of term. 18 pupils have opted to attend St. Mellons with the possibility of a further 4 out of district pupils. (Glamorgan)

1971
Nov. 19th Today the Motorway was officially opened by H. M. the Queen accompanied by H. R. H. the Duke of Edinburgh. The whole school attended the opening. I was introduced to H. M. the Queen by Mrs Hollings, Chairman of the Board of Managers.

1974
Jan. 23rd The glazier came – must return – he broke the glass.
Mar. 29th The last school day under the administration of Monmouthshire County Council.
Apr. 1st The school now under the administration of South Glamorgan.

Dilys Hughes' memories of St. Mellons' School

Mrs Lloyd's class was famous for its spelling lessons. Every day she would write down about thirty words on the blackboard and for the first half-hour every afternoon she'd point them out with a cane and we'd repeat them parrot fashion. The difference between 'their' and 'there' was never explained, but we must have been pretty smart as we all 'caught on'. In September the biggest boys would take a couple of large zinc baths up to Quarry Hill where they were filled with lovely yellow pears, courtesy of Lord Cope. These were then shared out among the pupils and there was never any jostling.

A tale about St. Mellons School that amuses me is one that my Great-uncle loved to tell. When he was a pupil-teacher, he had occasion to keep the two Morgan boys in after school. They lived in

142

the Fox and Hounds public house. About a week later – my uncle having to pass the pub on his way home – Mrs Morgan called to him, "Mr Thomas, could I see you for a minute?" She showed him into the little taproom on the right and she left, closing the door. He heard the key turning in the lock and Mrs Morgan's voice, "Now, Mr. Thomas, we'll see how you like being kept in!" After a while, although the window was small, he managed to escape through it.

School Sports

The first local Sports Day for the Elementary Schools in the Wentloog District was held at Walk Farm, Castleton, in September 1923, when children from the schools of Rumney, St. Mellons, Castleton, Bassaleg, Michaelston, Peterstone and St. Brides took part.

St. Mellons School rugby team c.1924, teacher Mr. A.H.Williams.
Back row: l-r Charlie Linter, Gordon Shepstone, Leslie Jones, Raymond Taylor, Oswald Thomas.
3rd row: Arthur Davies, Alec Shand, Noel Ivins, Billy Wheeler, Peter Thomas, William Harris, George Dando, George Cox.
2nd row: Jacky Martin, Gordon Addis, Bryn Thomas, Gwyn Jones, Fred Williams.
Front row: Henry Harris, Dinny Williams, John Glover.

143

Nipped-in waists for the ladies and boots for the children were the order of the day. Children include Edith Hulbert, Eunice Capel, Hilda Sydenham, Jack Williams and Courtney Williams.

Back row: l-r Arthur Davies, George Cox, Raymond Taylor, Gordon Shepstone, Leslie Jones, Brynley Thomas, Oswald Thomas, Gwyn Jones.
3rd row: Alec Shand, Edith Roberts, Thurza Monk, Clarice Thomas, Doris Wheeler, Maisie Monk, Doreen Shepstone, A.H.Williams.
2nd row: May Martin, Ann Ballinger, Phyllis Hughes, Enid Thomas.
Front row: Gordon Addis, Jack Martin, Dinny Williams, Fred Williams, Charlie Williams.

145

St. Mellons School children and teachers photographed on the Ton - c. 1910

146

Back row: l-r Peter Thomas, Cliff Thomas, Cliff Smith, Bertie Adams, Jack Lever, Philip Thomas, Trevor Cox, Bertie Stickler, Aubrey Sadler.

Middle row: Wally Davies, S. Jenkins, Reg Dando, Doris Taylor, Peggy Ballinger, -Dando, Doreen Morgan, Lorena Shand, George Dando.

Front row: Anne Harris (Howells), Dilys Hughes, Nancy Thomas (Leeburn), Olive Lever, Miss Williams, Edna Gerrish (Potter), Mabel Dando, Alfie Dando.

147

Back row: l-r Ann Sydenham (Turner), Pat Evans, Jean Thomas, John Sydenham, Marcia Welch, Lily Macmanus, Linda Miller.
Middle row: John Morgan, Malcolm Wilbraham, Alec Wilbraham, Gordon Shears, Pauline Cronin, Sylvia Davidge, Sheila Bird.
Front row: Gweneth Thomas, Ann Holloway, Ken Webber, Eleanor John, Jimmy Taylor, Terry Watts, Brian Shears, Esna Lloyd, Mary Thomas.

148

Back row: l-r Malcolm Webber, Peter Benson, Rhydian Jones, Mervyn Davidop, Tony Blake, Jane Urquhart, ?, Desmond Hughes, Marion Maggs, ?, Sheila Cawley, Wendy Potter, Stuart Williams.
Front row: Susan Higgins, Susan Noel, ?, Susan Jones, ?, Susan Noel, Frances Williams, Susan Jay, Pat Wilkinson, Judith Hale, Elaine Adams, June Saunders, June Wilbraham, Kay Fowler.

149

Back row: l-r Roy Clease, Dennis Bird, Peter Burchell, Nigel Evans, ?, Gerald Owen, David Wilbraham, Howard Duggan, Glyn Davey.

Middle row: Robert Webb, Jimmy Pike, Ian Benson, Isobel Kendall, Catherine Rocyn-Jones, Roger Walkey, Paul Walkey, Peter Rees.

Front row: Sandra Wheeler, Janet Taylor, Angela Maggs, Gillian Evans, Margaret Durston, Vivienne Davidge, Judith Morgan, Jane Sydenham, Marilyn Nurse, Rosemary Simpson, Anne Buckner, Mary Russell.

150

Mr Davies Class. c 1967/8

Back row: l-r Guy Morgan, Cathy Wilkinson, Gavin Jones, Adrian Godfrey, Lee Morton, Patricia Lewis.

Front row: Christine Jones, Karen King, Elizabeth Morgan, Susan Parr, Susie Lowe, Jane Crowdice, Tina King.

151

SPORT AND RECREATION.

Tradition has it that in the eighteenth century there was a *Shrove Tuesday football match* between Rumney and St. Mellons. The goals were the respective churches of the two villages. The ball, an inflated pig's bladder, could be kicked or carried (a mixture of soccer and rugby). Everybody could take part if they were prepared to risk life and limb, for the number of participants was immaterial, with the victors enjoying free samples at one of the beaten village's pubs.

In 1794, one of the Rumney players died from a skull fracture and the match was then discontinued for a number of years. In later years, the object was to score at either the Carpenters Arms, Rumney or the Blue Bell at St.Mellons with the start-line established roughly half-way between the two villages.

In the late nineteenth century a more serious sport, with entry fees and money prizes and known as the Powderhall races took place in Rumney. Athletes from far and wide competed.

Powderhall racetrack on the lower part of Cae Glas Road.

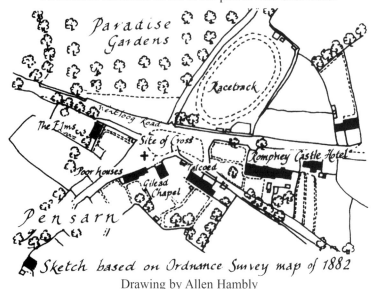

Drawing by Allen Hambly

The first written record of sport in Rumney and St. Mellons was an article in the *Countryside Magazine* in the early 1920s which stated that a *cricket* team had been formed in 1888 at St. Mellons. In the 1920s, sport began to flourish with a number of clubs and teams taking part in sporting activities. The Squire of Llanrumney made some of his parkland available at the Lodge Field and the recreation ground. The communities of Rumney and St. Mellons used the fields and most of the local gentry were very supportive. There was keen rivalry and competition between all the villages in the area. Local schools had annual sports days. Rumney had three football teams: the Athletic Club, the Brotherhood and the Sports Club, whilst St Mellons produced two *hockey* teams from the Women's Institute and the Red Triangle Club.

Little is recorded about *soccer* in St. Mellons in the early 1920s. At that time Rumney Athletic ARC was admitted to the Fourth Division of Cardiff and District League and in 1924, played a game against the Moorsmen (Rumney Moors) at the Ball Farm field. Ivor Batten kicked off and Len Rees refereed. Rumney won the match by two goals to one, the scorers were Spencer Penny and Tom Hurley, whilst Clifford Ward scored for the Moorsmen.

In 1928 Rumney Sports Club came into being and included a soccer team which had a new set of jerseys in the Squire's racing colours, (green and white). The clubhouse was erected on the western edge of Ball Farm, adjacent to the former market gardens on one side and Highcroft on the other. Later, other sports were introduced such as *rugby*, hockey, cricket and *tennis*. In the mid 1930s, *baseball* was introduced and became very popular with both sexes.

Sporting activities in St. Mellons had also begun to flourish. The cricket section under the auspices of the Red Triangle Club became a force to be reckoned with and the team included three of the Walkey family plus Ray Hughes, W. Solly, Tom Adams and W. Ballinger.

Hockey was very popular and the village fielded three teams from the Triangle Club and one from the Women's Institute. It is reported that there was much rivalry between the two clubs. On one occasion in 1921, the W.I. refused to join forces with the Red Triangles for a match against the Shell Mex Company side. The

Women's Institute teams were affiliated to the Monmouth County Hockey Association and to the All-England League. Their organiser was Miss Muriel Davies and the standard of hockey in both clubs must have been very high because men and ladies were selected to represent County and Country.

In 1928, after a long search, the Red Triangle Club secured for their hockey team, the pitch at Ty-To-Maen Convalescent Home, through the kindness of Cardiff Royal Infirmary. This was one of the best hockey grounds in South Wales, but sadly in the following year they had to cancel fixtures due to lack of players.

Rumney hockey team was experiencing similar difficulties and it was agreed that they would combine with St. Mellons, which led to a wonderful revival of the game one year later. It was then possible to field teams on Wednesdays and Saturdays. Among the players for the combined Rumney and St Mellons team were Miss Muriel Davies, (Team Captain) Max Budgen, (Vice-Captain) Vena Williams, (Vice-Captain) Muriel Buckland, Mary Gerrish, Elsie Toozer, Mary Tugwell, Bernice Tugwell, J.Mundy, Miss Lockley, R. Lockley, Reg. Prosser, Reg. Jones, Connie English and George Parish.

Rumney Ladies' hockey team c1920.

During the season 1937/38, a difference of opinion arose in Rumney Sports Club. Plans to revive the soccer team would necessitate the team playing alternate weeks on the rugby pitch. Rugby players strongly objected since the playing of rugby would be adversely affected. The Rugby Club elected to move out and the Squire came to their rescue once again, offering them the use of a field near Llanrumney Hall.

A decision was made to change the name of the team to Rumney and St Mellons R.F.C., based at the Fox and Hounds in St. Mellons, where the outhouses were used for changing rooms. During the summer of 1939, the Rugby Club gained permission to use a building in the market garden between Old Hill and New Hill St Mellons. It was old and in the process of being refurbished in readiness for the following season, but the outbreak of World War II brought their efforts to an end.

St. Mellons Linnets' rugby team 1921.

155

Rugby had been played in Rumney for about one hundred years, but it was not until the 1930s that it gained in popularity when there were at least two teams. During WWII and until 1950, no rugby was played. By dint of the hard work of Emlyn Davies, Shony Davies and Mr. Sullivan a new club was formed. Tom Jones was appointed fixture secretary and later passed the job on to his son Alfred. Between the two of them they gave over thirty years' service to the club. Monkstone Dancing School was very helpful in allowing them to use its garage for changing and washing facilities. The school also supplied hot water.

By the late 1950s, a second XV had been formed. In 1964, a youth XV was formed due to the untiring work of Viv Davies, Terry King, George Burgess and brothers, Peter and Dennis Murphy. In the same year the second XV won the first trophy for the club. The Rugby Club progressed rapidly and by 1974 owned their clubhouse at the Riverside Park playing field. Councillor Sam Parker had worked tirelessly to acquire the clubhouse site. The next big task was to obtain Welsh Rugby Union status, which was achieved in 1987. Great service to the club was given by Ken Gooding, Con Ritchie, Graham McCormack and Dave Escott.

From 1921 tennis was played regularly in St Mellons on a grass court at Ty Bont, by courtesy of the Shellard family and later, on new tennis courts at Tyr Winch Road Playing Field. Matches were played against teams from surrounding areas, such as Penylan, Castleton, Whitchurch etc. In 1923, Miss Muriel Davies presented a tournament trophy. Regular players were Miss Lockley, R. Lockley, R.Prosser, Reg Jones, Olive Stevens, George Parrish, Doris Solly and others.Two hard courts, owned by Mr. Jack Baldwin were available in Rumney at the Grove, where regular players were Chris and Sally King, Gwyn Richards, Len Brown, Connie Hutchings, Geoff Thomas, Jack and Eileen Dunn, Joyce and Yvonne Trinnick and Eddie Humphreys. Tournaments were played at Rumney House and Rumney Court, by courtesy of Mr. W. Cubitt and Mr. Ivor Griffin respectively.

Baseball became very popular from 1930 and was played by both men and women. The ladies' team originally played on Batten's field which was later taken for housing development. They then moved to the men's site on the Lamby foreshore. Today there are a

156

number of clubs, mainly in Llanrumney, which have been very successful.

The bowling green at Rumney Hill Gardens was opened by the Lord Mayor of Cardiff in 1957. It was built on the site formerly designated for use as a cemetery but was found to be unsuitable for this purpose. *Rumney Bowling Club* was formed in 1957 and since its inception members have gained a number of prestigious awards.

In the early 1900s, St. Mellons had a thriving cricket team under the auspices of the Red Triangle Club which was affiliated to the Y.M.C.A. Games were played on the Lodge Field at the top of St. Mellons Hill and they enjoyed a good reputation. Tom Adams had been their captain for twenty years up to 1932 when the club was disbanded due to lack of interest. Sports clubs in those early years were not only places for sporting activities, they also became venues for dances, card games, skittles and dominoes. The following players of international fame have resided in or played for Rumney and St. Mellons during their successful careers; Ian Robinson, Nigel Walker, Steve Ford, Robert Norster and snooker player Mark Williams.

St. Mellons Golf Club was formed in 1937 and was then called the St. Mellons Golf and County Club. It was a privately-owned club, managed by the St. Mellons County Estates. The Club was owned by Mr. Gwyn Davies of Vaindre Hall, the big house adjacent to the 14th green. In 1963, Mr. Davies died and part of his estate, including the golf course and clubhouse, came onto the property market. The executors of Mr. Davies' Estate offered to sell the club to the members for £34,000, not a lot of money by today's standards, but a fortune in 1964. Most of the 1,000 social members did not want to know, but it was a different story with the 160 golfing members. A consortium of senior members was formed including Colin Smale, Tom Phillips, Viv. Williams, Ralph Kemp, John Crouch and others, who proposed that the golfing members purchase the club and raise the £34,000 purchase price. By March 1964, the Club came into the ownership of the members and was renamed the St. Mellons Golf Club (1964) Ltd.

Since 1964 the golf course has been extended, together with major improvements to the clubhouse. St. Mellons Golf Club currently boasts of having three Welsh Internationals, two at Senior level and one at Junior.

157

Rumney football team c. 1930. Back row: l-r Roy Williams, Edgar Scrivens, Trevor Williams, Harry Webb, Emlyn James, Trevor Trevarthen, J. Toozer, Frank Clatworthy, Jack Farmer.
Middle row: Arthur James, Spencer Penny, Lawrence Davies, Billy Sullivan, Ludwig Peterson, ?
Front row: ?, Tommy Elliot, Lesley Hurley.

Rumney football team c. 1950s Back row: l-r Nobby Wyllie, Bill Barrett, Bobby Fowler, Tom Radford, Trevor Bolt, ?, Mickey Brown, Arthur Thomas, Cyril Thomas.
Front row: Brynley Cottrell, John Keenan, Alban (Nobby) Mahoney, Eric Ridout, David Davies, Bobby Foulkes. In front: Robert Bolt.

Rumney Ladies' baseball team 1936/7. Back row: l-r Peggy Reynolds, Joan Prankard, Phyllis Livermore, Eileen Dunn, Gladys Mears, Betty Gerrish, Eve John, Dilys Richards. Front row: Violet Hutchings, Connie Hutchings, Olwen Dennison.

Rumney and St. Mellons rugby team 1938/39.
Back row: l-r - Dawnay, Mr.Jones, Ernie Waters.
Middle row: Referee, ?, Jack McKinnon, Doug Maplestone, Dennis Bedford, Stewart Sheppard, Ernie Higgins, Ken Johnson, Don Johnson, Geoff Thomas, Arthur Sheppard.
Seated: Alan Walkey, John Davies, Tom Cobner, Ron Doddington, Ossie Dawnay, Geoff Merrett, ?
In front: Jack Dunn, Eddie Humphreys.

159

St. Mellons cricket team 1921

St. Mellons men's hockey team 1920s

THE COUNTRYSIDE MAGAZINE
(Including Social & Cultural Life)

The Countryside Magazine was published monthly, at a cost of one penny from February 1921 until 1936, initially serving Rumney and St. Mellons, later including other parishes of the Wentloog area. The magazine, which was edited by Mr Harold Coombes, reflected the whole panorama of life at that time and reported important local events. In the early years of the publication, the *South Wales Echo* was very complimentary, stating, 'It is of unusual interest and value. It is something more than a chronicle of small beer and village gossip, for it deals with the antiquities of the district, gives nature notes, presents news of all the sports and social activities.'

JULY, 1921. No. 5. Vol. I.

Harold Coombes, who lived with his wife in Rumney opposite the present police station on Newport Road, was a man dedicated to his community, a keen sportsman and interested in all aspects of local life. Mr. Coombes was voluntary editor of the magazine for the whole fifteen years of its existence.

As with most publications today, this magazine depended on income from advertisers. The advertisers were not only from Rumney, St. Mellons and Castleton but many were from Roath, Splott, the centre of Cardiff and a few from Newport. The retail trade was certainly beginning to understand the power of advertising. The following is a selection of some of the items and services advertised.

161

162

163

In 1921, one big event recorded in great detail, was the visit of HRH the Prince of Wales. The editor, responding to readers' requests, produced at 'enormous' cost, a Special Souvenir Edition. In his editorial he wrote, 'Such an opportunity could not be lost, let the expenses be what they may. Never was such a day in St. Mellons as that on which our charming Prince Edward, Heir Apparent to the Throne, visited it. The auspicious occasion demanded a comprehensive record of all that happened on that memorable day, June 7th 1921.'

There were many photographs and reports from those involved. Mr. T. Ifor Jones produced an article entitled *The Full Story of the Prince's Visit.* He had read, some time earlier, that the Prince would be motoring from Cardiff to Newport and as the Independent Chapel had recently been secured as an Educational Centre, he thought it a good idea to ask His Royal Highness to visit St. Mellons and inspect the local Ex-Servicemen and the Sports and Social Club buildings.

'This was the beginning of weeks of preparation, painting, polishing, cleaning, planning who should attend, making refreshments etc. The occasion was obviously a great success. There was a chorus of cheers as the Prince arrived. "Jumping out of his car, a lithe, clean-cut type of sporting Britisher, he was received by L. Forestier Walker Esq., M.P. Immediately the Band of the 2nd Batt. Royal Welsh Fusiliers played the National Anthem, the Parade of Ex-Servicemen sprang rigidly to attention and the public stood bare-headed." The report lists those people introduced and men and women to whom the Prince spoke, such as Sgt. Hinton, who had lost a leg in the War. Sgt. Major James Vincent of Rumney, probably the oldest veteran, also caught the eye of the Prince, who, recognising his medals, asked him about his Sudan War experiences.

Inside the building, introductions were made to lady helpers and photographs of various teams and fixture-lists of cricket, billiards, athletics, lawn tennis and boxing were given attention. The Prince then relaxed with a cigarette and two cups of tea, with the ladies dancing attendance. He thanked the ladies and moved outside to the enclosure, where he stopped and praised the children for their hearty singing and was presented with a small bunch of roses by a coy Thurza Shepstone. The one hundred and fifty Ex-Service men

164

then passed in single file, Mr. T. Ifor Jones introduced them to the Prince, who had a word with each one as he shook his hand. As the Prince left, a Guard of Honour was formed by Boy Scouts from Cardiff. St. Mellons Boy Scouts were at the entrance to the enclosure where the band struck up the Welsh National Anthem. The party proceeded to the road in a hurricane of cheers where he met Miss Ann Davies, one of the oldest inhabitants. With the aid of the Ex-Servicemen to hold back the crowd, he walked, cheers ringing in his ears, the hundred yards to the Chapel. On his arrival, the Treasurer Mr. Reg. Jones opened the doors and HRH The Prince of Wales entered, thus opening it informally.

The Prince of Wales shaking hands with ex-servicemen.

Proposed classes for the new educational centre were listed, debating, choral, lectures, children's lantern lectures and Women's Institute Classes. As the Prince was leaving he was asked what he thought of the buildings and the work being done. "I think it's splendid," he replied. "I am only sorry there are not more of these places as I go around the country, I have rarely heard of such a building being taken over in a village like this for such classes. I really think it's a wonderful piece of work and I wish you and all who work with you every success." Cheers followed him up St. Mellons Hill as he went over the hill-top. Many of those present said,

"He arrived as the Prince of Wales, he left in the golden sunshine as our Prince of Hearts!" Everyone agreed that it had been a day to remember.'

Another special occasion recorded in the Countryside Magazine, was the unveiling of the Cenotaph and the opening of the Memorial Hall in Rumney on 19th March 1924. The Foundation Stones had been laid on September 22nd 1923, by Mrs Ivor Griffin of Rumney Court and the Squire, Mr C.C. Llewellyn Williams of Llanrumney Hall. Fund raising continued in order to meet the cost of £2300.

'At 3 o'clock on the opening day, everything in the village appeared normal and undisturbed. As 3:30 approached, the whole scene changed as if by magic. Villagers gathered from all quarters and visitors came from various parts of the locality. Rumney was about to honour its heroic dead. The beautiful Cenotaph was to be unveiled and the magnificent Memorial Hall opened.

The spirit of Remembrance was manifest everywhere. Silent thought and reflection supplanted vocal utterance. The quiet of this auspicious occasion was infinitely more expressive than a myriad of chattering tongues. Some two thousand people were present. The platform held a worthy assembly, which included the Marchioness of Bute, Lord Tredegar, Mr. L. Forestier-Walker M.P., the Venerable Archdeacon of Monmouth, Mrs Ivor Griffin and Mrs Fred Howell.

The ceremony began with the singing of "O God our help in ages past" which the people sang with fervour. Then followed a scripture reading and a prayer said by the Rev. Sorton Davies B.A. The reading of the names of Rumney's thirty-five fallen men was delivered in silence. Lord Tredegar then unveiled the Cenotaph and addressed the gathering. He pointed out that over two hundred and ninety Rumney men had served their country during the War and he very much regretted that thirty-five of them never came back. The Archdeacon, assisted by the Vicar of Rumney, pronounced the dedication and a bugler sounded the "Last Post" from the Hall Tower. Wreaths were then placed on the Cenotaph.

The Chairman, Mr L. Forestier-Walker, then called upon the Marchioness of Bute to formerly open the Memorial Hall which she did with a golden key. The Marchioness then made a short speech, finishing with, "It seems to me that we need no memorial to the glorious dead – they are ever in our thoughts. What we need, rather, is something tangible to remind us, who are still living, not to fall short of the ideals for which they laid down their lives – honour, justice, freedom, truth. So may this Hall, which I am privileged to open to-day, be a token to all around, that the people of Rumney are carrying on the principles for which their loved ones died."

Opening of the Memorial Hall Rumney, The Marchioness of Bute with Mr. William Jones, (Highcroft) on the left and the architect, Mr. W. T. Gough on the right.

People then filed into the newly-opened Hall where further formalities continued, including more speeches and hearty votes of thanks to all those who had contributed to the achievement of the building of the Memorial Hall and Cenotaph. Mrs Fred Howell opened the bazaar, promising a subscription of ten guineas towards the fund. Further votes of thanks followed, ending with Mr. Wm. Jones (Highcroft) earnestly appealing to all those present to allow the stallholders to relieve them of every penny they could afford. The debt remaining on the Hall, he wanted cleared as soon as possible. Tea was then served, after which the stallholders got down to business, showing good salesmanship. Money they wanted and money they got! The cause was the thing that mattered!'

Social and Cultural Life.

With the facilities provided by the Sports and Social Club and Educational Centre in St. Mellons and the new Memorial Hall in Rumney, social activities in the area increased including those of the Women's Institute.

The **Women's Institute Movement** had been formed in Stoney Creek, Ontario Canada in 1897 by Mrs Adelaide Hoodless. Mrs Hoodless was brought up in a rural community. Later she married a business-man from Hamilton and one of their children died from drinking contaminated milk. Consequently she sought to introduce domestic science to schools and colleges and to women living in rural areas. The Women's Institute aimed to teach rural women hygiene and childcare and help them to improve their local communities.

The W. I. Movement spread throughout Canada. Mrs Alfred Watt from British Columbia had been an adviser to the Department of Agriculture assisting in the formation of new branches. When her husband died she decided to move to the U.K. Her early attempts to establish the W.I. were unsuccessful. In February 1915, she met Mr Nugent Harris of the A.O.S. (Agricultural Organisation Society) a government body set up to help rural communities cope with rapid changes taking place at that time. Men were abandoning the land to work in factories and other urban developments. The A.O.S. worked to help farmers and smallholders set up co-operatives to buy and sell at better prices; also they became involved in projects to revitalise and improve the quality of village life. The idea of the W.I. movement appealed to Nugent Harris and consequently the A.O.S received funds from the Treasury to promote the new W.I.

The first Women s Institute was established in the U.K. on Anglesey in North Wales at Llanfair P.G. in September 1915. From the outset it was envisaged as a non-political and non-denominational organisation. The first meeting of St. Mellons W.I. was held at Llanrumney Hall on 13th October 1919 with Mrs Maud Williams, wife of the Squire as the first President. Many W.I. members were mothers and daughters and the first half-year joining fee in 1919 was one shilling. Other W.I.s were formed in the area and reports appeared regularly in the Countryside Magazine. One describes the visit to St. Brides W.I. of the other Institutes in the

168

Group: - St. Mellons, Rumney, Marshfield and Peterstone. The occasion was the annual picnic on 18th August 1927. It was held on the beach at St. Brides and with the exception of a few heavy storms, it was a moderately fine day! Tea was served in the Waverley Restaurant and a very happy crowd chatted away. After-tea games, organised by the Misses M. Davies, I. Cubitt and G.M. Stanley, were held on the beach. A tug-of-war between the various Institutes caused much fun, the 'Invincibles' being St.Mellons.

Members St.Mellons W.I. in the 1950s.
In background: Phyllis Taylor, Rose Wheeler, Gwen Winmill, Carrie David, Florrie Bailey, Muriel Davies, Polly Rock, Eva Gerrish, Annie Jones, Margaret Thomas, Mimi Winmill, Hilda Evans, Celia Jones, Olive Jones.
Kneeling: Vera Edwards, Ada Addis, ?, Connie Nurse, Megan Edwards, Eluned Hale, Muriel Wilson, Violet Brazington, Ann Inseal.

Reports on meetings, sometimes weekly, gave an account of varied activities. There were talks on diverse subjects, e.g. - The life of a lady reporter from the "Echo" and on local history. Mr. A. H. Williams, a regular speaker on the Institute circuit, spoke on all aspects of local history. Another regular speaker was Miss Muriel Davies, often speaking on 'wild life'. One such talk on *Summer Visitors in the Bird World* was accompanied by lantern slides lent by the National Museum. This type of meeting was often open, with men and children invited. As a result of a talk on the King Edward VII Welsh National Scheme, of which Cefn Mably Hospital was a part, many members volunteered to make clothes for the patients.

There were demonstrations of upholstery, cookery, flower arrangement, antiques and their preservation, cake-icing, (by Mr H. Gosling, the local baker) fruit preservation, sewing techniques and many more.

There were reports of numerous fund-raising events by members for the W. I. movement as well as other charities. Concerts, community singing, charades competitions, bazaars, raffles, whist drives and socials raised substantial amounts. Educational courses were organised by the W.I., basketry, quilting, dressmaking and butter-making to name but a few. The instructor for butter-making came from the Monmouthshire Agricultural Institute. Drama competitions were held annually, the winner of the local group going forward to compete in the County. The performance of these one-act plays was once again open to all as were any special lectures, if the subject was of general interest to men and women alike. Amateur theatrical nights were organised by the W.I., with other groups also putting on short plays in the Rumney Memorial Hall.

1933 - Memorable *Festival of Drama* at Rumney......'The County Drama Festival of Monmouthshire was held in the Memorial Hall Rumney. This revealed the following: -

   i.   that there is histrionic ability in abundance in the villages of Rumney, St.Mellons and Castleton,

   ii.   that there is growing enthusiasm for good drama in the area and

   iii. that the competition spirit, encouraged by the League achieves the desired object – that of demanding the very best work from the players taking part.

Rumney had produced four plays, Castleton three and St. Mellons one. "The Lovely Miracle" by Rumney and "The Old Bull" by Castleton were selected for the final programme of the competition to be held in Abergavenny.'

During the mid 1920s, Rumney Male Voice Choir and Rumney Wesleyan Choir were formed. St. Augustine's Sunday School theatrical productions also had a wealth of talent. These three groups were to provide many members for the Rumney Amateur Operatic Society. In 1933, the Operatic Society decided, after three years of not over-ambitious operettas to tackle the ever-popular Gilbert and Sullivan. Their production of 'Pirates of Penzance' was a remarkable success and according to the report in the Countryside

Magazine, 'Rumney has every reason to be proud of such a combination of talented performers, this production has placed them in the front rank of amateur operatics.'

The Rumney Amateur Operatic Society went from strength to strength. The venue for the operettas was the Rumney War Memorial Hall and the performances ran for a week. They were performed in authentic costume with a full orchestra resplendent in evening dress. The stage must have had an apron-extension to accommodate the full cast. In front of the stage were the orchestra, the piano and the conductor. The hall was full each night with standing room only towards the end of the week. Young people from St. Mellons were brought over by coach on the Monday evening and admitted free of charge on dress- rehearsal night.

The shows were extremely popular in the life of the village and indeed there was a wealth of local musical talent, including that of Cliff and Fred Pritchard, Bill Hann, Sam Hague the local chemist, Ivor Jones, Bert Hewitt, Les Jones, Ivy Napier, Frank Everson, Gwyn Richards and many more. Annual productions included: -

1933 The Pirates of Penzance
1934 H.M.S.Pinafore
1935 Iolanthe
1936 The Mikado
1937 The Rebel Maid
1938 Tom Jones

The President was Mr. O. L. Bailey, the pianist Miss Olwen Beavis and later Miss Audrey Sheryn. The Society was quite a matrimonial agency as several members were either 'courting' when they joined or met there and later married. Frank Everson married Mabel Wilcox, Les Jones married Edith Tugwell. Other couples were Bill Chapman and Edna Powell, Winnie Prankard and Frank Lee, Eileen Greenway and Alfie Powell, Elsie Williams and Stan Charles and Chris King and Sallie Snell. The Society disbanded at the outbreak of WWII and was not re-established.

Rumney Annual Eisteddfod

In wartime, 'homegrown' talent was much encouraged in such events as **Eisteddfoddau** which took place annually in many villages in Wales. These events included competitions for singing, recitation, piano-playing and of course for the famous male-voice choirs and mixed glee parties. Rumney had its own Eisteddfod Committee, President and a host of Vice-Presidents. Adjudicators were invited from outside the area and competitors came from far and wide to take part in a full day and sometimes evening of music and poetry.

GRAND FESTIVAL ALL TROPHY COMPETITIONS

RUMNEY EISTEDDFOD COMMITTEE

(Chairman.—A. SMITH, Esq.)

THE EIGHTH

Annual Eisteddfod

will be held at the

Rumney Junior School Hall

Saturday, September 22, 1951

Closing date for Entries Thursday, September 20th, 1951.

President :—S. W. HAGUE, Esq., M.P.S.

Vice-Presidents :

Councillor Dr. C. A. BENCE.	Alderman FRANK CHAPMAN.
Councillor W. J. HARTLAND.	Mrs. S. W. HAGUE.
Mrs ERIC EVANS, J.P.	Mrs. C. A. BENCE.
C. C. LL.-WILLIAMS, Esq.	R. WILLIAMS, Esq.
J. A. BILBY, Esq.	EWAN G. DAVIES, Esq.
ERIC EVANS, Esq.	H. GOSLING, Esq.
B. W. EDWARDS, Esq.	G. R. HUTCHINGS, Esq.
W. HANN, Esq.	W. JONES, Esq.
IVOR C. MOORE, Esq.	T. J. E. PRICE, Esq.
G. G. SAUNDERS, Esq.	C. ROLFE, Esq.
WILL SHUTE, Esq.	E. G. THOMAS, Esq.
A. SHUTE, Esq.	

*Conductor :—*J. A. BILBY, Esq.

Adjudicators :—

MDM. LILY RICHARDS, B.A., L.R.A.M., A.R.C.M.

EDGAR J. REYNOLDS, L.R.A.M. (Caerphilly).

Accompanists :—

Miss MARION WILLIAMS, L.R.A.M., A.R.C.M.

Miss AUDREY SHERYN.

J. H. GREEN, M.MUS (Wales)., L.R.A.M., A.R.C.M, L.T.C.L.

Light Refreshments available at Moderate Charges

Eisteddfod programme

172

Rumney Operatic Society — The Pirates of Penzance, 1933.

St. Mellons Agricultural Show.

In the reign of Elizabeth I, the annual St. Mellons Fair came into
being. It was an hiring fair, when the men of the district put
themselves forward to be hired for the coming year by the local
farmers. There would be fiddlers, drummers, perhaps a harpist and
wandering pedlars selling ribbons and trinkets. This Fair was held on
St. Melo's Day, 22nd October on the Ton below the Church. On the
main coastal route from South Wales to London, St. Mellons was a
convenient meeting-point and gathering-centre for drovers. Herds of
cattle were collected at the village forge where they were shod with
wooden slippers in preparation for their long journey.

In 1863, the first Ploughing Match was held in the great field
at Llanrumney Farm. The St. Mellons and District Farmers
Association was formed in 1871, taking over the running of the
Ploughing Match. This was the birth of the St. Mellons Show. Men
of the district participated enthusiastically with eight or more teams

of horses taking part in this annual event, which attracted as many as five hundred people. Local people wanted something more than a ploughing match, so it developed and by 1880 the show had grown to include classes for horses, cattle, sheep, pigs and root-crops. A dairy section was introduced by 1891 which involved cheese and butter competitions.

The Show continued in unbroken succession until 1913. There was no event between 1914 and 1919, but the St. Mellons and District Farmers Association continued their activities by supporting the War effort. Their hard work resulted in the provision of a motor-ambulance for service at the Front. A total of £2,000 was raised during the War years.

Members of St. Mellons and District Farmers Association, smartly dressed for the 'big occasion' of St. Mellons Show

In 1920, the Show restarted with record entries. A feature was a military tournament. A new section was provided by the St. Mellons Women's Institute. The W.I. had their own tent in which they displayed flowers and other homecrafts. In 1923, despite the fact that farmers were going through a depressed period, the number of entries doubled to more than five hundred and a total of twenty silver cups were awarded as prizes. For the first time the Show was held in Llanrumney Park itself and was most successful.

The 1927 Royal Show, organised by the Royal Agricultural Society of England, was held at Newport and the St Mellons Show Committee sent a donation of fifteen guineas. St. Mellons and District Agricultural Show had now established itself as a major event and attracted visits by the Lord Mayor of Cardiff and the Mayor of Newport. New attractions were introduced such as a jazz band as well as competitions in needlework, dairy-produce, homemade wines etc. By 1931, St. Melo's Day had long been forgotten and the show date changed to September. It was now the premier local event of the year. The attractions included the parade of Tredegar Farmers' foxhounds, show-jumping, pony and rider musical chairs and the dairymen's float competitions with the wonderful action of their horses. All made for a pleasant day out. The Show continued unabated until WWII and recommenced in 1946.

Parade of Tredegar Farmers Foxhounds at Llanrumney Park.
l-r Huntsman, Tom Cavanagh, Master of Foxhounds, Marjorie Stone, (Druidstone Road) and Whippers-in, Edgar Scrivens and Cyril George.

The venue remained at Llanrumney Park until 1952, when the Show was forced to move because of housing development. In succeeding years the venue changed a number of times; first Quarry Hill, followed by the Vaindre, both in St. Mellons and after a break in 1956, due to Foot-and-Mouth decease it returned to Quarry Hill between 1957 and 1961 then moved to Duffryn Farm, Coedkernew in 1962. It was at Duffryn Farm that the Centenary Celebration was held in 1971.

Young Farmers Club and Vice-presidents at the Show 1954. l-r Robert Baker, Vernon Barber, Peter Smith, Colin Thomsett, Charles Wright, John Lewis, Margaret Prosser, Dilwyn Prosser, Valerie Addis, Ann Pocock, John Neal, Mary Evans, Edgar Scrivens, Marjorie Addis, Pat Hegarty, ? ,John Baker and Wynford Prosser.

In 1980, the Show moved to Cefn Mably Park where the beautiful setting contributed to many years of successful social and family events. Once again because of development the venue had to change; in the year 2000 the grounds of Tredegar House in Newport became the new site for the Show. Foot and Mouth regulations caused cancellation of the show in 2002. In 2004, the show was again cancelled due to the National Eisteddford being held on the site.

Rumney and St. Mellons Horticultural Society held their first annual August show in 1913. Classes included fruit and vegetables, dairy produce, poultry, needlework, schoolchildren's classes and allotment and cottage gardens. The Horticultural Show continued for fifteen years, the last one was held in 1928.

Rumney Horse Show started in the late 1930s. A small group of horse-lovers, Herbert Jenks, local councillor and landowner, George Wadsworth, haulier, Ivor Clode, shipping chandler and George Moon, corn and hay merchant, set out to provide something for others who felt as they did about horses. Meetings, at first, were held in a small hut to the rear of the Carpenters Arms. The pub at that time was also the farmhouse of a farm owned by Herbert Jenks. Competition classes included Hunters, Welsh Cobs, Shires, Welsh Mountain Ponies and Hackneys; three classes for these, which was quite a feat. When these competitions were over at the end of the day, the atmosphere changed for the galloway races. Spectators gathered on the inside of the ring and competitors raced around the outside. Herbert Jenks' grandson Clive Handford remembers entering these races and recalls falling off on more than one occasion!

The show was held on an invariably wet August Bank Holiday Monday and attracted competitors from a wide area, for competition was keen. During WWII the venue for the Horse Show moved to Ball Farm, also owned by Herbert Jenks. His son Trevor remained at the Carpenters Arms and was by now very much involved with the Show. Replacing his father as Chairman when Herbert died, Trevor's special interest was show-jumping and this became the main attraction. Some of the 'big-time' showjumpers used to do the South Wales circuit during August Bank Holiday week; Rumney on Monday, Pontypool Park Tuesday etc. Well-known competitors included, Wilf White, Allen Oliver, Ted Edgar and Fred Broome, later joined by his son David, daughters Elizabeth and Mary and later Fred Jnr.

After WWII, committee meetings were held in the Carpenters Arms. Much-appreciated financial support was given by Hancocks Brewery of Cardiff. Profits from the show were given to several charities; the Institute for the Blind, the Sunshine Home for Blind Babies, Nazareth House and Cardiff Royal Infirmary. Hospital beds were donated and a small plaque noting the donation from the Show, was placed above each bed. After housing development in 1952, it was necessary for the venue to be changed once again. Sophia Gardens in Cardiff was the site chosen and when in 1955, Cardiff became a City, the name also changed to the City of Cardiff Rumney Horse Show. The Show continued successfully for a number of years, but gradually became less popular with well-known competitors and after Trevor and Olive Jenks left the area, the show returned to Rumney, to Greenway Park. In 1983, after almost fifty years, the show came to an end.

Trevor Jenks started riding at an early age; he is seen here outside the Carpenters Arms, before the First World War.

Social life centred around the churches, chapels and a variety of activities which included choir, garden parties, fetes, lectures, social evenings, dances, hunting and whist drives. The Christmas Whist Drive was known as the Poultry Drive, with poultry and other Christmas fayre donated by local farmers and businessmen. Most of these social activities were fund-raising events and included raffles with prizes of coal, live poultry, plants and other useful items. In 1925, the first cinema show came to the Rumney Memorial Hall and was arranged by Mr Fred Howell of Tredelerch House.

178

Rumney Baptist Sunday School 1921. Adults: Olive and Ivy Stephens, Pupils: Mary Gerrish, clutching handbag, with Edith and Bernice Tugwell to the left and right of her. Mary Tugwell is at the top right-hand corner.

The Townswomen's Guild was founded in 1929 by Dame Margery Corbett-Ashley. Due to the demise of the Rumney branch of the Women's Institute, it was decided to form a Townswomen's Guild. At a very successful meeting in 1938, Councillor Mrs. W. Mathias was elected President, Mrs. D. Williams, Chairman, Mrs. G. Evans, Vice Chairman, Mrs. D. Evans, Secretary and Mrs. N. Wills, Treasurer. The group quickly became very popular and outgrew its meeting-place in the Baptist Church Hall. It became necessary to cap membership and create a waiting list. The popularity of the Guild was, in most respects, due to its ability to cater for various groups of interest such as Arts and Crafts, Music, Social Studies and Drama. In due course, a music-group developed and formed a choir under the baton of Mrs. J. North. The group performed at concerts in the Memorial Hall locally and at other venues throughout Cardiff. From its inception the choir was accompanied by pianist Mrs. M. Hughes.

In 1970, the Federation of Townswomen's Guilds decided to close down the **Llanrumney Guild** and to form, under the guidance of Mrs A. Middleton, the **Wentloog Guild** as a replacement. The two Rumney organisations have worked very successfully, giving support to each other in their various activities. The **Rumney Guild** has been recognised as the biggest of its kind in Wales and possibly in the whole of the United Kingdom.

RUMNEY AND ST. MELLONS
The Area at War

Many old publications give details of men from villages around this area, who served their country in wars. For example, a gravestone in St. Mellons Churchyard, records the death of Evan Thomas, late of the Grenadier Guards, who fought at the battle of Waterloo and died, aged 80 years, on 3rd April 1870. The War Memorials in St. Mellons and Rumney indicate that both villages suffered substantial losses relative to the size of their population, during the two great wars of the twentieth century. In the 1914 - 1918 War all men who went to fight, were, in the main, volunteers. Any young fit men left behind, were given a hard time in the community and referred to as cowards, often receiving white feathers through the post, or pinned to their front doors. Evidence of this attitude lies in a letter sent by a Private McFarlane from the trenches in France to a former employer in St. Mellons. He states his disgust at the cowardly young men who had failed to volunteer for the armed services. The writer of the letter came through the war unscathed.

A copy of the Letter: 13883 Lcpl. Ralph Macdonald
                                     C. Coy. 5thBatt. S.W.B. (Pioneers)
                                                B.E.F. France
Dear Mrs. Williams,   13th April1916
          No doubt you will be surprised to have this letter from me. I think I promised you a line when I left there. So now I have a bit of time, I think it's my chance. Perhaps I won't have the time later on as the fine weather is coming and thank God for it. We have been looking forward for it for a long time I can tell you. We have had a long cold and trying winter over here and by all account you have had some very rough weather around there. I had a letter from the Secretary of my club. He told me it blew a lot of the telegraph poles down, so I am sure you had a rough time of it. Now I hope this will find you, Mrs Williams and all your family in good health. I am thankful to say I am in the best of health and spirits at present and you know that's a good thing to say over here. Well, I must tell you I have had marvellous luck up to now, I can tell you it's a hot shop at times, it makes the hair on your head stand up straight you know. When you get a lump of iron whizzing past you, it makes you feel very uneasy and plenty of bullets flying about. Still, we are getting quite used to it now.

          Well, this is a great agricultural district where we are at present, or other words it used to be, but my word it has been ripped up by shell fire

180

and one thing and the other. I don't think it will ever be the same again. It's a shame to see the villages and their fine old churches levelled to the ground. Just fancy a peaceful little village like St. Mellons or Castleton razed to the ground. I can assure you they will have to suffer for it later on. The place has got a weird look about it, especially at night-time. It gives me a creepy feeling going over the ground in the dark. Well I do hope this will be the last year for us over here, no doubt they are beginning to feel the pinch now. Mind you, they were well prepared for it and I think they have invented every possible thing they can think of for the destruction of human life. They are a crafty, cunning, ingenious lot to deal with. Of course, it will take a bit of time yet before they are conquered, which they will be. I am afraid it's going to be a dear job yet you know. We can't expect to have it all our own way. I am sure we have got the upper hand of them now.

Now I suppose it's a bit quiet about there now and by what I hear, there are any amount of young men at home now, I call it poor spirit on their part, they ought to be over here and faced what we have and seen the sights we have. I think it would rouse them up a bit. I wonder what would have happened if we had been the same as them. I am afraid it would have been a bad job for a lot of them I can tell you. I am proud I came when I did. Well, there is not much more I can tell you this time, you know we are not allowed to say what we like on our letters. If I have the luck to come out of this job, I shall be able to give you an account of my travels and doings over here and I hope it will be soon. Everybody seems to think this summer will see the end of it and what a blessing it will be for us all to see the end of this terrible conflict. I am sure everybody at home are eagerly waiting for the day to come. Now you must please remember me to all at Maes-y-Crochan, tell them I am still going strong. I had a letter from there about a fortnight ago, they were all laid up then. I hope they are all got well again. Now I will draw to a close with best of wishes to you all and living in hopes of seeing you soon. I remain,

Yours sincerely, Mac.

Ben Howells, Jim Ward, and Edgar Elias, on the day they enlisted to fight in the First World War.

WWII was a much different affair, for everyone was involved in some way. At the time of the outbreak of war, some local men who were already in the Territorial Army, were at annual camp in Locking and were immediately transferred to the Regular Forces. Amongst them were the Higgins brothers, Eddie Humphreys, Geoffrey Thomas and Gerry Trinnick. Women also became liable for conscription into some form of National Service. This resulted in the formation of the A.T.S. now known as the Women's Royal Army Corps, the W.A.F.S., the Women's Royal Air Force Service, the W.R.E.N.S., the Women's Royal Naval Service and the W.L.A., the Women's Land Army. Men and women who stayed behind because of reserved occupations or unfitness for active service, volunteered their services in the Auxiliary Fire Service, Air-Raid Precautions, Red Cross Nurses, Women's Voluntary Service etc.

The Rumney A.R.P. and Red Cross Post was at Whitehall on the corner of Church Road, and the St. Mellons post is believed to have been at the old Village Hall. There is a story that one very efficient A.R.P. warden in Rumney, whose duty it was to make sure that nobody showed any light which could be seen from above, used to smoke his pipe upside-down so that enemy aircraft would be unable to see the glow from his burning tobacco.

Red Cross training. The nurse on the left is Trudy Inseal.

The Auxiliary Fire Service for Rumney was based at Baldwin's yard in the Grove and for St. Mellons it was housed at Llanrumney Hall. Fred Bird, in his recollections, recalls being a member of that service. He remembers a few occasions when the Auxiliary Fire Service was called into action at Llanrumney and St. Mellons. On one occasion whilst dealing with a barn fire caused by an incendiary bomb, one of his crew fell into the farm pond and had to be rescued. Another episode was just as he was leaving the White Hart there was an almighty explosion and he swears that he saw the roof of Mrs Scully's house 'Brynhyfryd' lift off a few inches amidst a cloud of dust before settling back in place. He did admit "I had been drinking rather late." A survey the next day, however, did confirm what he had seen - a bomb had exploded nearby. A second unexploded bomb was discovered in the vicinity, which had to be dealt with by an army bomb-disposal unit.

Bombs intended for Cardiff Docks occasionally missed their targets and landed in Rumney and St. Mellons. Upper Newton Farm, Rumney was severely damaged on one occasion and Rumney Court was another casualty. The Pottery suffered blast damage, as did a number of houses in the area of Rumney Hill. Cows were killed in a field at Greenway and damage was also caused to the sewer outfall pipe on the foreshore.

Left - the result of a direct hit on the cowshed at Upper Newton Farm and right - the badly-damaged house. In the years after the War, it collapsed and only recently has been replaced by a new house.

David Williams, whose father was the local Police Sergeant in Rumney, remembers his childhood when he lived in the Police Station at 766 Newport Road. At various places in the village, large round tanks of water were placed for use in emergency fire-fighting and a public air-raid shelter was built near the Carpenters Arms. His mother was in the Red Cross, so in the event of an air-raid, both parents had to go to their respective posts, leaving David and his brothers alone in the Anderson shelter at the end of the garden. He vividly recalls a day when the siren went whilst he was on his way home from school. Looking up to the sky he saw an aircraft flying very high. Suddenly the heavy anti-aircraft guns at the Maerdy gun site opened fire and the noise was deafening. Many people recall this day when Cardiff Power Station was hit. On another occasion, during the night the siren sounded and his parents jumped out of bed to go to their posts. They had hardly gone downstairs, when there was a huge explosion somewhere behind where the Police Station now stands. A piece of shrapnel came through their roof and through the bed where his mother had lain just a few moments earlier. David has vivid memories too, of the times leading up to the landing in France on 'D- Day', June 6th 1944, when there was a constant stream of military traffic going past his home on Newport Road. On that day he recalls that the sky was full of various kinds of aircraft, many of which were pulling gliders.

Earlier, the Allied Forces on the Continent had suffered a massive defeat at Dunkirk. Our own British Expeditionary Force was decimated and thousands of troops were killed or captured. So, with the enemy facing Britain just twenty miles across the Channel, the Government asked for volunteers to join what later became the Home Guard. Norman Williams recollects that at the outset, Rumney volunteers who met at Rumney Court, were armed with just one privately-owned shotgun between them. The rest had sticks, staves, hay-forks etc. Their duties included patrolling the foreshore to watch for any possible incursions from the sea, manning dug-outs at Caer Castell to watch out for possible airborne landings and occupying guard posts along Newport Road. Other known volunteers included some of the North brothers and the late Bill Hann. Today, the T.V. series 'Dad's Army' treats the Home Guard as a comedy. Although the Home Guard was a bit farcical due to its lack of equipment in the early days, it later became a force to be taken seriously.

The St. Mellons Home Guard was under the command of Major T. Ifor Jones with headquarters at the Village Hall. One of the look-out posts was on the top of the Church Tower. When going on duty one night, having bolstered his courage at the Blue Bell Inn, a member of the Home Guard, whilst climbing the tower, grabbed a rope to steady himself and rang one of the bells. As the ringing of bells was prohibited, except as a warning of invasion, this was taken as a serious matter and the offender, Tom Bird, was discharged from further service. Other members of St. Mellons' Home Guard were trained to use the anti-aircraft guns at St. Brides Camp. Among them was Reg. Ford, market-gardener from the Began, Fred Williams from Maes-y-Crochan Farm, and Cyril Jones, well-known auctioneer. Later in the war, as fear of invasion dissipated, the Home Guard was allocated other responsibilities such as guarding bomb-damaged buildings to prevent looting and assisting at local gun and anti-aircraft balloon sites.

Rumney Platoon Home Guard 1941

There were several British military bases around the area - Colchester Avenue in the West, Maerdy Camp in the South, Druidstone House in the north and St. Brides in the east. Later, American forces were based at what is now the St. Mellons Hotel and Country Club. They also occupied a specially-constructed stores and supplies depot, adjacent to and south of the railway line between Rumney and St. Mellons, now Wentloog Business Park. These sheds, A, B, C, and D were huge in comparison with other buildings in the area at that time. It was known as the 'Sorting Depot' and the Sea Transport Stores. Supplies came in by sea from the U.S.A. to be sorted and despatched to areas where they were needed. The sheds were also used for the storage of the remains of U.S. military personnel who had been killed in action whilst serving in Europe. Bodies were stored in the sheds pending repatriation to the United States for interment.

The sheds and grounds have been put to several uses over the years by the Rover Company, Curran steel fabricators and others. The open area adjoining the railway line, now the Freight Depot was used for the sorting, storage and despatch of pit-props.

In both World Wars, the William Nicholl Convalescent Home in St. Mellons, now St. John's College, was a major location for the nursing back to health of many wounded service-men.

Soldiers at the William Nicholl Convalescent Home in St. Mellons.

As a result of men being called up for military service, farms, which were providing as much food as possible, were short of labour and Land Army girls were recruited to help out. They came from all walks of life; daughters of the wealthy and working-class, nannies, secretaries, clerks, housemaids etc. They worked in all weathers on farms and market-gardens. Other girls, but none locally, became forestry workers and were known as the Women's Land

186

Army Timber Corps. Hostels were set up for these girls such as the one at Witla Court in Rumney and another at White Lodge, St. Mellons. Miss Muriel Davies of Greenfield, St. Mellons was appointed Area Welfare Officer for the W.L.A. The cook at the Witla Court hostel was Anne Inseal who lived in the now-demolished Highcroft Cottage. As the war progressed, first, Italian and later German prisoners of war were brought in to supplement the work done by the Land Army girls on the farms. The prisoner of war camp was on the site of the present Wyevale Garden Centre at Castleton.

Land Army girls at Witla Court.

The Women's Land Army.
' Back to the land we must all lend a hand
To the farms and the fields we must go.
There's a job to be done, though we can't fire a gun.
We can still do our bit with a hoe.'

The Observer Corps, whose duty it was to watch for enemy aircraft and report to the military, on type, number and direction of flight, manned an observation post at Caer Castell. Persons known to have been members included John Lewis, Harry Woodbury, Hywel Richards, Eric Dolman, Ernest John, Watkin Thomas and Emlyn Thomas.

Dr. J. B. Williamson 1923-1998

Dr. John Boyd Williamson, known to all as Dr. Jock, was a Scotsman born and bred, a much-respected village general practitioner and a resident of St. Mellons from the early 1950s until his death in November 1998. He lived with his wife Hazel and their six children at Mainbrace in Druidstone Road. Many villagers will remember sitting in Dr. Jock s hallway, exchanging village news and gossip whilst waiting to see Dr. Jock in his surgery. Naval photographs and pictures, plus the tartan curtains in the hall, were heart-warming evidence of Dr. Jock s earlier life and ancestry.

Jock joined the Royal Navy at the age of 18 years and served on the battle cruiser H.M.S. Penelope, known to many sailors as H.M.S. Pepperpot, on account of the number of bullet-holes which riddled the ship's outer plating. H.M.S. Penelope sailed on convoys to Malta and it was on this ship that Jock was wounded and subsequently received the Distinguished Service Cross for his bravery in action. Jock then saw service in the submarine H.M.S. Truncheon in the North Atlantic. He often joked that he went into submarines because the pay was better and gave him a better chance of 'socialising' when he was on leave. It is well known 'that all the nice girls love a sailor' and a kilted sailor was certainly someone special! Hazel met Jock at home in Cardiff when she was 16 years old and he was 18 and they saw each other when he was on leave. She joined the W.R.N.S. when she reached 18, so leave was then a special time for both of them. Romance blossomed in wartime!

When WWII ended, Jock was demobbed and became a medical student in Edinburgh where he trained and later qualified. Although students are notoriously impoverished, he and Hazel decided to marry and their first two children were born during their time in Edinburgh, the remaining four children arriving later in Cardiff.

Dr. Jock was a man of the people and was very much involved in community life. He served as a Community Councillor, a member of the Village Association Committee, a Parish Church Councillor and as a Governor of St. Mellons Church in Wales School. Dr. Jock and Hazel's home 'Mainbrace' was the scene of

188

many parties, including Trafalgar Night celebrations and Conservative Party receptions, where villagers and patients were welcomed as friends. Dr Jock was a man with a deep love for his wife and family and he treated his patients and villagers as though 'they were his own'. His death left a great void in the village.

Mac. Potter. 1914-2004

Marcus Griffiths Potter, universally known as Mac., a resident of Began Road, St. Mellons until his death in 2004, had a long and distinguished career in the R.A.F. Having joined R.A.F. Haltern as an apprentice at the age of 15½ years, Mac achieved his ambition of becoming a pilot in 1938 and flew virtually every type of aircraft before ending up permanently in Blenheim bombers

He served throughout WWII in France, North Africa, India and Palestine. In 1940 he found himself in France, having to fall back in the face of the swiftly advancing Germans. Squadrons of aircraft had to be moved north in order to avoid capture or destruction, so Mac's squadron, having more pilots left than planes, was sent to man the aircraft of a squadron that had its planes intact, but had lost its pilots. They successfully saved the Blenheims, flying north to a small village called Vreux in north-east France. Some weeks later, Mac and his crew were ordered to evacuate the station and fly north again. They flew the last aircraft out of Vreux and a monument was set up in the village, next to the war-memorial, bearing an inscription which notes the names of Mac and his crew. Every year since WWII, the people of Vreux invited Mac and his wife Edna back for a reunion and they attended on numerous occasions. At the time of Mac's death, the Mayor sent condolences and prayers were said for him in the village church.

Towards the end of WWII, Mac trained Polish pilots near Carlisle. They nicknamed him the Führer since he was known as a hard taskmaster, but they were happy to drink with him at the local pub. This probably accounts for the high reputation that Polish pilots had after such severe training.

Mac's accumulated conduct of operations during WWII resulted in the award of the Distinguished Flying Cross in 1944, presented to him by King George VI at Buckingham Palace. He

189

rarely spoke of it, for he was a man of great humility and was never one for 'blowing his own trumpet.'

John Charles Lever. 1919 -1986.

John Charles Lever, known as Jack , born in St. Mellons, attended the Village School until he was 14 years old when he left to become a gardener at the William Nicholl Convalescent Home which was then an annexe of Cardiff Royal Infirmary. During that time he helped build the Village Hall and took part in many of the boxing matches held there.

Jack joined the Territorial Army and was sent to Northern Ireland for training. WWII was declared whilst he was away so Jack did not return to the village of St. Mellons for many years. He became part of a very elite unit, the 'Commandos,' who made many raids in Norway. Following further training in Yugoslavia, he was transferred to Burma. Jack was badly wounded in Burma and owed his life to the 'Ghurkas' who carried him for 48 hours, travelling only at night.

After spending 18 months in hospital in India, Jack returned home to St. Mellons and in 1946 he married Elsie. Three daughters were later born to them. Jack became a member of the Commando Association and of the Burma Star Association and on meeting up with Rumney man Ted Morgan, who had been with him in the same 'dug-out' in Burma when they were both wounded, it was discovered that their injuries were identical. Both were extremely glad and fortunate to return to their home villages.

Secret Army WWII

When Britain faced her darkest hour in WWII, a select band of Welsh clergymen and other civilians were designated Special Duties agents. They would have been at the forefront of Churchill s last-ditch plans to eject Hitler from these shores. Their orders, in the event of an invasion, were to spy on the Germans and radio their intentions to British High Command from churches which had aerials hidden behind lightning conductors on their towers.

Among Welsh clergy recruits was the Rev. Cecil Gower-Rees of Llanarth – later to become Vicar of St. Mellons. He was part of the U.K.-wide resistance movement, a covert force similar to the

Resistance in occupied France, whose members were sworn to secrecy and who operated without alerting the suspicion of their communities. Intelligence experts at M.I.6 recruited agents from the ranks of people whose jobs allowed them to travel around the countryside without arousing suspicion. They were doctors and bus-drivers, milkmen and midwives, - and a multitude of vicars.

Members of the secret army of 3,000, were trained to operate as a guerrilla band which would emerge at night to wreak havoc on the enemy. Individual units were also issued with a .303 calibre rifle, the telescopic sight and silencer to be used for the chilling job – had the invasion succeeded – of killing anyone in the locality who was found to be collaborating with the enemy!

In 1995, a reunion dinner was arranged for everyone involved in the National Special Force and it was not until then that details emerged publicly of Britain's 'Secret Army'. A few families, however, when sorting through the property of deceased relatives, had sometimes come upon scraps of notes, descriptions of troop movements and drawings of battalion insignia, which were curiously out of keeping with other personal effects. This was how the family of the Rev. Richard Sluman, head of the secret cabal of seven Special Duties agents which included the Rev. Gower-Rees, learnt of their father's war-time activities.

Rumney and St. Mellons must have had similar units operating at that time, but their oaths of secrecy remained as constraints and many courageous civilians must have gone to their graves taking their secret with them.

November 11th Remembrance Sunday at the War Memorial St. Mellons.

191

The Homefront

One organisation which was very active wherever help was needed, was the Women's Voluntary Service or W.V.S., later the Women's Royal Voluntary Service or W.R.V.S. They could be found giving out cups of tea to firemen and rescue workers in air raids and giving help and comfort to the rescued. Mrs E. Thomas and Mrs. F. Beese both of Ty Fry Road, Rumney were leading local members.

The area played host to evacuees from the London blitz and about twenty children were given safe shelter at Llanrumney Hall. Ada Wyatt helped care for those at Llanrumney Hall. Melba Crabtree, nee Loftus, of St. Mellons, was a Girl Guide at this time and earned one of her war-service badges by helping with the children. Melba was awarded a second badge for helping the war effort by collecting waste materials, such as paper, rags, scrap-metals, silver paper etc and delivering them to a collection point. This kind of activity was carried out by school children throughout Britain and was mainly organised through the schools. There was a further influx of evacuees in 1944 when some 100 children arrived in Rumney from West London and were billeted with families in the area.

Whilst children were doing their bit for the war effort, their mothers were also very much involved. As well as working hard to keep a home together for their families, coping with rationing of food, clothing, coal, etc. they still found time to knit warm gloves, socks, and balaclava helmets for men on active service. Additionally, ladies organised jumble sales, sales of work and flag days for the 'Spitfire Fund' which helped to provide funds to build fighter planes.

Mothers and wives who received the dreaded telegram informing them that their son or husband had been killed in action, were heartbroken. Some who received more than one telegram were devastated. Sadly this happened to the Thomas family who lived on Rumney Hill. Two sons were lost. One family named Hicks, who had close connections with Maerdy Farm, lost three sons and a memorial to them can be found in St. Augustine's Churchyard in Rumney.

Food Rationing

The amount of food varied from month to month depending on the supply of any particular item; the following is the allowance for an adult each week: -

Meat - to the value of 1s-2d (6p). Offal was originally not rationed but sometimes formed part of the meat ration. Sausages were not rationed but were difficult to obtain.

Bacon and Ham - 4oz (100g)

Butter - 2oz (50g)

Cheese - 2oz (50g) sometimes 4oz (100g) or even 8oz (225g) if supplies were available.

Margarine - 4oz (100g)

Cooking Fat/Lard - 4oz (100g) often only 2oz (50g)

Milk - 3 pts (2.04 ltrs) sometimes 2pts (1.36 ltrs) Dried milk 1 pkt every 4 weeks.

Sugar - 8 oz (225g)

Jam/Preserves - 1lb (450g) every 2 months.

Tea - 2 oz (50g)

Eggs - 1 shell egg a week when available. At times, 1 egg every 2 weeks. Dried egg 1 pkt every 4 weeks

Sweets - 12 oz (350g) every 4 weeks

In addition to individual rations there was a points system: - 16 points per person per month e.g. 16 points = 1 can of fish or meat or 2lbs (900g) of dried fruit or 8lbs (3.6kg) of split peas. Welfare Clinics distributed concentrated orange juice and cod liver oil for babies, pregnant and nursing mothers with priority milk, which was also available to invalids.

Provision of school meals was started during the war-years to ensure that school children had the best possible meal once a day. Many mothers were working long hours for the war effort. In July, 1939 the government started to issue public information leaflets giving advise on *'Your Food in WarTime.* Food and Health advice was also given over the 'wireless.' Marguerite Patten was a regular contributor on Kitchen Front on B.B.C. early in the morning. Recipes were given to make the best use of every possible ingredient that was available such as preserving fruit and vegetables and making economical pickles and chutneys. Meat, sugar and fats were in short

193

supply and more homegrown fruit and vegetables were eaten. (cf. Food advice of today) The Radio Doctor, Dr. Charles Hill, also gave advice on health matters, telling children to take their cod liver oil and malt and to go to bed early!

Identity Card.

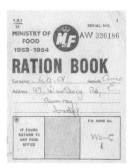

Ration Book.

End of WWII and people were delighted to celebrate with a V.J. children's party in Linden Grove, Rumney.

At the end of the 1914/18 War, a group of people in Rumney decided that a fitting memorial should be built in memory of all those who had lost their lives. A public meeting was called to discuss the proposal. A decision was made to hold weekly collections in the area with a view to building a hall. A piece of land was donated by Mr. T. Batten of Church Farm and eventually in 1924 came the official opening of the Rumney War Memorial Hall in Wentloog Road. For many years it served the communities of both St. Mellons and Rumney. The Memorial Hall has been and still is a living reminder of the sacrifices made by previous generations. The names of those from Rumney who lost their lives in both conflicts are commemorated on the memorial in front of the hall.

Cardiff City Council decided in the early 1950s that the Earl Haigh Homes in Beaumaris Road, Rumney should be the City memorial to the dead of the WWII and a commemoration stone on the land in front of the houses was unveiled by Field Marshall Lord Montgomery. It is now normal practice for the Lord Mayor to visit Rumney on Remembrance Day and lay a wreath on behalf of the City of Cardiff.

The St. Mellons War Memorial which is situated at the bottom of St. Mellons Hill shows the names of the fallen in both World Wars. The annual parade from St. Mellons church to the War Memorial follows a Remembrance Day service held in the church.

Thoughts of Jennifer Spackman after visiting the grave of her Great Uncle Walter Hughes of St. Mellons.
'In November 1999, I saw for the first time, the letter written by the padre to Walter's family, informing them of his death in May 1916 in the Arras region of Northern France. The information section of the British War Graves Commission was able to provide information and directions to his burial place and in March 2000, we set out to find Grave 6, Row E, Plot 1 in the grave-yard at Tilloy-les-Mofflaines. Driver Walter Robotham Hughes of St. Mellons and of the Royal Field Artillery was buried there.

We are fortunate to visit France frequently and are familiar with the street names, plaques, monuments, bridges and beaches where those killed in the Second World War are remembered. Never before had we visited a First World War Cemetery. As we drove along the country roads in search of Tilloy-les-Mofflaines, it became apparent that this had been an area where considerable fighting had taken place. There were numerous sign-posts to graveyards for French, Commonwealth and British soldiers. Like many war

195

cemeteries the one at Tilloy is in the countryside.

The Cemetery itself is strangely beautiful and impeccably maintained, with not a weed or scrap of litter amongst the row upon row of headstones. The atmosphere was very, very moving and we moved quietly along the rows reading the inscriptions, the dates, the ages and the messages, carved beneath the insignia of Regiments, often long since amalgamated or even disbanded. Regardless of rank or status, the stones are exactly the same in size and shape. Officers, men, doctors, engineers and some who could not be identified, other than as "a soldier of the Great War", lie together, the sincerity of inscriptions and precision of row upon row emphasising the terrible losses incurred.

Protecting the cemetery is a wall of local stone and it was here in a waterproof safe that we found the most loving memorial of all - *The Book of Remembrance,* where every soldier buried in Tilloy is mentioned, who they were, where they came from and how they were killed. There is a room for visitors to write their messages or thoughts and we felt humbled to read and add our own. There was also a photograph of a smiling soldier. Who was he and who had left the photo behind? The messages did not say and the photo was unsigned.

There were no other visitors that day and the silence was broken only by the birds and the wind in the trees. Across the road is the local football pitch and it seemed appropriate that on match days the noise of young men enjoying their games would be audible in the cemetery at Tilloy-les-Mofflaines. The young men buried there, had undoubtedly enjoyed their soccer, before the "War to end all Wars" robbed them of the chance ever to play again.'

VILLAGE LIFE IN THE 20th CENTURY

When older residents of Rumney remember the village of their childhood, they describe it as a beautiful place to live; stone-built thatched cottages and farmhouses surrounded by countryside, apple orchards and cows grazing in the fields. Today, people choose to preserve some of those houses and to convert old farm buildings into dwellings.

In the early 1920s, on the old village road in Rumney below the Rompney Castle was the cottage of Jimmy Dunn the fisherman. Opposite the Grove, was Dai Marsh's Bakery and behind the nearby houses were orchards and the market-gardens of Mr Bolt and Mr Tugwell.

The Rompney Castle, modernised now, still stands. In the area where the Gospel Hall and the Library now stand, were the Talcoed Cottages (demolished in 1946) and the parish houses with their half-stable doors. In one of the parish houses lived Miss Mary Edmunds, a lovely old lady, who used to wear a pink cotton bonnet with a frill framing her face. Local children used to buy ginger pop from her, re-using the old glass pop-bottles with a marble under the stopper. Where the chemist and other shops now stand, was a beautiful old house called *The Elms*, named after the trees that surrounded it.

In the 1920s, the farms close to the village began to change hands. When Mr. Baker moved out of his farm at the corner of Ty Mawr Road and Brachdy Lane, it was taken over by a shipping company, William Hurford & Co. who imported Irish cattle and fattened them for the market. This became common practice for butchers from Cardiff with land in Rumney and St. Mellons. Walter Prosser, had a butcher's shop in Clifton Street and he had grazing rights on the Lamby. When Fred Miles moved from Church Farm to St. Mellons, his farm was bought by Tom Batton, a butcher in Salisbury Road, Cardiff. Mr Batten no longer farmed the land but used it to graze cattle and finish them prior to slaughter and sale in his butcher's shop.

After the 1914-18 war, as Cardiff was gradually expanding, old houses were condemned and modern new houses were built. In 1923, Henry North and Sons had 10 new houses under construction.

Wentloog Road 1920s.

One pair of houses was built on the site of Jimmy Dunn's cottage. Other builders included, Mr. Griffiths, Mr. Truscott and Mr. Bailey. In the Countryside Magazine it was reported – 'On the main road, Rumney's Bungalow Town is thriving tremendously, new buildings being produced with the speed and dexterity of a conjuror's hand.' Mr Batten of Church Farm had given land for the building of the Memorial Hall whilst the remainder of the farm was later used for houses and for shops near the Memorial Hall; Mr Harries in the paper shop, Horrell's Dairies, the Fish and Chip shop and Prince the drapers.

Early in *1933*, Rumney Parish Council met to discuss the Parish Council Houses near the Village Green. They were described as follows 'in a tumbledown, insanitary condition, which does not enhance the rural beauty of the parish. To retain them would only be on sentimental grounds. From a hard, matter of fact business point of view, they should have been pulled down years ago and substituted by modern houses of a similar type, the revenue from which would be far in excess of that obtained from the present buildings. To make the cottages really habitable would involve huge expense. The Sanitary Authorities have recently issued a provisional Closing Order, leaving the present occupiers in an unfortunate predicament. The Parish Council, a very human body, is naturally sympathetic, but is seriously considering whether, in the interests of the village, the buildings should be demolished or not. A decision will be made when a sub-committee has been appointed and reports back.'

A sketch by Allen Hambly showing THE GREEN, RUMNEY, as it might have looked at the end of the 19th Century with Talcoed Cottages on the left, Gilead Wesleyan Chapel in the centre and the Poor Houses on the right.

Administration

Research has shown that Rumney and St Mellons have, over the centuries, been included mostly with Monmouthshire or sometimes with Glamorgan. Magor and St. Mellons Rural District Council was the administrative body for a large part of the 20th century. The local parish councils bore the brunt of villagers' complaints and suggestions and councillors passed these on to the appropriate bodies above them.

Rumney Ratepayers Association was formed in 1926. The first reference to Rumney being taken into the Cardiff boundary was in 1927. Residents were considering what advantages were to be gained, for, at that time Rates were low and were expected to remain so for some time. Rates continued to be a big issue along with the condition of the roads. By 1933, a deputation from Rumney attended a meeting with Cardiff City Council to discuss the transfer of Rumney into the control of Cardiff. Parish Councillors reported back to the Parish Council where a heated debate took place. Villagers were asking if they would be better off and if rates would be increased. Generally they seemed to be in favour of *Absorption* but against *Urbanisation*. By 1937 these differences had been resolved and Rumney came under administration by Cardiff.

Local people were impatient for improvements, both inside and outside their homes. Roads were a problem in the early 20th century and continue to be so in the 21st century. In the letters column of the Countryside Magazine of January 1929, a resident of Ty Mawr Avenue wrote to complain about the attitude of Councillors and conditions in his road and others in Rumney. 'They are an eyesore, a positive danger to life and limb and a great detriment to the value of the properties.' He berated Councillors who lived on the comparatively comfortable main road, saying, 'Let them set off from Ty Mawr Road to attend a function in town and see what sort of state they get in later, when they return on the last bus to find every street light out. They would have to grope their way along the slushy uneven surface that serves for a road!'

Charabanc outing: c 1920. Most people on this outing seem to be members of the Rumney Baptist Chapel. Why are they outside a cider and perry makers?

Transport

The 20th century has seen changes from horse-drawn vehicles and bicycles to the traffic chaos of today. Imagine the excitement of a charabanc outing in the 1920s! A day-trip to the Wye Valley, Porthcawl or Cowbridge Common would have been a real adventure!

By the 1920s there was a bus service between Cardiff and Newport, but by June 1932 people were dissatisfied with the service. A newspaper report records 'a deputation representing the Parish Councils of Rumney, St. Mellons, Marshfield and Coedkernew attended a meeting with Cardiff Corporation Tramways and Buses Committee, making a strong case for an improved service between Cardiff and Newport. They expressed the dissatisfaction of people in country districts, pointing out the need for additional early morning buses and the issue of cheap workmen's tickets, season-tickets and cheaper fares. They referred to the discomfort caused by overcrowding on the late buses from Cardiff. All their comments were favourable received, the committee promising to give the matter their consideration.'

St. Mellons Charabanc outing. All in their Sunday best. 1920s.

The Coastline or Red & White Bus was always on time, 'you could set your watch by it.' It left Newport on the even hour and Cardiff on the odd hour, except for the last bus which left Cardiff at 9.15pm. After leaving Cardiff, it was not allowed to set down passengers within the Cardiff Corporation Bus boundary and when coming from Newport, it was not allowed to pick up passengers in Rumney.

Farmers and other residents used the *Coastline* to go to Newport Market on a Wednesday, or to shop or attend meetings in Cardiff and Newport. The service was discontinued in the mid 1960s.

Housing

Through the 1930s house-building continued. *Newcombe & Co. (Cardiff) Ltd.* were advertising that a subsidy of £75 had been arranged for purchasers of small houses which were to be erected on the main road sites at Rumney.

After the 1914-18 War, there was a shortage of houses, but after WWII the problem became more acute. It was common practice to live 'in rooms' sometimes with parents, sometimes in rented accommodation, often sharing the kitchen. The old army camp at Maerdy Road was used as temporary housing whilst new council houses were being built. Frank Hennessey, well known Welsh entertainer and broadcaster lived at Maerdy Camp until he was three years old and he remembers being surrounded by ducks and chickens.

Self-build houses

Due to the post WWII housing shortage, ex-servicemen throughout the country took it upon themselves to band together to build their own houses. The first self-build society was formed in Brighton in 1948. By 1955 there were five self-build groups in the Cardiff area.

An article in the Daily Mirror by "Ruggles" describing the self-build idea, had been seen by Douglas Roberts. He and his brother-in-law, Douglas Hutchings, a local butcher, failed to be accepted by any of the Cardiff groups, so they decided to form their own. During January 1953, they had informal discussions with other ex-servicemen, who were also building craftsmen. Having decided to go ahead, the first formal meeting was held on 1st February 1953.

The group, affiliated to the National Federation of Housing Societies was formerly registered as *The Rumney Housing Association Ltd.* All members agreed to work 21 hours per week and one week of their summer holiday. The men were, J.A.Burge, master builder and carpenter, W.E.Jones, sales representative, E.T.Humphries, local government officer, B.D.Waite, plasterer, W.A.Watts, plumber, E.E.Stoodley, bricklayer, A.E.Bell, bricklayer, J.R.Evans, carpenter, V.D.Hutchings, butcher, D.T.Roberts, fitter

202

and turner, A.E.Colledge, fitter and glazier, and W.B.Lane, transport driver.

Cardiff City Council leased land directly to the individual members for the erection of ten, semi-detached bungalows in Lynton Close and two in Lynton Place. The work to be carried out was usually arranged, on site, by Jim Burge and Basil Waite, during the tea-break on a Sunday afternoon. There were some early problems with bad weather conditions and shortage of bricks. Despite this, the first two were occupied in October and November of 1954 and the last two in July 1957.

A few minor jobs continued until March 1958. The twelve original members had remained throughout the project and arranged for dissolution of the Association later in 1958.

Tea-break: Men l-r:Eddie Humphries, Alfie Burge,Billy Watts, Basil Waite, Billy Jones, Barry Lane plus interested children and a visitor to the site.

St. Mellons

Changes in St. Mellons came about much more slowly than in Rumney. Houses, four pubs, shop, post office and police station were all clustered around the church and most of these still remain. Doreen Shepstone, born in 1913 at Sea View Stores, remembers – 'At the end of the Great War, there were prisoners of war working for the church cutting trees and bushes in and around the churchyard.' Doreen and other village-children enjoyed their childhood, walking through the 'plantation', an area with beautiful beech and oak trees between the old school and the church. In autumn, the leaves seemed to be up to their knees. The children had a 'bogey', made from wood and old pram-wheels. They dragged it to the top of a track near the church, then rode on it down the track to Newport Road. After the service on Sunday evenings, people from the churches and chapels of Rumney and St. Mellons gathered in the parish church for community singing. They were conducted by Mr John of Church Lane. Doreen stated, 'I particularly enjoyed the Hallelujah chorus from the Messiah. I remember buying fish and chips in winter and ice cream in summer from Mr John. I also enjoyed watching a little steam train, which carried the pipes for the Rhymney Valley Sewer from Began Road to the work-site where they were needed.'

Children playing on the Ton, St. Mellons village.

The Rhymney valley sewer was the forerunner of many changes. Men working on the sewer used St. Mellons as their base. Construction took two and a half years and was completed by Christmas 1921. During this time, the men, mainly Irish, were housed in large wooden buildings erected on Druidstone Road near

204

the house called High Mead. The men were on strike for seven weeks in 1920 but after this, relations between staff and workmen improved.

A controversial issue was reported in *August 1932* issue of the *Countryside Magazine*. There were both objections and support for electricity pylons to be erected at intervals throughout the countryside. Opinions were divided. 'They mar the countryside' or...'the alternative would be more damaging still to our rural beauty' or.... ' it would necessitate the cutting-up and spoiling of many miles of countryside' or....'They may not be visions of elegance but are not very ugly either and at times seem to have the power of fascinating the eye.' Alternatively underground cables could be laid. Similar controversies arise today about wind farms.

It was reported in *January 1933* issue of the same magazine that a scheme to install street lights in St. Mellons had been put forward by the South Wales Power Company. The plan and estimates were turned down, 'for the present', by the Parish Council.

The South Wales Power Co. moved into unfinished offices on Newport Road, St. Mellons at the end of 1939. There were no doors on the individual offices, but if they hadn't moved in, the War Dept. would have commandeered the building.

Thornber's Hatchery – packing chicks on the despatch line.

In 1954, Thornber's Hatchery was established in the orchard of Wern Fawr House off Wern Vawr Lane St. Mellons. James McManners who had worked for Thornber in Yorkshire from the age of 14 came to St. Mellons to manage the new business.

A few farmers in the area entered into contract with Thornber. They were provided with stock to produce eggs for the hatching of hybrid chicks by Thornber. Day-old chicks were sent, usually by train, all around the U.K. Local customers also collected their day old chicks. James McManners wife Isabella, who now lives in Marshfield, recalled that the monks of Caldy Island were customers. On one occasion after collecting the day-old chicks from St. Mellons a storm blew up when they were returning by boat to the island; unfortunately due to the heavy seas all the chicks were lost.

Happy days when motoring was leisurely.

Log-books of St. Mellons school have given an insight into village life. One thing that was spoiling life in the village in the mid 20th century was the increasing number of cars and lorries passing through on the A48, the main trunk road from London to West Wales. In November 1971 the M4 was opened and this relieved traffic congestion in St. Mellons and Rumney.

Another significant year for St. Mellons was 1973 when the village came under the administration of Cardiff City Council. The South Wales Echo reported in March 1974 an ambitious plan to turn a big new housing estate into a mini-town, with its own railway station and shopping centres!

In 1984 the South Wales Echo reported that housing development was now taking place on a much bigger scale. A new ward of Trowbridge had been created; this was mainly within the old parish boundary of St. Mellons. A target of 5,000 homes had been set. Compare this with about 630 homes in St. Mellons at that time. House prices in the old part of St. Mellons then ranged from approx. £25,000 for a terraced cottage to £45,000. for a three-bedroomed semi. House building continued along with a new school, pub, police station and health centre. In a deal with Cardiff City Council, Tesco agreed to build a supermarket and to finance a community centre. Building had started in October 1981 and by November 1982 both were in use along with other shops and a hairdressing salon.

In 1986, land surrounding the old William Nicholl Nursing Home was put up for sale by South Glamorgan Health Authority. Housing development was planned on the 19 acre site. Objections were made by residents in the old community of St. Mellons and by the Community Council. They did not want another big housing development springing up on their doorstep so soon after the sprawling new housing estates of St. Mellons. In spite of objections, development went ahead. Beechtree Park is now a very pleasant area of the village.

In July 1987, local builders G. B. Coffin Ltd. applied for outline planning permission on a twelve-acre site between Began Road and Druidstone Road St. Mellons. An action group was formed to oppose the development and fierce opposition came from villagers and Community Council. This time the protest campaign was successful, for proposals for 100 houses were rejected and following an appeal, a proposal for 14 luxury houses was also rejected. Since then there have been regular applications for individual houses in that area but no major building has taken place.

In 1988, application was made to build sixty-three houses on a site off Old Hill, St. Mellons. Once again there was fierce opposition, the Community Council protested, but building went ahead albeit with a reduced number of houses.

In July 1988, St. Mellons Community Council protested that the rural aspect of the village was in jeopardy when a planning application was made for twenty-five homes on land bordered by Eastern Avenue, Tyr Winch Road and Bridge Road. Planning was granted however and Ruperra Close came into being.

Some time after the destruction by fire, in June 1989, of the former Poor House and Village School building at the Ton, planning permission was granted to build new town Houses on the site. It was stipulated that a team of archaeologists should undertake a field valuation, as the area might contain material of archaeological importance.

In 1989 an application was made by St. Mellons Community Council to Cardiff City Council to re-name the area known as St. Mellons Ward as either St. Mellons Village or Old St. Mellons. The latter name was chosen.

Old St. Mellons Village Association. (OSMVA)

The Old St. Mellons Village Association, successor to the St. Mellons Sports Committee, was formed on June 12th 1974 with the aim of holding a day of sports and fancy dress competitions, followed by a dance, at the Playing field in Tyr Winch Road, St. Mellons. Since the field had no running water, toilets, lighting or power at that time, the committee, made up of keen community councillors and active villagers, had to use lots of imagination and its full powers of persuasion. On July 5th 1975, efforts were rewarded when the first very successful Sports Day took place.

The Committee, led by its first Chairman Viv. Parr, was then encouraged to hold a Halloween Party at the Athletic Hall (known as the Tin Hut) in the Village. The hall was suitably decorated to create a dark and murky atmosphere and the event was another success. This was followed by an Outdoor Carol Party on December 22nd 1975. Both events provided funds for activities and records show that fund-raising became a specific objective. In 1976, the Committee adopted a Constitution and spent some of its funds on football and cricket equipment so that the Junior football team and local cricket enthusiasts could enjoy playing at the Sports Field. That year too, a Village Party was held, with cabaret provided by the Women's Institute. Investigations then began into the provision of changing facilities and toilets at the Sports Field and as a result, a large railway container wagon was purchased and sited there.

In Jubilee Year 1977, the Committee was very active organising the Village Party, Village Fete and soccer competitions.

The cricket pitch was also prepared for summer fixtures. Financial help was given to repair the tennis courts at the William Nicholl Home and the idea of forming a tennis club was well-received. By mid-1978, soccer, cricket and tennis programmes were well established with the help of funds raised by a succession of village social activities. Then came the news that St. Mellons Community Council was about to purchase the Sports Field for the village and in October 1978, outline planning permission was sought for a pavilion at the field. Fund-raising was increased and one response was the formation of the 100 Club in late 1979. In April 1980, the St. Mellons Sports Committee was able to fund the foundation works and base for the pavilion and later supplied volunteers to fit the kitchen and plant shrubs around the pavilion.

The Electricity Board's Rotunda Theatre was used, in 1982, for several successful social events and the need was recognised for improvement of the Village Hall. It was at this time that the St. Mellons Sports Committee became the St. Mellons Village Association. On July 19th 1982 alterations to the Village Hall were started and £2500 was donated to the Community Council for Village Hall redevelopment. The emphasis in 1983, was on fund-raising to support work on the Hall. Activities included a Quiz Evening, Coffee Morning, Auction, Sports Day and Fete, Bingo, Ladies Football, sponsored Badminton, Choir Evening, Village Raffle, Village Dance plus the ongoing 100 Club. Further donations of £2500 and £1000 were made to the Community Council.

In 1984, a further £1000 was donated to the Community Council and the Village Association prepared itself for another busy year starting with the first Race Night, aptly named 'The St.Mellons Renovation Race Meeting.' Two very successful book publications, *The St. Mellons Cook-book* and *The Story of St. Mellons* were also supported. Members volunteered to work on finishing the Hall, by assisting with painting, tiling and cleaning. During one such cleaning session, Jimmy Saville, who was appearing in Cardiff at that time, happened to be running past the hall and was invited in by Scouts who were working outside. The ladies were thrilled to say that they had met Jim of *Jim'll Fix It* fame. Jim later agreed to be photographed with Vera Booth, secretary of St. Mellons Village Association and the South Wales Echo recorded his unofficial visit.

In September 1984, after further donations to the Community Council, the St. Mellons Village Association organised a dance to celebrate the opening of the redeveloped Village Hall. The Hall and its amenities were much appreciated and all the more so because so many villagers had played a part in the renovation work. Whilst the focus of attention had been on redevelopment of the Village Hall, sporting activities had continued, particularly with the Junior Soccer team and the Tennis Club, so much so that the Association agreed to fund-raise for a second tennis court at the Sports Field. Contracts for this court were eventually signed in late 1986 at a net cost of £9,200 including an initial deposit of £3,400.

Local dignitaries at St. Mellons Village Fete, early 1980s.

In 1987, the Association upgraded stage facilities at the Village Hall and then started what was to become *The Entertainers* by presenting a Variety Show in November 1987. This Amateur Dramatics Group currently stages an annual Spring Show and a Pantomime in late November/early December. Tickets are always much in demand. Fund-raising then continued through a wide range of much-enjoyed events and this enabled the Association to contribute £8,000 to the Community Council, to help fund an extension to the side of the Village Hall in late 1990. In 1991, a further £5,000 contribution helped meet the cost of an extension to the rear of the Hall.

During the 1980s and 1990s the Village Association always looked favourably on requests for financial assistance from the Scout Group, Parish Church and St. Mellons Church in Wales School. Examples of aid given included Insurance for the Scout minibus, aid for churchyard maintenance, help for funding for fencing at the Church in Wales Village School and with sports equipment and team-strips.

In early 1993, £3,000 was raised for repairs to the Hall roof, whilst mid-1994, saw £1,000 raised towards work in the kitchen. In 1995, in conjunction with *The Entertainers*, the Association invested £2,000 in new sound equipment which enhanced stage productions and still gives a very professional touch to village shows. In 1996, mindful of the wonderful use made of Village Hall facilities, the Association contributed £1,000 for tables at the Hall and renovations at the pavilion in the Sports Field and £2,000 went towards general purposes. Village Hall events are usually enhanced by use of a bar and this was upgraded at a cost of £1,000 in 1998. During the same year, £1,500 was raised towards the cost of an improved ventilation system at the Hall.

The year 2000 was to herald the new Millennium and in 1999 and early 2000, much planning went into preparations for Village Celebrations. In advance of the celebrations £1,000 was donated for general purposes in 1999 and a further £1,000 was spent on refurbishing the stage-curtains tracking system to theatre standard. A wonderful mid-summer full week of events involved many community groups and in Aug/Sept a most successful local history exhibition lasted five days. Local people were begging for more. Early in the year 2000, a contribution of £5,000 was made towards the gas central heating system at the Hall with a further £2,000 in late 2001, towards improvement of Hall security. Yearly donations continued to be made, for in 2002, the Association project-managed and secured grant-funding for the complete refurbishment of the Hall kitchen at a cost of approx. £11,000. Renovation-work on the disabled toilet at the Hall took place in 2004 and folding doors were installed in the side hall to enclose stacked chairs. The Association – now known as Old St. Mellons Village Association continues to fund-raise for further projects.

For many years, local benefactor Cyril Rogers gave much

support to OSMVA in his role as Honorary President. In 2004, Vera Booth, an extremely hard-working and long-serving past-secretary was elected President. Four Vice-Pesidents, namely Malcolm Booth, Edna Potter, Myfanwy and Eric Williams, were elected, in recognition of their contribution to the community over many years.

The Community of Old St. Mellons is a thriving mixture of young and old, committed to working, playing and enjoying life together. OSMVA works hard to support social and sporting activities and to improve amenities in the village of Old St. Mellons.

Cyril Rogers and a relative of Helen Rees at the presentation of a picnic table in memory of Councillor Rees.

Getting Around

Before WWII, very few families had their own car. Transport to and from work or for pleasure was by bicycle, bus or 'shank's pony'. The motor car has given us independence and freedom and has extended our horizons. Instead of waiting for a bus in the rain, struggling up Rumney or St. Mellons Hill on a bike, or trudging on foot to school from the Moors in all winds and weathers, the car has given us comfort and convenience. It has also given so much pleasure, enabling us to travel at our leisure to places only dreamed of by our forebears. This has, however, brought problems. Before the Eastern Avenue by-pass and M4 were built, traffic heading to Cardiff, Swansea and beyond passed through St. Mellons and Rumney. At the time, it brought misery to people living on the main road and it was a great relief when new road systems were introduced. At the

212

beginning of the 21st century, traffic has once again increased and with it the stress of waiting in queues. Misery and worry about exhaust fumes is now experienced on minor roads. Maybe the days of horse, bicycle and walking were indeed the healthier good old days.

The type of bus used on the Cardiff to Newport run in the 1920s.

The Good Old Days?

Were they really so good? No toilets, no hot and cold running water, no bathrooms, no washing machines, no central heating, no TV nor many more things that we take for granted today.

Homes in Cardiff and Newport had water piped into the houses some time before those in the outlying villages, where rain water was collected from the roof for washing and cleaning purposes. A trek to the village pump or water spout was the routine for obtaining drinking water, though some people were fortunate enough to have their own well.

In the first half of the twentieth century, bathing- only once a week- was in a galvanised bath, in front of the fire. Wash-day was a regular Monday morning ritual. The whites were often boiled in a wash- boiler, a large cast- iron bowl over a fire, often in an outhouse. The washing was rinsed several times in cold water, with a blue bag

213

added to the last rinse to make the whites appear whiter. A good drying day called for light wind and sun on the clothes which were pegged on a long high line outside, supported by a wooden clothes prop. On wet days, the washing was either hung on a line in an outhouse, or on a wooden clothes-horse in front of the fire.

The pump in Church Road Rumney, one of several in the village.

In 1897, **Sunlight Soap** produced a small book, described as 'a treasury of useful information of value to all members of the household.'...'Sunlight soap purifies and whitens; the clothes washed with it never have that peculiar and unpleasant smell imparted to them by soda and coarse soap. The house, instead of reeking with the smell of washing, is scented as with the perfume of hayfields.-For carpet, apply Sunlight Soap freely with a loofah or soft brush, wash off with clean water and dry with clean linen cloths.'

Things useful to remember:-

    i.   Washing done with Sunlight Soap only takes half the time and quarter the labour that would otherwise be necessary.

    ii.   You will sleep better if your bed is well-aired in the morning.

    iii.   Salt is an excellent thing to clean the teeth with.

    iv.   A little sugar, sprinkled on a fire that is nearly out, will often cause it to burn up bright.

v.   The old-fashioned remedy of tallow rubbed on brown paper and worn on the chest, is an excellent one for colds.

vi.   A little castor oil rubbed into your boots occasionally will make them last much longer.

vii.   Potato peelings and cold water are excellent for cleaning glass decanters, etc.

viii.   Dry salt, sprinkled over a carpet before it is swept, will help wonderfully well to brighten the colours.

i.   Five minutes spent in darning a thin place will most likely save an hour's work later on.

ii.   A wise woman will always welcome any friend of her husband and strive to make home the "loveliest spot on earth" to him.'

Milk churn, butter churn, a cream setting pan and a pair of butter beaters, used to extract moisture from butter.

Other advice – '*The Duties of parents* include protection of their children, care of their health, morals and manners, provision for their wants, advise, encouragement, kindness, good example and anxious effort to have them educated and trained for the honourable discharge of the duties connected with the station of life to which they belong. Parents are responsible for the performance of these duties to the best of their abilities and means. They are responsible to God who gave them children, responsible to the children whose misery or happiness in after-life depends on the fulfilment of the duty, responsible to society of which their children will form a part when grown up and responsible to the State to which they are subject.

Children should show their parents – all respect, obedience, esteem, gratitude and love and should be kind and gentle towards one another. There are few lovelier sights than a family moving harmoniously to the impulses which speak in every glance of the eye, in every expression of the countenance, in every word and finds its happiness in all gentle and loving ministries of one toward the other. But to realise such a happy condition as this, principles must be cultivated which should govern and mould every family.

i.   The principle of mutual respect and deference.

ii.   The principle of mutual love.

iii.   There must be mutual activity.

iv.   There should be no selfishness, no disposition on the part of any member to concentrate his thoughts and wishes in himself, independently of the comfort and interest of those around. The happiness of one should be that of all, and all should desire the happiness and enjoyment of each other.

v.   To crown the whole, the fear of God should be the grand principle to sustain, elevate and mould all.

These principles will be, to every family, of far greater worth than the most precious jewels. Families, everywhere, should remember that without such principles to enlighten, guide, direct and purify, there can be no real, no permanent happiness, however well educated or wealthy they may be. It is good principles alone, which make a virtuous and happy home.

Contrasting lifestyles from Sunlight Soap Book.

216

Cycling for women and children

There can be no doubt in the mind of any unprejudiced person that cycling, if not carried to excess, is one of the healthiest forms of recreation that can be indulged in, and, where it is possible, I would advise every woman and child who is old enough, to become the possessor of a machine.

Nowadays there are so many makers it is difficult to know who to patronise, but the best plan, if you wish to purchase one, is to try as many different makes as you can and choose the one that suits you best, being careful to see the saddle is comfortable, the crank-throw the right length and the handles the proper height, before finally deciding on the machine.

The next thing will be to learn to ride, for this is not by any means as easy as it looks. The quickest way will be to take lessons, and there are plenty of schools where these are given, but it is not everyone who cares to go to the expense.

This being so, a quiet country road, where there is little or no traffic, should be chosen for the first few attempts and attended by a good-natured brother or kind friend, the learner may make a start. A good deal of practice will be necessary before the balance, steering and pedalling are acquired, the learner must take great care not to overtire herself, since at first it will be found extremely fatiguing.

In France women cyclists are rarely, if ever, seen in anything but knickers and a blouse, but this inelegant style, I am glad to say, has not 'caught on' with our English sisters, nor is it necessary. A short plain skirt and coat, tailor-made if possible, with a sensible hat that is not easily affected by wind or rain, is all that is required.

The hair should be neatly arranged, any short strands that are likely to get out of curl and blow about, being pinned securely back, for if a girl wishes to look well on a bicycle, she should be neat and trim, anything fussy or flimsy here being quite out of place.

Toilets

The toilet of course was another matter................

A certain person living in Rumney is known to have played a trick with his cousin on their sisters, who often went 'up the garden path' together. The boys waited for their sisters to be settled in the toilet, then they crept up behind the toilet, quietly opened the access door, that was used to remove the buckets, and pushed stinging nettles through the door, stinging the girls' bottoms! The girls went running and screaming back to the house whilst the boys disappeared for the rest of the day. They knew they would be in deep trouble. Needless to say, it didn't happen again!

When the tai bach was at the end of the garden or in the orchard, on a cold dark night, company was always a must.

A two-holer.

Looking Back ......Thoughts of a group of War-babies i.e. Products of the 30s and 40s...and earlier!

218

We were born before television, penicillin, artificial hearts, frozen foods, Xerox, contact lenses, videos and the pill. We arrived before radar, transistor radios, Rock and Roll, credit and diner cards, split atoms, laser-beams and ball-point pens; before dish-washers, tumble-driers, drip-dry cloths, air-conditioners, electric blankets, pantyhose or tights; bar-codes, T.V. remote control, automatic lifts, polio-vaccine, Watson and Crick's description of the double-helix D.N.A., Sputnik and before man walked on the moon.

We got married first and then lived together. (How quaint!) We thought 'fast-food' was something eaten in Lent, a 'big-mac' was an over-sized raincoat and 'crumpet' was something we ate for tea. We existed before house-husbands, computer-dating, dual-careers, at a time when a meaningful relationship meant getting along with relatives. Sheltered accommodation was where we waited for a bus and 'going all the way' meant staying on the bus as far as the terminus.

We were before disposable nappies…only large terry-towelling ones for us, whilst day-care centres and retirement homes were non-existent. We had never heard of F.M. radio and for many of us, it was paraffin lamps and gas-lighting with regular trips to buy an accumulator for the wireless, paraffin for the lamp or gas- mantles at the hardware shop. 'Hardware' meant nuts and bolts and 'software' wasn't even a word.

Girls did not use crimpers or straighteners, we relied on a Toni home-perm and Amami setting lotion on a weekly bath-night. Boys used Vaseline or Brylcreem, for gel did not exist and young men did not wear earrings! Tizer and Corona pop were real treats or it was home-made lemonade or ginger-beer, instead of today's Coca-Cola. Mums produced home-made cakes and meals… no ready-made boxed shop stuff for us nor sliced bread.

In our youth, 'made in Japan' meant junk, the term 'making-out'referred to how you did in your exams i.e. scholarship exam followed by Grammar School and 'O' levels, or Secondary School and leaving at age 15. We listened to 78 r.p.m.records on wind-up gramaphones, for compact audio-cassette tapes did not exist. We wrote with scratchy-nibbed wooden stick pens in Primary school and liquid ink for the ink-wells was made up from ink powder and water. Later we used fountain pens and bottled Quink. What a treat!

Pizzas, Mcdonalds, T.G.I. Fridays and instant coffee were unknown to us. In our day, cigarette-smoking was fashionable, though most people could only afford 5 or 10 Wills' Woodbines. 'Grass was mown, 'coke' was kept in the coal-house and used on the open fire ... no central-heating for us. In bed it was bedsocks and hot-water bottles (pottery variety) which kept us warm. A joint was a piece of meat you cooked on Sundays and used for a base for a stew on Mondays, whilst 'pot' was what you cooked the stew in ... sometimes on the fire, if not on the stove. 'Rock music' was a baby's lullaby, 'Eldorado' was the name of an ice-cream, a 'gay' person was the life and soul of the party and nothing more, whilst 'aids' meant beauty-treatment or help for someone in trouble.

Over the past sixty plus years, life has changed dramatically so we and our contemporaries have had to make countless adjustments, and it's time to enjoy a 'rest' in our retirement, at present 60 for women and 65 for men. How sad that our children will have to work even harder to 'get on the housing-ladder' and more years to reach retirement! Our world has 'expanded' and modern times have brought many advantages such as greater longevity and improved living-conditions. With the advantages, however, have come disadvantages such as pollution, less time for family and religion and greatly increased stress.

By the grace of God, we have survived into the new Millennium.

Looking back at the Millennium Exhibition.

220

RAMBLES AROUND RUMNEY AND STROLLS AROUND ST. MELLONS

William Booth who lived at 99 Newport Rd. Cardiff, was the author of *Rambles around Rumney with Camera and Sketch-Book*. This book was presented to Cardiff Library at the time of his death in 1928. Between 1890 and 1928 Booth had recorded his observations, made sketches and taken photographs of Rumney and the neighbouring villages. The following are a few extracts from his book.

'The village of Rumney is straggling, decidedly straggling, there is no particular High Street or Boulevard and the Marine Parade or Sea Wall is some distance from the village. The houses are built in threes and fours at the end of lanes that finish up in ditches Ty Fry Road to wit.

Once upon a time, about a hundred years or so ago, (1790) there was an enquiry in Parliament about the state of the roads in Wales and Monmouthshire. The member for Monmouthshire stated, that so far as Monmouthshire was concerned, they had no roads, they travelled in ditches. Walking up Rumney Hill if you look over at the road running at the side of the present improved gradient, it looks as if the said member was correct. It must have been like, 'Jordan, a hard road to travel I believe. Perhaps in wet weather, soft road would be more appropriate.'

Booth refers to Cardiff as a neighbouring 'village' but then goes on to say that *'most villagers of Rumney, do their shopping in Cardiff on Saturday market-day. The walk home across the Moor, when there is a good east wind blowing, is appetizing'.*

He describes the farmers as follows --- *' One or two of the farmers breed horses and cattle but most of them supply Cardiff with flowers, vegetables and milk. Very few of them are troubled with corn and other cereals.'* He also tells of walking through the pottery and fields to get to the quarry *'where the extensive view takes in the sea, the Somerset coast, the Holms, Cardiff and Penarth, not to mention the brickworks and the power station.'* He continues along the path over the stile into Ty Mawr Lane and *'Hey presto without any magic carpet we are transported into a shady Devonshire lane, the scenery has quite changed, we are in a delightful dell, but there*

221

is so little of it, about half a square mile. We are then on the Wentloog Level among the dykes and marshes, the ducks and geese.'

The advent of the motor car made main roads dangerous for pedestrians, *'the only way to take a walk is to dodge down back lanes and across the fields. There are two or three ways of getting from Rumney to St. Mellons. One is to take the stone stile at Rumney Green and across the fields under Ty Fry Road, which brings you out on the pretty lower road to St. Mellons. Another way is down Mill Lane across the common of Llanrumney Park to the river, just there as Parson Hugh Evans would say, a shallow river, to whose falls, melodious birds sing madrigals, a delightfully cool and pretty place it is. Then across fields and along ditches with a prospect of Llanedarn Church on the hill across the river, reaching St. Mellons at the back of the Church, a road that would bother the most murderously-minded motor-man.'*

Ty Mawr Road - the lane to the right leads to the quarry

222

Today, standing on the Rhymney River Bridge during the rush hour, looking west towards Cardiff, what would William Booth think of the scene? One sees not only cars of every description, but vans, lorries, buses, motor cycles - all negotiating the roundabout, changing lanes, blowing horns and drivers waving fists. Overhead, the fly-over takes more traffic down to the South of Cardiff and Cardiff Bay.

The present Rhymney River bridge under construction in 1910.

Rhymney River itself has changed – fisheries, trade and black coal dust have disappeared. An official document dated 1770, shows that goods were landed from boats at Rumney Bridge, with a Customs Officer in attendance. The river bridge itself is the latest of a number which have stood on the site or adjacent to it. The crossing was originally a ford but, as noted earlier, a bridge was there by the second half of the 12th century. Further bridges were built and repaired during the following six hundred years. In 1805 an Act of Parliament was passed for a new bridge to be built. The Act included details for the administration of the bridge by the Trustees and for

223

toll-charges. It was in the process of being built when in 1809, *'in a sudden rise of the floods, the materials constituting the said Bridge were, from the violence and rapidity of the said flood, carried away'.* Consequently in 1810, a second Bill presented to and passed by Parliament, amended the previous Act.

The amendment describes the bridge as *'a convenient and commodious communication between that part of the United Kingdom called England and the Principality of Wales.'* It further describes *'the dilapidated, ruinous and decayed state of the old bridge, which passage across that part of the river is rendered very incommodious and dangerous to passengers, cattle and carriages, and it is expedient that another bridge should be erected forthwith.'* The Trustees were given further powers to raise money and increase the toll-charges. The bridge remained in place until the present one was opened on 12th January 1912.

Looking towards Cardiff, the commercial development that has taken place on Rumney Common, has replaced the old ponds and clay pits. In the 19th century, brickworks were the only buildings on the Common, to be followed in the early 20th century by Connies and Meaden's steel-processors. At one time the road was a wet and muddy track which was later raised to give a better road across this low-lying flood-plain. During the early part of the twentieth century, the road was about five or six feet above the level of the ground on either side. After WWII the level of the Common as a whole was raised by the tipping of hardcore from bomb-damaged sites and other demolished buildings.

At Rumney Pottery, the bridge toll-house once stood on the neatly-trimmed grass between the house and the present road. The driveway down into the pottery from the road is the only remaining visible sign of the old Roman road. Looking east towards Newport, all the houses on the right of Newport Road up to the Ty Mawr Road junction have been built in the 20th century on former orchards and fields. To the left where Castle Avenue and Castle Crescent are sited, stood Rumney House and Lodge. Rumney House was the home of William Cubitt and his family, who were great benefactors of St. Augustine's Church, Rumney. In the 1901 Census, William Cubitt is recorded as a mechanical engineer and an employer. He and his wife, born in Middlesex, had eight children aged between one and

224

twelve years. There were seven servants, a butler, governess, nurse, nursemaid, cook, housemaid and kitchenmaid. His coachman, Henry Pacey lived in the Lodge.

Rumney House, home of the Cubitt family.

The next building, once called Castlefield, was in 1891, the home of Philip Hacquard. In 1901, William Galloway, a mining engineer, lived there with his family and employed four servants. The house, during the 1920s was the Rumney Hill Private School for Girls with about one hundred pupils. A *Countryside Magazine* reporter attended a party for children at the school given by the Principal, Mrs. Reynolds. He reported that the school had started with only a few pupils and now represented a triumph for private enterprise. He was impressed by the polished manners of the children. This house is now the Conservative Club.

Next door, Morgans Restaurant was formerly known as 'The Oaklands.' It was for many years, the home and surgery of the late Dr. Clifford Bence a former Lord Mayor of Cardiff. In 1901, 'The Oaklands' was the home of Joseph Heald, a rolling-stock manufacturer. He had eight children and two servants. On the brow of the hill stands the Hillcrest Care Home, formerly Tredelerch House. Lascelles Carr, a journalist and later, owner of the Western Mail, lived there in the late 19th century. In 1901, J. E. Gunn, a chartered accountant, occupied the house with his wife, seven children and two servants. These houses, built in the countryside and near the site of the old Rumney Castle, must have been impressive at the beginning of the 20th century.

Continuing along Newport Road, all the houses on the left were built during the 20th century on green-field sites. Rumney Hill Gardens, set back from the main road and running behind the houses, were once designated as a burial ground but found to be unsuitable. At the junction with Ty Mawr Road, prior to 1965, stood a small cottage which was once the lodge of the Great House. The cottage itself, during its lifetime, was a school, where pupils paid a penny per week to learn elementary reading, writing and arithmetic. There was only one room and a bed on pulleys was raised and lowered morning and night. Almost adjacent to Ty Mawr junction are three pairs of cottages below road level. These cottages, originally known as Rectory Villas, back on to the new Vicarage and are believed to be much older than other nearby properties. After passing the entrance to the Vicarage there are two groups of terraced houses; in the middle of these is the entrance to Beili Bach. Behind the church there were formerly six stone cottages dating from the 17th century, of which only three remain.

Continuing along Newport Road, the small terraced properties up to the Walk were known as Hillsborough Terrace where an old milestone can be seen. The properties as far as Whitehall Parade are of more modern design. On the opposite side of the road the Police station now occupies the site of a former bakery which changed hands a number of times over the years. The earliest known owner of this site was a Colonel Deane and the last owner before the police station was the Country Maid Bakery.

Set back from the road is the Pen yr Heol guest-house which is on the site of the old Pen yr Heol Farm. Pen yr Heol played an important role in the affairs of the parish over many years, because it was there that the Parish Council often held their meetings, as did the administrators of the Poor Law and a number of other committees. It was also in this building that the Independent Breakaway Movement from the Established Church held their first gathering and later became Wesleyan Methodists.

At the top of Widecombe Drive stood the corrugated iron-clad parish hall. Next door was the famous old alehouse still known

226

as the Carpenters Arms. In 1901 it was also a farm. In the census return, one Richard Jones describes himself as a farmer and innkeeper. His daughter worked in the pub and he also employed a farm bailiff, a waggoner and two domestic servants. This public house is fondly remembered by locals and old Cardiffians. This fondness resulted from the time when Cardiff public houses were closed on Sundays whilst Monmouthshire pubs remained open. Cardiff inhabitants became frequent Sunday visitors to Rumney pubs. Drinkers who over-imbibed, found the journey home a little overtaxing and lay down on the grass on the common to sleep. They were known as the 'Sons of Sleep.' The Carpenters Arms was an important watering-hole and references to it can be found in a number of old diaries and publications.

Newport Road, (the top road) looking towards Newport. The Carpenters Arms to the left and Rumney Hill Garage to the right.

Adjoining the Carpenters Arms was the blacksmith's shop. Set back from the road was Rumney Court, a large red-brick house built by Richard Travell, described in the 1881 census as a Gentleman. In the 1891 census he was a Retired Hotel Keeper aged 66. In 1901 the house was unoccupied, but there was a gardener living at Rumney Court Lodge. The lodge stood about half-way along the present-day parade of shops. This building was demolished brick by brick and rebuilt just below the Rompney Castle in Wentloog Road. At one time, the main house was the home of

227

Richard England, a wholesale potato importer. At the present time it is the Royal British Legion Club.

The entrance to Ball Lane was at the side of the former Rumney Court gardens. On the other side of the lane was another blacksmith's shop and at one time a wheelwright's shop. This was attached to the end of the Cross Inn. In various census returns the occupiers of the Cross Inn have been described as innkeepers, publicans and, often as wheelwrights. The 1891 census lists five wheelwrights and a blacksmith.

Stuart Scrivens recalled – *"In the wheelwright's shop they made all the usual farm wagons and floats as well as wheelbarrows and many lesser wooden implements. I have often stopped, as a boy, to see old Thomas the wheelwright, start with a piece of elm, to shape and cut out the hub of a wagon wheel. I might perhaps pass a few days later and he would have inserted the spokes and the wheel was taking shape. I was interested and would go again and would see the valleys and the wheel complete, ready for the banding which would contract tightly onto the wheel as though a magician had been at work."* Some years later it was in this small blacksmith's shop that John Hodson, known locally as John the welder, started repairing farm machinery and other implements. He then moved to Pwll Mawr Farm in Wentloog Road where he rented former cowsheds and started the Rumney Welding and Engineering Co.

It had been reported in the Cardiff Times and Weekly News, April 18th 1903 – 'A Rumney Inn. At Newport County Police Court on Saturday, Mr. Parsons, barrister, submitted plans of the re-building of the Cross Inn, a thatched house in a tumble-down condition on the roadside in Rumney. The house, a pre-1869 beer house was in an unsatisfactory condition.' This explains the difference between a photograph in 1896 and one in 1906. The well-respected landlady Mrs Elizabeth Rees died, aged 82 years, in June 1932 having been the licensee for 62 years. She was held in high esteem by all who knew her kindly smile and sweet disposition. The Cross Inn is now owned by Brains Brewery and has recently been refurbished.

On the opposite side of Newport Road, at the junction with Whitehall Parade, stands Rumney Hill Garage. The garage has existed since 1924; petrol was sold at the time but this was discontinued due to new rules and regulations. It has been a car sales and repair business since 1967. On the other side of Whitehall Parade on Newport Road stand more shops that have changed hands many times – Lipton's, Maypole, Duggan and James, Rolfe's agricultural stores, Hague's the chemist, later Boots the chemist.

Newport Road - The Cross Inn on the left.

Opposite the Cross Inn and at the junction of Wentloog Road and Newport Road, Wentloog Court, a new block of flats stands on the site of the former County Cinema, which itself replaced the house known as the Firs. The cinema opened on Boxing Day 1939 and provided many years of entertainment for local people including Saturday morning matinees for children, with Roy Rogers and Hopalong Cassidy. During the 1960s, cinema audiences dwindled and finally in November 1974 the County Cinema closed.

County cinema, Newport Road, Rumney.

Continuing towards Newport, the shops to the right were built in the 1960s. County Builders, Godsalls Bakery and Les Jones, newsagents were some of the early occupiers. At the junction with Maxwell Road stands White Lodge Residential Home, formerly the home of Henry Budgen, a prominent surveyor. The Monkstone Inn, set back from Newport Road, housed a school of dancing. Fairfield House and Lodge occupied the site of the later Guide Dogs for the Blind Centre, now moved elsewhere. Fairfield House was the home of brother and sister Bill and Fanny Simons. He had strong connections with the Dowlais Iron & Steel Works and she was an authoress. Miss Fanny, an erstwhile President of Rumney Drama Club, was better remembered for her great display of patriotism during WWII, when people were encouraged to support the war effort by mending and making-do. She was often seen shopping wearing mismatched stockings and old shabby clothes. She and her brother were charming people.

   The next house on the right was Witla Court, built in 1850 on the site of a small cottage known in 1841 as Witla. At that time it was occupied by an Irish agricultural labourer, father of eleven children. By 1871, it was called Witla House and a Mary Ann Davies lived there with her two sons and two daughters. They employed a gardener. By 1891, the status of the house had improved again. It was then known as Witla Court. Henry Heywood, mineral importer, born in Nottingham, lived there with his wife and three children. They had a cook and two housemaids. At that time it became the first place of worship for Roman Catholics in Rumney. During WWII, as noted earlier, the house was used as a Women's Land Army Hostel. Some years later, it became a pub, prior to being demolished for housing development.

Witla Court. circa 1900.

Returning to the Cross Inn, on the left hand side of Newport Road our journey continues eastwards towards St. Mellons. The ground on the left was formerly market gardens worked by the Shute brothers and the Shepstone brothers. The next piece of ground was known as the 'Rec.' or the Rumney Sports Club playing fields. These backed on to Ball Farm and the former farmhouse still stands in Ball Road. Playing fields and the Eastern Leisure Centre now occupy that land. The next house is High Croft, originally a farm and in 1901, the home of Elizabeth Lewis, 48, a widow and grocer. Living with her, were her brother and sister, Thomas and Alice Small, single and of private means. High Croft was later the home of William Jones. He was affectionately known as 'Baggy' Jones because he had started a

231

company making paper bags. This business developed over the years and his great-grandson is still associated with the Company. More recently High Croft was used as a police station.

Further along on the right-hand side are two schools; Rumney High School, opened in 1954 as Caer Castell and St Illtyd's Roman Catholic High School. The latter is near the boundary with St. Mellons and built on the site of an old Roman settlement.

Crossing the boundary into St. Mellons, the first property is Quarry Hall Nursing Home, known until recently, as Quarry Hill House. It is situated on a hill overlooking the lower reaches of Wentloog and the Bristol Channel and has magnificent views of the Severn Estuary and the Somerset and Devon coasts. The house used to have extensive gardens with an orchard running down to Greenway Road. Quarry Hill House was built about 1850 by Benjamin Joseph Hemmingway, who, at that time, was the contractor building the Rhymney Railway. He died in the house in 1856. In 1861, a widow, Elizabeth Thomas lived there with her three sons, all described as brewers. They had five employees, a cook, handmaid, housemaid, gardener and farm servant. In 1868, Mr & Mrs William Collingdon became the tenants.

Quarry Hill House.

Mr Collingdon was a tobacco importer and manufacturer. This was the beginning of the Cope family connection with the house, for Mrs Collingdon had been a Miss Cope. The family continued to live there until 1873, when the house was purchased by the father of Mathew Cope. Mathew Cope, who was a Colliery Proprietor, moved into Quarry Hill House and lived there for 60 years until his death in 1933. By this time his son Sir William Cope and family were also living there and they remained until the death of Lord Cope in 1946. Sir William had been created a Baron in July 1945 on the recommendation of Prime Minister Winston Churchill. He chose the title Lord Cope of St. Mellons.

During WWII the house was let to the Joint War Committee of Monmouthshire, to be used as an auxiliary hospital by the Order of St John and by the Red Cross. Originally, the intention was to use Quarry Hill as a hospital for male service personnel. The plan was changed and it was used as an auxiliary hospital for women service personnel. The hospital opened on 28th May 1942. In the 1950s, the house was acquired by Cardiff City Council and was used as a residential home for the elderly. From the early 1970s, the house fell into disrepair until the late 1990s, when it was developed as a private Nursing Home. It is now known as Quarry Hall.

Sir William Cope with members of staff at Quarry Hill Auxiliary Hospital, where women of the Forces recuperated.

233

Mount Pleasant House, stands on the right-hand side of the road and Greenfield, the former home of the Davies family, stands a little further on.

View of Fox and Hounds, including cottages now demolished for car park.

The Fox and Hounds
Leaving Newport Road and walking down the old St. Mellons Hill, to the right stands the Fox and Hounds Pub. Records show that in 1812 it was part of forty-one lots auctioned at the Angel Hotel in Cardiff. The property was Lot 16, 'cottage, smith's shop, beast-house, (cow or cattle shed) garden, yard and pasture land.'

It was not sold that day but was sold for £400-0s-0d in 1814 to Farmer Edward Rowland of St. Mellons. He leased it to Thomas Lloyd. The property then passed to a Thomas Edmunds, and to a Catherine Lewis and by 1870, it was the Fox and Hounds Inn owned by a Thomas Lloyd. A bakehouse had also been purchased and added to the deeds. Thomas Lloyd sold the Inn to John Lewis for £600. Brains Brewery purchased it in 1933 and since then, it has had many landlords. Jean and Terry Jenkins took over the Pub in 1984 and in 1988 and 1990 won Pub of the Year Award. Brains Brewery who still own the Pub have recently refurbished it. The pub remains a popular eating and drinking place in St. Mellons. At the bottom of St. Mellons Hill and opposite the Fox and Hounds stands the War Memorial commemorating men of the village who died in two World Wars and in the Falklands Conflict.

Squire Williams opening the model railway at the Village Hall St. Mellons.

Old St. Mellons Village Hall

The Village Hall, originally built by villagers in 1936 and affectionately known as the old green tin hut, lies on the left-hand side of Newport Road. Many residents remember the model railway in the grounds, with its little steam-engine manned by Mr. Jones of Acuba Lodge, Druidstone Road, who gave rides to children in the 1950s. The Hall was renovated and developed from 1982-1984 as a joint venture between the Community Council and Old St. Mellons Village Association. Work was done under the Youth Opportunities Scheme.

The Hall has had a varied history. It has been used as schoolrooms, youth club, a children's nursery and as a meeting-place for Community Council, Village Association, W.I., Youth Club, Scout groups, Brownies, Guides, Whist Club, Thursday Lunch Club for Senior Citizens, Table-Tennis, Amateur Dramatics and for many family gatherings. The Hall continues to be the very hub of social life in Old St. Mellons.

The Star Inn

   The earliest mention of the Star is in the Business Directories of 1876, but for ten years prior to this, there was a beer retailer and shopkeeper in the village, but no address was listed. It is more than likely that it started as a Front Room Pub. After 1881 it appeared on the census returns as the Star Inn. 'In 1910, Thomas Scrivens gave notice to the Overseers of the Poor and the Superintendent of Police that it was his intention to apply at the next Special Session for permission to transfer the Licence of the Star Inn in St. Mellons to Walter Witts of Church Lane St. Mellons.'

   In the 1920s the Star was a popular meeting place for those employed on the construction of the Rhymney Valley Sewer. These employees even had their own magazine *The Sewerage Times!* In 1921, a report tells of a very pleasing function which took place at the Star. 'A presentation was made during the course of a smoking concert.' The concert was followed by refreshments. The Star remains a popular-meeting place, particularly for punters at the nearby betting-shop.

Left to right — Village shop and Post-Office (until 1926) on the corner of Church Lane. The Building became a private dwelling, which was demolished in the 1950s.

Did you know … ?
The blacksmith's shop was at the Forge opposite the present Village Hall. Children loved to warm themselves at the fire and watch horses being shod. No.1 Rose Cottage, around 200 years old and stone-built, was the site of the Wheelwright's shop with tea-rooms next door. In Maesycoed, Joseph Pearce ran a bake-house delivering bread by horse-drawn vehicle. The village rugby team used the stables as changing rooms utilizing hot water supplied by the bake-house. To attend surgery at No.1, Sea View Cottages, the first Doctor rode his horse from Llanishen. A District Nurse lived in Llandaff Square, her wages paid by villagers' subscriptions.

The White Hart

The White Hart is an 18th century coaching Inn. Outside still stands the mounting block used by horsemen. It was a coaching-stop on the long journey from London to Milford Haven. The journey took 27 hours for the 151 miles between Bristol and Milford Haven. The coach had four changes of coachmen with thirty-minute stops. Dinner was taken at New Passage Inn Ferry, supper at Cardiff and breakfast in Swansea, at 3.50am! Travellers had to possess great stamina to undertake long journeys by coach.

The White Hart Public House and garden is shown on the 1847 tithe map of St. Mellons as owned by Margaret Pearce. In 1876, the Inn with stables, garden and cottage was sold for £1,220 by William Pearce, innkeeper, to George Croft Williams of Llanrumney Hall. Squire Williams' family owned the Inn for 45 years and there were many tenant managers. From 1891-1897 the innkeeper was John Rees. In 1895, this John Rees bought the adjoining freehold land for £100 and 'messuage, garden and three cottages adjoining, for £325.' The messuage, (a term used in deeds to signify a dwelling house and the surrounding property,) was Wellfield House and the three cottages were nos. 1, 2 and 3 Church Lane. Wellfield House was, at one time, the old Post Office and was itself later demolished. The land on which it stood is now part of the White Hart car park.

Mrs Louise Watkins bought the Inn in 1921 and after many lean years sold it in 1936 to Mrs Elvira Roberts. Mrs Roberts also purchased Wellfield House and cottages in 1937 and in 1940 bought White Lodge Cottage, also known as Myrtle House. Mrs Roberts was a highly-successful landlady, especially during the War, when American Servicemen enjoyed the company of local people at the White Hart. In November 1945, Mrs Roberts sold the Inn to the White Hart Inn (St. Mellons) Company Ltd.

For 21 years it was once again managed by several Innkeepers. It was leased out from 1966 to 1973 when it was sold to Welcome Inns. Since then ownership has passed to many companies.

The Blue Bell Inn

The legend of the name, The Blue Bell, is included in the history of Llanrumney Hall. The Blue Bell Inn is a listed 500 year-old building standing in the centre of Old St. Mellons at the junction of Newport

Road and Tyr Winch Road. The old Pilgrims' Way or Roman Road along the line of Tyr Winch Road and Druidstone Road, continued over Penylan to Bassaleg and thence to Newport. The Blue Bell was a staging-post for coaches which rattled into the yard at the back of the building. Horses were changed and travellers entered the Inn to eat and rest during their long and often dangerous journey to and from London. The very popular Blue Bell – now known as 'The Bluebell' is currently undergoing renovation and refurbishment.

Ty To Maen House

Ty To Maen, now St. John's College, was originally a farm. In 1871, the house was occupied by Richard Allen, a corn merchant and one of the founders of Spillers Mill in Cardiff. Mr Allen was a Somerset man and his wife was born in Australia. They had a cook, two nurses, a housemaid and groom. Richard Allen had the building constructed in 1885 at a cost of £15,000. This attractive late-Victorian house was built in stone with Bath-stone dressings and has many impressive features, including a castellated tower with gargoyles. There are some fine interior features such as fireplaces and ceilings in the style of William Burges and an example of this is a ground-floor large canopied fireplace. The house is now a Grade Two Listed building.

Ty To Maen House.

238

Richard Allen occupied the house until his death in 1901. Later occupants were Sir John Gunn and Mr. J. C. Gould followed by Sir William Edgar Nicholl, Chairman and Managing Director of Spillers Mill, Cardiff and nephew of Richard Allen, who had built the house. On 24th April 1926, the mansion, in twenty-four acres of enclosed land, was presented to Cardiff Royal Infirmary to be used as a convalescent home. It was then known as the William Nicholl Home. The convalescent home was used by the Cardiff Royal Infirmary until the 1970s, except for a period in wartime and just after, when soldiers recuperated and were treated there. It was then taken over by the Area Health Authority and used as a branch of Whitchurch Hospital. In 1995, the house and grounds were purchased by Barratt Homes and on the same day, by prior arrangement, the house and five acres of ground were sold to St John's College. This Independent School, which has 500 plus pupils, takes children from nursery-age to sixth form.

St Mellons Hotel and Country Club
The house has had several name changes during its history. It was originally called Llwynarthan and was the home of Franklin G Evans, an eminent physician who died in 1904. It was then occupied by Sir Henry Webb, Baronet, Junior Lord of the Treasury and a coal-owner, who converted it to a Military Hospital during the First World War. In the early 1930's Mr Gwyn Davies, a Cardiff solicitor, who resided at Vaendre Hall, purchased Llwynarthen House, the surrounding land and associated buildings. He developed the estate in stages with the house becoming at first the Blue Horizon Country Club, a fashionable night-club. Facilities included horse-riding and tennis and of course dining and dancing. Horses were stabled in the buildings, now the golf club and grooms and hotel staff were also accommodated there. During 1937 the St. Mellons Golf Club was formed as a private club and became very successful with about 1000 members, of whom only about 160 were golfers.

In 1938 Mr Davies started to develop further land as a golf course and stables and other buildings became the Golf Club House. Plans were hindered by the outbreak of WWII when the house and land were taken over for war purposes and troops were stationed there. Anti-aircraft guns were mounted on the land sloping towards the A48. On the death of Mr. Gwyn Davies in 1964, his executors placed all the land, buildings and equipment up for sale.

The County Club

After WWII, the house, then known as the County Club, was the venue for many annual balls and dinner-dances for groups such as the St. Mellons Show, the Farmers and Dairymen's Association and Tredegar Farmers Hunt. Auctions of local houses, farms and agricultural land also took place there. The house is now known as a Best Western St. Mellons Hotel and Country Club. It has a frequently used Fitness Centre and is a popular venue for weddings and receptions.

Straying from Newport Road there are other houses of note. One of these is **Began Farm**, off Began Road. In his **Monmouthshire Sketchbook,** Fred Hando tells us the origin of the name Began, as taken from a booklet published in 1879 entitled **Welsh Royalists,** by J. Rowlands. The name is tied to the history of the Kemeys family. Edward, one of the first Kemeys, 'is said to have married Nest, the heiress of Andrew de Beauchamp, or, according to the Welsh pronunciation of the name, de Began and had with her the estate of Beganslegh or Began in St. Mellons. Beganslegh was a manor of Wentllwch held by the service of one-fourth part of a knight's fee. It is supposed that the original Began, half a mile from

240

the present house, stood on Coed yr Hen Cwrt – Old Court Wood'. In 1392, Beganslegh was held by John ap Henry Kemeys and the Kemys families of Newport, Rogerstone, Bedminster, Cefn Mably, Caldicot and Rumney are descendants of the Began-based family.

The present house was erected in the fifteenth century. Until recently, there were two shields on either side of the central upstairs window, unrelated to the Kemys of Cefn Mably coat of arms. J. Rowlands described the shields as follows – 'the outer shield contains three circles and supports two crosses, while the inner shield has two hearts and one cross.' Further explanation is then given 'on the front of Began House are two armorial plates; a female stands at the left corner, and a male at the right; inside are two human hearts and a star at the bottom. The inference is that the parties are standing in place for the performance of their nuptials. The hearts have a striking coincidence with the motto of the Bardic chair of Cemes, Pembrokeshire, "Calon wrth Galon" – Heart to Heart – and the star in the heraldic device denotes the third son.' David Kemeys' third son married a member of the Llewellyn family of Cefn Mably.

After the Kemeys family moved to Cefn Mably, a younger son, born at the turn of the 14th century continued to live at Began House.

Photograph of Began Farm taken by William Booth in 1890. This shows the shields on the wall and the old tile roof.

Began Farm with slate roof, after modernisation. The end centre gable has been removed.

Llanrumney Hall

Llanrumney Hall was originally an Elizabethan mansion and was rebuilt in 1825. The Hall and Estate were acquired by Charles Croft Williams of Roath Court circa 1859 and remained in his family until purchased in 1952, by Cardiff City Council, for housing development.

    The mansion has had many alterations over the centuries. It once stood in a well-wooded park near the Rhymney River. In one of the upper rooms, there is a chimney-piece bearing the date 1587 and the coat-of-arms of the Morgan family, who acquired the house after the Kemeys family.

    Many myths and legends abound concerning the house. During the 12th century the monks of Keynsham Priory were the owners of a small manor in the area. The house was built on the site of a cell or grange of that Priory. Legend has it that the monks used to organise an annual sport or jollification day to celebrate St Malo's feast day, 22nd October - now St.Mellons Day. This was a race on foot from the monastery to St. Mellons Church. The Blue Bell Inn is said to have been built on the site, below the Church, where the race finished. The winner of the race was presented with the monastery's bell which had a blue and white clapper and it is from this bell that the Inn took its name.

Ancient manuscripts assert that the headless body of Llewellyn, the last Welsh Prince of Wales, was interred at Llanrumney Hall. In 1282, after Llewellyn was killed in a skirmish with some English soldiers near Builth Wells, his head was dispatched to King Edward I who was staying at Conwy Castle. The headless body was brought secretly by the monks to Llanrumney Hall, which in those days was known as Little Keynsham, on account of its close association with Keynsham Abbey in Somerset.

A statement by the granddaughter of a Mr. Moggridge, who once owned Llanrumney Hall, notes that her grandfather's workmen discovered in the vaults of the Hall, a stone coffin placed in the very thick wall of the monastery, which was thought to have contained the remains of Llewellyn, whose body had never been found. The historian, Professor Freeman, who once resided in Llanrumney Hall, also believed that the remains found there, were of Llewellyn, last Prince of Wales.

Freda Williams moved into Llanrumney Hall in the spring of 1953. She described the view from her window in the top flat. 'On my first day I looked out of my window and saw some twenty new houses lined up on the right. At the front there was a wonderful greenness to be seen, dotted with daffodils, rhododendron bushes, cherry trees and a marvellous massive oak tree in the middle of the green. Its trunk was so thick, it must have measured many yards around. Some stupid fool set fire to it and it is no longer there. Further off, just below the hill, there was a lily-pond full of goldfish. A narrow bridle path led to it with wooden seats at intervals. You could imagine horses walking home after a day with the hunt.

Behind the house were the stables and a magnificent kitchen garden. Half a mile square, it contained peaches, nectarines, plums, apples, pears, raspberries, strawberries, and every description of currant, herbs, vegetables and flowers. I treasured for years a lovely peony which grew the most wonderful red blooms, until, with the passage of time and the builders shovels, it just disappeared. At the side, was a wonderful bank of tulips, black as jet and a small summer house.

The thick walls of my flat were part of the building, reputedly a monastery more than five hundred years ago. When building work was taking place, a crest dated 1573, was found over

243

the fireplace. Doorways were knocked out and mercury, said to ward off evil spirits, flowed from the walls. Once my flat housed all the servants and I am told that a butler murdered his wife in the large storeroom which has a low ceiling.' Freda told of hearing creaks and seeing monks in the house, but other people did not have the same experience.

Llanrumney Hall

The Rompney Castle, in Wentloog Road Rumney, appears on early 19th century tythe maps and in the 1851 census, was recorded as **The Pear Tree** with 19 acres. The inhabitants were described as farmers and victuallers.

There is a story that the Pear Tree became the haunt of a gang of smugglers who operated from the River Rhymney, with the wealthy owner of a local manor house as their leader. The landlord of the Pear Tree was said to have been in league with the gang, but they were never caught and there is no written evidence to prove their guilt.

Near the end of the 19th century the Pear Tree was purchased by the American Consul in Cardiff. He made many changes to the property, including the building of a mock-baronial hall (now used as the public bar) and is credited with changing the name of the inn to the Rompney Castle.

On May 6th 1890, the property was put up for auction and was described in the catalogue as having 'extensive views over the Bristol Channel with ample stabling accommodation laid out in attractive grounds.' A map to guide prospective buyers, shows that the Rompney Castle was set in open countryside, with only a few neighbouring farms and private houses.

Drawing of the Rompney Castle as it appeared on the sale catalogue of 1890.

When the Welsh Sunday Closing Act was introduced, the village of Rumney was still a part of Monmouthshire, where public houses opened on Sundays. Many people walked out to Rumney to drink on Sunday nights and the situation became so bad that David Lloyd George, Prime Minister, once declared that "Rumney was like hell on earth on a Sunday." After many complaints from licensees and local residents, this state of affairs was quickly put in order by

245

the police and Rumney returned once more to rural tranquillity. Was it always so tranquil? The Rompney Castle had its regulars who often called in on their way home from work, or from delivering goods or milk. If they had a 'drop too much' it didn't matter, as the horse knew the way home. Local lads were often on the lookout for amusement. The Rompney Castle used to have tall wrought-iron gates and on several occasions when one of these 'regulars' had gone into the pub, leaving his horse and cart outside, the boys set to work. Their favourite trick was to remove the horse from the cart, close the gates with the horse on one side and the cart on the other. They would put the shafts of the cart through the gate, put Dolly the horse back into the shafts, then hide behind a hedge. When the unfortunate owner came out of the pub, a little worse for drink, he was totally unable to understand how poor Dolly had got through the gate!

The Old Vicarage (Maesllan) Church Road Rumney
One of the earliest references to the existence of this building is recorded in the *Notes on Parishes in the Llandaff Diocese.* In 1531, the Abbot of St Augustine's leased 'the farm in the parsonage of Rumney in the Lordship of Wentlooge' to Thomas Baker and Thomas Jones for the sum of £5-12s-1d. In 1558, the Vicarage is referred to in Bishop Kitchin's Report of the Diocese of Llandaff and 'phelipp powel clerke vicare there is resydente upon his vicarage'. In 1746, 1780 and 1796 the Vicarage received grants from Queen Anne's Bounty amounting to £600, a large amount of money in those days.

In AD 1763 the Diocese of Llandaff sent out a questionnaire to the vicars of seventeen of its parishes. The Vicar of Rumney declared he did not live in the Vicarage at Rumney, since the house was described as 'being a little poor thatched cot not fit for a clergyman that has a family to live in.' The sexton lived there instead.

On May 14th 1813, the death of the Rev. W. Green Humphrey, Vicar of Rumney, was recorded in the Court Rolls of the Manor of Rompney. Apparently at his death 'there became due to the Lord of the Manor, a Heriot of the best quick beast he had (when he died) within this Lordship and if he had no such quick beast then the best Gaffer with 4 legs that he had and if he had neither Beast or

Gaffer above the value of 5 shillings then 5 shillings in money in lieu thereof.' In AD 1835 it was styled a Vicarage worth £88 gross and the Dean and Chapter of Bristol were the Patrons and Impropriators.

In 1901, the Dean and Chaptor of Bristol decided the house was 'not only inconveniently situate but unfit for a residence-house and that it would be inexpedient to expend money in improving the same.' It was then sold by the church to a private individual, the Rev David Joseph Davies for the sum of £300 and from then on became known as the Old Vicarage. Meanwhile, the incumbent vicar of St. Augustine's Church had moved into a brand new Vicarage on the other side of the churchyard.

The Old Vicarage in Church Road, Rumney.

Today the house is certainly not 'unfit to be a residence!' It still has its old world charm, but it has the luxury of central heating, electricity and modern plumbing. Residents of the 20th century have added their modernising touches, but without destroying any of the former character. The house still has its bare stone walls, its beautiful oak-beamed ceiling, big open fireplace with bread-oven and original flag-stoned floors. The roof, originally recorded as thatched, then having stone tiles and now conventional slates has changed a lot, as has the size of the house. It started life as a one-up-one-down cottage, but as families grew, rooms were added through the generations – the kitchen and dairy in the 18th century, the east side extension in the late 19th century and a small extra kitchen and bathroom in the 20th century. Church Road has also changed dramatically. In 1901 the Old Vicarage stood on its own, snuggling next to the church in a leafy country lane, known as Church Lane, but now it is in a road of many houses.

Whitehall is marked on early 19th century maps and the use of the English name Whitehall, instead of a more usual Welsh name, suggests that it was a building of grandeur and status.

White Hall was owned, in 1804, by John Wood, who was born in Carmarthen in 1755. Wood, at that time, was living at Roath Court and had leased White Hall to Lewis Thomas. Wood was a successful figure in the Cardiff mercantile society at the end of the 18th century. He married Mary Nicholl, daughter of William Nicholl of Cae Maen, Llanvythin in 1779 and served as treasurer for the County of Glamorgan, under-Sheriff between 1787 and 1806 and Clerk of the Peace from 1798 to 1815. He was a Barrister-at-Law at Lincoln's Inn, London, partner in the banking firm of Wood, Evans & Co. and became a junior partner in the Cardiff Bank in 1812. It is likely that Wood Street, where the Cardiff Bank building once stood, was named after him. John Wood died in 1817, aged sixty-two years.

Whether White Hall, now Whitehall, was built in its present form during the 18th century or on the site of an earlier structure possibly incorporating a part of it, is not clear. The proportion and layout of the principal rooms, the symmetrical arrangement of the front façade together with the relatively low pitch of the roof and wide soffits suggests a late 18th century date. The bulk of the fireplace-wall in the ground-floor room behind the parlour (drawing-room) indicates earlier building work, with possibly a gable-entry next to the fireplace. It could be the site of a bread-oven which was reached from the fireplace. The house now boasts two fine fireplaces. The parlour fireplace is believed to have come from the old Cardiff Building Society offices in St. Mary Street or from the Cardiff Bank in Wood Street; if the latter, it would be coincidental that a feature so

248

closely associated with John Wood should find its way back to the house that Wood once owned and after a gap of more than 170 years! Upon his death in 1817, at the age of 62 years, the house was left to one of his sons, John Jnr.

Twentieth century records and Ordnance Survey maps describe the house as Whitehall instead of White Hall. Together with a group of outbuildings it was used as a farm during the nineteenth and early-twentieth centuries, subsequently reverting to use as a single dwelling, now completely surrounded by the houses of Church Road, Whitehall Parade and Wentloog Road.

Whitehall House.

Farms and Farmhouses

The largest farm in Rumney was Ty Mawr Farm. In 1851 it comprised 235 acres. Llanrumney Farm and Wern Vawr Farm in St. Mellons each had 200 acres in 1871 and 1881. The acreage on the farms varied with each census, some increasing, some decreasing. Farms with 100 acres or more were : -Vaindre Vawr, Tyla Mawr,

249

Pandy, Tyn-y-Parc, Pen Peel, Wern Gethin in St. Mellons and Penyrhoel, Greenway, Lower Newton and Church Farms in Rumney. There were many more with 100 acres or less.

These farmhouses, mostly dating from the 16th and 17th centuries, were built of stone, their walls up to four feet wide at the base. They had wide chimneys, with a bread-oven to one side and a black oven-grate for all the cooking and heating of the water. From about 1910, many of the old houses with thatched roofs were being condemned and improvements had to be made. The thatched roofs were replaced with slate ones; these were raised to give more head-room on the lower and upper floors. Longcross Farmhouse in Rumney is the only house in the area with a thatched roof today.

Cadw listed buildings.

In the 1970s, a number of Rumney and St. Mellons farmhouses were listed by Cadw as being of Special Architectural and Historic Interest.

- Rumney, Greenway Farm - Old farmhouse. C18 or earlier, 2-storey building with thick walls of stone, gabled slate roof, formerly thatch. With wide straight staircase of 18th or early 19th century; former bake-house to east of cross passage.

- Rumney, Middle Newton – Outbuilding; adjoins west end of house, 18th century or earlier, 3 bays, stone rubble walls, slate gables roof, roof trusses with joint collar and tie beams. House; an altered early 16th century farmhouse of 1 storey and attic; slate gabled roof (raised, formerly thatched). Fireplace and part of stone staircase have been removed but house and outbuildings together graded II as one of the very few remaining farm-units within the city of Cardiff.

- St.Mellons, Vaindre Vawr - Moated site. Farmhouse of 17th to 18th century. Two parallel ranges, north-western range bombed and rebuilt above ground level. South-east range of three storeys; its south-east elevation of three bays, cement-rendered cladding, tarred slate roof with flanking yellow brick ,stacks. .... South-east ground-floor room with stone-flagged floor. ..... Late 19th century style stair to first floor, wood newel stair to attic. Stopped and chamfered beams on first floor. Attic or second floor with queen strut roof and with run-out stops to principal rafters.

- St.Mellons, Faendre Hall - Mid 19th century, dated 1850 externally. House of two storeys and attic with external walls of ashlar cut stone and slate roofs; ashlar stacks, 17th century Gothic styles.

(ashlar = square blocks of cut stone or thin dressed stone to face a wall) .... Semi-octagonal structure resembling an external medieval kitchen projects from North-west elevation of house. South-east garden elevation of four bays. From North-east end, first bay with parapet, with paired sash-window on first floor and with French casement on ground floor, second bay projects and has a crowning gable, a three-light transom and mullion window on the first floor and with French casement on ground floor, window on ground floor........

Above: Ty Mawr Farm. Below: Longcross Farm 1891

251

CHARACTERS, PERSONALITIES AND MEMOIRS

William Thomas was a Vicar at Peterstone Super Ely in the Vale of Glamorgan, near Cardiff. He kept records of local gossip and in his diaries are some interesting snippets about people who lived in or had connections with Rumney or St. Mellons.

Extracts from the *William Thomas Diaries* and other records.

The following are snippets about people who lived in, or had connections with Rumney, in the 17th, 18th and 19th centuries.

Llancarfan parish register records a marriage between Catherine Collins and George Watkins of Rumney in 1724. This lady was the daughter of Henry Collins (Gent) of Treguff, Llancarfan. In his will dated 26th July 1724, he left Catherine £10 in lieu of 20 sheep which had been left to her by an uncle and which he (her father) had sold. He also left 20 acres of land in Rumney to his son Henry. This Collins family members were descendants of a line of copyholders who are recorded in manorial records in Rumney. Catherine died just three years after her marriage on 19th March 1727, followed immediately by her four-year-old son and they are buried together beneath the floor of Rumney Church. William Thomas records that her widower husband, George Watkins 'on 3rd February 1766 was buried in Cardiff. George Watkins who had been in the market with his malt as usual that day, was making up his accounts at home when a fit came over him and he died with his pen in his hand in the 62nd year of his age.'

The Rowbotham family was a substantial yeoman family who held land in Rumney as well as in Llanedyrne and the Vaindre, St. Mellons, in the 17th and 18th centuries. Rowbothams could be found in all sorts of trades and situations. In 1695, Mary Rowbotham had kept a brothel in Cardiff, which, it is reported, was much resorted to by the prisoners in the gaol. She was buried in Rumney in May 1733. In 1702, John Rowbotham, a barber in Cardiff, was prosecuted with others for wearing oak leaves on the Pretender's birthday.

Jonas Stephen of Roath and Alice Edwards of St. Mellons were married by special licence on 21st July 1750 at St. Mellons. On the 1st July 1751 a son, Thomas, was baptised and sadly, just three days later, was buried on 4th July 1751. Another son, Jonas, was baptised in Roath seven months later in February 1752. A further son Edward, was baptised in 1755 at Rumney. Jonas was buried in Roath in 1759 aged 7 years, only a month after the death of his mother. The father Jonas remarried a Mary Lewis of Michaelston-super-Ely by special licence in 1761 but he died a year later. It is recorded as follows:- '7th June 1762 was buried in Roath, Jonas Stephen, a farmer from Rumney from six days' sickness, his death struck him in Llandaff's fair on Monday ye 31st May past. He died of ye present fever which has raged and been ye death of very many in London and other parts of England and Wales. Do often strike them in their heads and sweeps many in 2 or 3 days and 7 at the farthest. Another fever in manner of a cold do rage in many places but few dies of it - ye imposture broke within him about 48 hours before he died. About 32 years of age and married to his second wife this 13 months past, who is big with child, having miscarried before. He was a man who loved to live high but not much before ye world being in and about £200 in debt. On 21 June 1762 was sold in Rumney ye goods and chattles of the late Jonas Stephen deceased and ye household stuff sold very dear.' His wife's own sister had to buy her sister's curtain box and trunk and give 10s.6d for her gown and cloak.

Old Richard Thomas of the Ball House died on Tuesday 17th September 1751. 'He was a preacher with ye Methodists, a good and learned man.' His burial is not recorded in the registers however, nor in Bishop's Transcripts and it cannot be found in the St. Mellons or Llanedern registers. On July 4th 1762, the wife of Thomas Evans of Rumney, was buried, 'since ye month of May last, from a long lingering disease she took from his drunkenness and abusing her. She was no more than 30 years of age.'

On 21st June 1764 a son was born (his fifth child alive) to Charles - Madam Morgan's Coachman - and Peggy his wife. Madam Morgan was the widow of Thomas Dean Morgan Esq., of Llanrumney Hall and she had leased St. Fagan's Castle where she was living. She took a number of her servants from Rumney and St. Mellons to live in St. Fagans.

The Wentllug Marshes had a very evil reputation for malaria. This disease was fatal mainly to men who worked in the fields, where contact with mosquitoes was more likely. Their wives often died in childbirth. From the turn of the 15th century there was a well-known piece of advice given in Glamorgan, that young females with eyes on a quick fortune should go to the Wentllug Marshes and marry a rich widower. In 1763, John James, Vicar of Rumney, Marshfield, Peterstone, St. Brides and Coedkernew, in answer to the Bishop's visitation queries regarding Peterstone, stated, 'I do serve Peterstone but do not live in the parish, there being no vicarage or parsonage house to live in. I do live in the vicarage house in Marshfield, the adjoining parish, Peterstone being all moorland, being judged unhealthy and the air being agreeable to but few constitutions.'

Two other frequently-occurring Rumney family names are Miles and Edmunds. In 1822, Thomas Miles, his son Isaac, age 21, daughter Rebecca, age five and a servant Mary, all of Red Barn Moor Rumney, were found 'dround' in the Yellow Pill. An entry in the church burial register rather points the finger at poor Mary. The Edmunds family, were fairly well-off, they resided in many places in Rumney including Ty to Maen, Longcross Farm and the Elms.

Memories of Rumney in the early 1900's Anon.

'Visiting Rumney from Cardiff centre meant either a walk or a very acceptable, if rather uncomfortable ride on a hard-seated tramcar, which had an upper deck with no cover from the weather and, of course, no lighting. This would take one to the Royal Oak Terminus. From there it was a long walk, or, if one had the money to spend, a horse-drawn brake. This would leave the Royal Oak Mews three times a day for St. Mellons, going over the Common, which was dimly-lit at night with gas-lamps, reaching the old humped-back bridge over the Rhymney River. This was not wide enough for two vehicles to pass each other.

Over the bridge, with Rumney Pottery on the right, there was a path to Rumney Village through fields, over stiles and over the quarry. This was all right if one was not afraid of a bit of mud. Going up Rumney Hill, sometimes one had to wait a moment while a pair of well-groomed horses, drawing a lovely polished carriage was driven out of one of the big houses on the left. After leaving the Cardiff boundary, there were no lights on the roadways.

Rumney and St. Mellons were very quiet country villages in those days. Most people in the villages attended one or other of the places of worship. Even if some men did not attend often, they had a very good excuse that it was a day of well-earned rest. During the week, most manual workers were at their jobs at 6 a.m. or earlier and did not get home until their children were in bed in the evening. Gardening, washing, sewing and haymaking were never done on Sundays. It was the day for members of the family to gather together. Shops did not open on Sundays. In Rumney only one grocer's shop, a converted front room, existed, whilst tobacco for the men and a few sweets for children were sold on weekdays from a little cottage on the Green.

No doctor resided in Rumney or St. Mellons, so if one was needed he had to be called from Cardiff or Newport. He would arrive on horseback or in a horse-drawn vehicle. One policeman looked after St. Mellons and Rumney. Many of the boys from both villages felt his stick. He would run after them over the fields and reens if he found them in someone's orchard scrumping apples, or playing rat-tat ginger on an old lady's door.

Many able-bodied parents would tramp to Cardiff on Saturday nights to buy food for the family. The Sunday joint could be bought from the village butcher. He usually killed one animal a week. On Saturday, his wife and children would deliver joints of meat to scattered homesteads ready for Sunday dinner. A lot of cottagers kept a pig for bacon. Cattle and sheep were a common sight around the lanes. Many men worked on one or other of the farms or market gardens.

Most children in those days went on an annual Sunday School/Whitsun Treat. There was little else to amuse them and a ride on a farmer's wagon was an occasion to be remembered. Children were not over- indulged in those days and what they never had, they never missed!'

Memories of Stuart Scrivens 1913 - 1982
In 1975, Stuart Scrivens wrote down his memories of the Scrivens family, local personalities and memories of his childhood. Harry Scrivens, Stuart's father, was one of a family of two girls and five boys who, in 1885, lived with their parents on their grandfather's forty-acre farm at New Church East near Shirenewton, Chepstow. The girls were working locally but as jobs were scarce, the family decided that there would be more opportunities for work

255

in Cardiff. They were from a farming background, knew about Spiller's Mill and hoped to find work there.

'Their westward trek took them through Rumney, just outside Cardiff. In those days, Rumney Hill was very treacherous, with no tarmac surface, only rough gravel. The wagons would have to stop at the top of every hill to put a "sprag" in the wheel, or a slide, as they called it. The sprag would be attached to one or two of the wheels, to act as a brake. The family looked across to what was then a beautiful old farmhouse, Ty Mawr Farm. - The boys suggested to my grandfather that there might be work at such a big farm, so he went across and knocked on the door. Having told the maid, who answered the door, what he wanted, he was invited in and eventually saw the farmer, a Mr. Turberville. It turned out that Mr Turberville had a vacancy for a bailiff - and an empty cottage. So he engaged my grandfather there and then and the family moved into Malt Cottage, now demolished, but it was then at the end of Brachdy Lane.'

The boys found jobs, two at Spillers Mill, one at the docks, one at Roath Park and one mining in the valleys. John, who started work as a gardener at Roath Park, later worked as a gardener at Rumney House. Eventually he took a cottage near the Maerdy railway bridge and this later became Spring Meadow Farm. Stuart continues :-

'I can remember the great ponds on Rumney Common, where they used to dig for clay. I don't remember the names of all of them but there was a Waring's Brickyard and as a boy my father worked there, driving old Waring about in a little pony and cart. There was a big stationary steam engine driving the clay "pugs", also providing steam for the brickyard, which was looked after by old Bill Shute. He was an elderly man with one arm, the other arm having a metal hook instead of a hand. My father and the other lads, wicked as they were, would root up the fire so that the engine would blow and old Bill Shute would chase after them, trying to grab their jackets with the hook. One time when they were working in a clay pit, near where the Power Station stood, now Allied Carpets, there was a huge explosion and the fly-wheel of the old engine flew through the air and landed in the pit, not many yards from where my father and his mates were working.

256

I have many stories of the brickyards, where they used to have thousands of bricks drying in racks, before being baked in the kilns. The sole drying agent was the wind, and there were shutters on the big drying racks, with louvres which had to be altered every time the wind changed. Old people used to talk a lot about the hard winter of 1894/5 when the Rhymney River froze over. (also Roath Park Lake) The frost went down 4ft to 5ft into the clay and the brickyards couldn't work for about 16 weeks. That winter there was skating on the brick-ponds.

In those days, Rumney was a beautiful old parish and I remember it in my own youth as a lovely village surrounded by cornfields. At threshing time, old Rhys Edwards of Llanederyn would travel the county with his threshing machine, calling on all the farms in Rumney, Ball Farm, Whitehall Farm, Ty Mawr Farm, Greenway Farm and Church Farm.

Sitting in school, we would hear the hum of the machine working away and see the smoke rising from the engine, as they threshed the corn not more than a few hundred yards away, at Ty Mawr, Whitehall and Church Farms. This was before there was any building on what is today Whitehall Parade and the Walk. Whitehall farmhouse still stands. A very different place Rumney was in those days. My grandfather used to cut the corn with an old mowing machine drawn by a pair of horses in the fields where the housing estate now stands.' (This would have been what was called a binder; it cut the corn and then tied it in bundles in one operation.)

He remembered his grandmother speaking in Welsh. Thinking that she was from near Chepstow, he thought this unusual. She was in fact from Nantyglo, certainly a Welsh-speaking area at that time. 'There is no Welsh spoken today, of course, or even when I was a lad, but my father told me that the Richards family who lived at Maerdy Farm, were, in his day, one of the last Welsh-speaking families in the parish. Their boys spoke English in school but once they got home they had to speak in Welsh. My grandmother had the "Cymraeg." There was a lady living near Malt Cottage, a Mrs Davies, who also spoke Welsh. Mrs Davies and my grandmother would go up for water together "Cymraeging" away. It was a sight which would be unbelievable today, for my grandmother never carried a pitcher in her hand, but on her head, which people would stare at, even in those days. The sows, for they always kept pigs, would very often follow her up the road and my father often told me he didn't think they understood any English. When he or my grandfather tried to get them in at night, they might curse and shout and the sows would take no notice, but old Gran would come out and speak Welsh to them, which would bring them, like children, into their sties for the night.

Woman with pitcher

Cutting hay from the rick.

What I remember most about my early days in Rumney was the poverty. But for all that the people were honest, decent and hardworking and there was happiness and contentment. My father had a large garden and gardening meant a lot to the people of those days, because we had little money to run to the shops for six pennyworth of this or a shillingsworth of that. Instead, we were able to grow our own potatoes, cabbages, beans, etc. and we had our own apple tree.

The gentry who lived in Rumney then, were also wonderful people, most of them now, of course, gone from the parish. There was Squire Williams of Llanrumney Hall, a fine gentleman, a good employer of labour and a very generous man to anyone who knocked on his door. In those days, when Squire Williams would pass on his horse and I was with my father and mother, we would have to touch our hats as a mark of respect. Great respect was shown also to the vicar, Vicar Davies and his daughter, Miss Davies. In many ways I am sorry that those days and ways have altered.

In the long summer evenings after school, there was no running about the roads for us, as there is today. There was work to be done. Very often when the weather was hot, as seemed to happen more often then, we village boys would go down to the river after our toil in the garden. When the tide came up to the banks, we would be swimming like otters. Every one of us learnt to swim in that river. Very often our father would take all six of us along the sea wall. It was peaceful and there was something in life worth living for. One summer's evening, we were on the sea wall when a three-masted yawl came in and anchored near the lynches. My father knew the skipper and we had great pleasure, in going aboard. She had brought 100 tons of stone from the Gloucester River, to form a breakwater. As the years went by we often saw that ship, the *Success of Bridgewater*. She would come right up beyond the pill, where we used to bathe, to the jetty just 200 yds below the railway bridge, bringing the stone which was hand-winched out of the hold and used to protect the river bank from erosion.

When he was a boy of 14 my father started working for a fisherman by the name of Jimmy Dunn. He lived in an old cottage, demolished now, in Wentloog Road. My father would be out on the mud flats, all times of the day and night, opposite the sea wall, when the tide was out, in his bare feet, trousers rolled up to his thighs, pushing a wooden sledge over the mud and getting the fish out of the nets. If the tide wasn't beyond the nets, they used a flat-bottomed boat, which they would paddle around in about a foot of water. They would get the fish up to the lynches, then carry them across the fields to the Maerdy Road and back to the old cottage. There they would boil the shrimps and sort the fish which were sold locally.

Jimmy Dunn also had a 28 ton yawl, as my father used to call her, which they used to sail down to the old Barry Harbour, give her a list on the beach there, then load her up with sand. That was the time they were laying the Pontypridd sewer through Rumney and Jimmy Dunn would bring the load of sand back from Barry Harbour and beat his way up the river to the old jetty. Some of the timbers of this old jetty can still be seen in the mud, just below the Penstaff Railway Bridge. (The railway bridge leading from New Road to the Park) That sand was used in laying the sewer and the price they got, as my father used to tell me, was one shilling a ton.

I remember our Sunday evening strolls over to Llanrumney, sometimes past the farm called Blackbird's Nest. Every time we passed that farm, maybe a dozen times that summer, my father would tell us the story of the murder in Blackbird's Nest. According to my father, it was a serving maid who was killed by the butler. From there, we would wend our way back to Earlswood Farm, across the fields known as the Acre fields at the back of Greenway Farm, ending up at an old stone stile on what is now Cae Glas Road, eventually getting home tired and weary. We would then take off our best clothes and have a cup of cocoa and perhaps some bread and jam. Sometimes if we were lucky there would be a piece of cake each before we went to bed, never without saying our prayers.'

A walk across the quarry fields on a Sunday afternoon.

Personalities remembered by Stuart Scrivens.

'One old character well-remembered and always respected by local lads was a gentleman known as Jim the Ditcher who lived down on the Moors below Skew Bridge. He frequented the Rompney Castle of an evening after his day's work. He would come up from the Moors, dressed in a dark jacket, sacking puttees on his legs and wearing a bowler hat. He earned his living by piecework, cleaning out the ditches or reens. He had two great baulks of timber, which he would ram down into the mud so many yards apart, thus sealing off a section of the reen, from which he would bale out the water as far as he could. He then got down into the empty ditch and with a straight spade, like a peatcutter, re-cut the reen banks. In this way, he progressed along the reens moving one timber baulk at a time. That was how Jim the Ditcher earned his living and got his nickname.

Keeping chickens pre-WWII.

Joe Chamberlain, Tom Woodman an old poacher and Harry High Stepper were all characters who frequented the Cross Inn. Alf Rees the landlord, was a stern man and a man of principle who would never allow a man to drink more than he could afford. Rough cider at 4d a pint was equal in strength to about four pints of beer today. Joe Chamberlain, who had a wicked sense of humour, went out one night when the trio were short of money, crept round the back of the Inn to the chicken coop and took out the best cockerel. Now Alf Rees prided himself on keeping a good breed of poultry, so Joe returned with the cockerel under his arm saying that he had collected it off a lorry passing through from Hereford. The bird was intended for delivery to a man down the village. Now Alf was struck by the bird right away, he could see it was quality and after a lot of

261

talk, the long and the short of it was that Joe sold Alf his own cockerel over the bar. There was total silence in the bar the following night when Joe was summoned by the landlord to pay back his ill-gotten gains, which he did immediately.

There was homely comfort in the pub in those days. The men would be there in their working clothes, telling their tales, smoking their old twist, rubbing the twist in their hands, cutting it with old knives and enjoying their pipe of baccy. Tom Woodman would invariably come in with 4 or 5 rabbits in his old poacher's coat,

"Want a rabbit for your dinner tonight?"

" Well I wouldn't mind, like."

"That'll be a pint of scrumpy. "

That was 4d for the scrumpy and the skin was worth 2d, when sold later to the rag and bone man.

In that same pub at the back was a little snug where Squire Williams' chauffeur, butler and gamekeeper would meet. In those days there was no Sunday drinking, but somehow or other in the countryside, as it was then, rules were very often broken and on Sunday morning the select few would be in the snug supping their ale, and the local lads knew this. They would hide in the bushes off Ball Road watching out for the gamekeeper, old Yorky Merritt and his mates to come up for their beer session in the Cross Inn. Once they had all passed by, the lads would be out with their nets and ferrets to have a good hour of ferreting on Ball Hill. They were good days and good people, full of character and fun.'

John Baldwin 1903 - 1987

John (Jack) Baldwin moved to Rumney from Splott at the end of the 1920s. He lived with his mother in Church Road. He married Dorothy Clarke and after acquiring a plot of land at the end of the Grove, he built a pair of detached, flat-roofed houses, one for himself and the other for his sister and brother-in-law. Jack was always full of ideas and established a joinery workshop alongside his house. Behind an area he had laid out with tennis courts, he set about building a swimming pool. On completion he was unable to carry out his plans for use of the pool, because the outbreak of WWII meant that the pool had to be used as a static water tank for the Auxiliary Fire Service.

In the post-war years he set about restoring the pool which he opened to the public. In addition to a block of changing-rooms, he laid out a terrace where customers could be served refreshments, prepared by his wife. This enterprise lasted only a few years and although a precise date cannot be given for its closure, some local folk can remember swimming there up to 1953.

A continual source of annoyance to Jack was the use of part of his land as a turning area for vehicles and he hit the local paper headlines on one occasion when he impounded a Council refuse-collection vehicle. All trace of this venture has now disappeared and the premises are used for motor vehicle repairs and as an MOT testing station.

Daisy Bolt 1907-2005

Daisy was the third of eight children, four boys and four girls. Her father was from Devon and her mother from Calne in Wiltshire. They both came to Cardiff to look for work. Mrs Bolt worked in service and Mr Bolt for Noah, Rees and Griffin, agricultural suppliers. Daisy thought that they had met when her father was making deliveries to the house where her mother worked. They had started married life in Splott before moving to Rumney in August 1914. The children, except Edith who had a weak heart, walked to Rumney, because there wasn't enough room for them in the cart. Daisy remembered 'it was a long walk on a scorching hot day.' They came across the Common and took a short cut over the Quarry where they had to ask the way.

Daisy remembered her father Ernest playing with the children every evening after he finished work. In the summer it was cricket on the village green, in winter, games in the house; draughts, ring-board and darts. With eight children, money was short, but it seemed to be a happy childhood. Their father sometimes threatened them at night when they were supposed to be going to sleep, 3 or 4 to a bed, squabbling instead of settling down.

It seems that her schooldays were overshadowed somewhat by the strict Headmaster, 'Dai Matt' from whom she had the cane on more than one occasion. Daisy was a bright child and was offered the chance to sit for a scholarship to Rhiwderin School. (pre-Bassaleg) Her father refused to let her sit the exam because he could not afford to pay for books and transport if she passed. Another childhood memory was of the boys, who, after coming from Band of Hope, would be ready to play tricks such as rat-tat-ginger, knocking on doors, then running and hiding. Another one was to make up a small parcel tied to a piece of string, then place it in the road and hide behind the nearest bush. When someone came along and went to pick up the parcel, the parcel moved. Try again, it moved again and so on.

On Saturday mornings, the boys worked in the market garden and the girls had jobs to do at home; brasso the stair-rods, clean the fender and other cleaning jobs about the house. In the school holidays, the girls would also work in the garden. That way their parents knew where they were and they couldn't get up to any mischief. As they got older, they went to dances in St. Mellons, not Rumney; this was too expensive. Their mother didn't like this much, not wanting them to mix with 'those rough boys in St. Mellons!'

The family lived in several houses in Rumney. In the 1920s they moved into the present butcher's shop in Wentloog Road. This was luxurious living as it had one of the few bathrooms in the village. They were there for less than ten years because Mr Bolt took Greenway Fach, on Greenway Road because it had large acreage suitable for a market garden. The lovely rambling old house was cold but had no bathroom! Daisy did not 'go out to work,' remaining at home at first, helping her mother and after her mother died in 1934, looking after her father and three brothers. This was no easy task, cooking for four hungry men, washing their muddy clothes and drawing all the water from the well.

In the mid 1930s, Ernest who had had a fruit and veg. round, rented the lock-up shop on the corner of Cae Glas and Wentloog Roads. Daisy worked with him in the shop. Violet, Daisy's sister, had lost a son to peritonitis in 1939 and in 1945, Violet also lost her daughter aged fourteen years, only twelve days before her daughter Vivienne was born. Daisy cared for her baby niece because her sister was neither emotionally nor physically able to cope.

Due to housing development, the land at Greenway Road was compulsorily purchased and the house demolished. The Bolt family moved into one of the newly-built houses and bought ground in Michaelston-y-Fedw for a market garden. In 1958, Daisy moved to 102 Wentloog Road, a purpose-built row of shops with living accommodation. Her father Ernest died a little later leaving the shop to Daisy, she continued in business there for nearly twenty years, when she retired and moved to her final home in Cae Glas Avenue. Daisy had a fit and active retirement and lived in her own home until shortly before her death, the day before her ninety-eighth birthday.

Len Hayes 1902-1998

Len was born 6th October 1902, in Strathnairn Street, Roath where his father ran a horse-drawn cab business. The family moved to Penlasgan Farm, St. Mellons when he was a boy. His father bought several properties in Rumney and St. Mellons. Len married Betty Williams in January 1947 and they had one daughter, Christine. They moved several times, finally settling at Penyrheol Farm in Rumney. Farming was Len's livelihood, but it was his work with horses that he loved best. Len had started to drive horses in his father's business when he was only thirteen years old and during his years of farming, he had a milk-round and entered local shows in the trade classes for horse-drawn milk-floats. He had never had a car and his horse and carriage proved useful during times of petrol rationing. For a number of years he was in regular demand for weddings and other special occasions. In his younger days, he often drove celebrities around the area, including Field Marshal Lord Montgomery when 'Monty' received the freedom of the town of Newport.

The feat that gained Len most publicity was when he took a coach and four-in-hand to London in October 1955. The idea started with Mr. Bill Probert, home on leave from Malaya, when he saw an old coach in Len's yard. As a result of discussion with Len and others, Mr Brian Wicks from Wiltshire, brought his 100-year-old stage-coach from the Bath Museum to carry Len and his party on their memorable journey. The old London stage-coach, still bearing *Cardiff to London* on its paintwork, with four horses driven by Len, left Rumney, bound for London. Accompanying Len and Bill Probert, on the coach, were Mr. W. Johnstone, a bus driver, who had been given leave to blow the 150-year old post-horn and Mr. Harry Atkins, former coachman to the late Squire C. C. Llewellyn Williams of Llanrumney Hall; Mr Atkins was to take care of the horses. Other travellers were Mr. Probert's brother Tom, Miss Deidre Roberts,

Miss Phyllis Morgan, Mrs Alma Shears, all of Rumney and Mrs Joan Miller of Tintern. They also took with them, in recognition of the 50th anniversary of Cardiff becoming a city, a Jubilee message to the Lord Mayor of London from Cardiff's Lord Mayor, Alderman Mr. Frank Chapman. Everyone was dressed in clothes typical of Victorian times.

The intention was to travel when possible on the old coaching-route. They had just left the Coach and Horses in Castleton, where they had stopped for refreshment, when, from the bushes on the side of the road, appeared a mounted highwayman. Dressed in red mask and black cloak and brandishing two long-barrelled pistols, he demanded that the coach should stop.

The men tried to hide their money, the agitated ladies offered their jewellery in exchange for a safe passage. The highwayman was only interested in a few bottles of liquor produced from the coach and grabbing his loot, he galloped off. Later that day, it was said that the police were anxious to interview Mr. William Jones of Tyn-y-brwyn Farm, Coedkernew. Mr Jones and his horse Spurnhead were well known on the point-to-point and National Hunt racing circuit. Both horse and rider had been seen in the vicinity that morning.

Stand and deliver!

Without further incident the coach continued on its journey, *Newport, Monmouth, Ross, Tintern, Cheltenham, Whitney, (Oxfordshire)* and after not too many problems arrived in London seven days later. The last fifteen miles had taken them five hours, due to traffic problems. They arrived at the Mansion House in London thirty minutes late and amid camera flashes and television crews, they handed greetings to Admiral Drew, private secretary to the Lord Mayor. They then proceeded to find lodgings for themselves and stabling for the horses, for the night.

Len Hayes said many times that his life began at seventy. This was when he had retired from farming and took up carriage driving full time. He continued to take bookings for weddings until he was ninety years old and was one of the first members of the British Horse Driving Society who met each year to celebrate Len's birthday. They would meet at one of the local pubs and then go for a drive. This continued until Len's ninety-fifth birthday, when he said that he always looked forward to these drives. In the latter years he was a passenger, but would have preferred to have been the driver.

Sadly on 21st November 1998, Len passed away. His funeral, arranged by his daughter Christine, was a fitting end to Len's life. A horse-drawn hearse was brought down especially from Gloucester, to take part in the funeral cortege. Crowds lined the road when his funeral procession moved from his home in Cae Glas Road to the Baptist Chapel in Tyr-y-Sarn Road. After the service, the highly-polished mahogany hearse with silver-plated lamps and cut-glass windows led the funeral procession via Roath Park to Cathays Cemetery. Len's ninety-one year old sister Winnie Hosgood remarked, 'Len would have loved this!'

Frank Hennessy born 1947

I was born three weeks early, during a blizzard, in February 1947. (My Mam says it s the only time I was ever early for anything.) Our first proper home was at Maerdy Camp at the bottom of Maerdy Road. For the first three years of my life I was surrounded by ducks and chickens until we moved to a new house in Ely. Mam couldn t settle there, so shortly afterwards we came back to Rumney, which was to be home for the next twenty years or so.

I remember the blacksmith's forge near the Carpenters Arms, the Old Saddlery, the coming of the first Café in Rumney.... with a juke box! A highlight was Saturday morning pictures at the County Cinema.... wonderful excitement. Gregory's Hairdressers was another regular place to visit.... for a threepenny-all-off. Before the Llanrumney Estate was built, we kids would roam the wild bluebell woods all summer long – our imaginations unbounded.

Happy days and all so important to my later life as an entertainer and broadcaster.'

Gypsy Lydia Lee about 1880 - 1981

Lydia Lee will be remembered by many people in Rumney. From her early days going from door to door selling pegs, to her later days, when she used to sit in the chip shop on Newport Road, wearing a brilliant white headscarf and apron trimmed with lace, telling fortunes and drinking tea. Lydia Lee, a native of Cardiff, had travelled all over Wales but settled at Leckwith, which had been a traditional gypsy camping-place. During the 1970s, when development was taking place on Leckwith Common, Lydia moved to Maerdy Farm in Rumney. Her last move was with her family to Shire Newton Caravan Site, Rumney where she ended her days.

The following is part of the obituary for Gypsy Lydia Lee which appeared in the *South Wales Echo*:- 'Romanies from all over Britain were in Cardiff on the 17th August 1981, for the funeral of South Wales' gypsy queen Lydia Lee, following her death at Cardiff Royal Infirmary after a long illness. Mother of a large family including her deceased sister's children, Mrs Lee was buried at Cardiff Western Cemetery, following a short church service attended by scores of relatives and friends. One mourner said: "This is the end of a great era and our way of paying respect and saying thank you to a fantastic old lady!"

A staunch campaigner for gypsy rights, Mrs Lee fought a series of local authority battles and court actions in Cardiff during the 1950s and early 1960s. She hit the headlines in 1959 after writing to the Queen requesting the reversal of an eviction order, forcing her off her former camping-site home at Leckwith Common. Four years earlier, Buckingham Palace had passed an earlier plea to the Minister of Housing and Local Government, who backed her call for alternative accommodation.

Lydia Lee was one of the city's oldest and best-loved characters. Gradually, old age forced her to abandon selling pegs and flowers for a living. Until several years before her death, resplendent in colourful clothes, she had made weekly bus-trips into Cardiff, to greet city shoppers and friends.

She once said, "I've had a good life . . . having so many friends proves it." In accordance with Romany tradition, relatives of Mrs Lee maintained an all-night vigil following her death.'

The late Canon Roy Hallett, Vicar of St. Augustine's Church Rumney from 1969 to 1987, officiated at the marriage of a great grand-daughter of Gypsy Lydia Lee, whilst he was parish priest to the gypsy settlement.

Walter Marshall 1932-1996

Walter Marshall was born in Rumney on 5th March 1932, the only son of Frank and Amy Marshall and brother of Edna and Amy. The family lived at 19, Ty Mawr Road. He attended the village school followed by St. Illtyd s High School. Walter showed exceptional talent in the field of mathematics. Gaining a First in mathematical physics from Birmingham University when he was twenty, he obtained his Ph. D. at the age of twenty two. He became Head of the Theoretical Physics Department at the Atomic Energy Establishment at Harwell in 1960. His career has been described as a high-wire act combining skill and showmanship. In 1974 he became chief Scientist at the Ministry of Energy and was in 1981, appointed Chairman of the Atomic Energy Authority by Margaret Thatcher. The following year he received his knighthood and for the next seven years was Chairman of the Central Electricity Generating Board. In 1985, he was created a Baron taking the title of Baron Marshall of Goring.

Anticipating the National Union of Minerworkers Strike in 1984/5, he took a strategic decision to prepare the Central Electricity Generating Board in terms of fuel reserves and planning, to ensure the security of electricity supplies. A year later, when the Chernobyl nuclear power station fire showed the disastrous consequences of getting nuclear power wrong, he was able to identify the design and

269

operating flaws of the Russian reactor type and to explain to professional and lay audiences what had gone wrong. Out of this disaster was eventually born the World Association of Nuclear Operators, of which he became the first Chairman, doing much to improve the safety and operating performance of nuclear plants worldwide.

His fortunes then took a downward trend as the government decided to withdraw nuclear stations from the planned privatisation. Once out of office he continued with his international work, particularly in Japan and also in insurance and as a consultant.

Throughout his life he had relentless energy of mind and spent many hours at night and on long journeys, pursuing the proof of mathematical theorems. Following his early death in London on the 20th February 1996, an article in the *Daily Telegraph* emphasised – 'a sharp wit and effervescent sense of humour which were formidable weapons in Marshall's armour - he was a man big enough physically as well as intellectually to be worthy of caricature, and he would happily exploit this in Johnsonian style by poking fun at himself - on public platform and in after-dinner speeches. Not only was he a lucid and vivid exponent of the most obtrusive technical issues, but he could reduce an audience of the dullest engineers, the most pompous businessmen and self-important politicians to helpless laughter with exquisitely-timed stories. Here he deployed his larger-than-life personality with its unapologetic egocentricity, his tortured vowels born of humble Welsh origins and brilliant university education in Birmingham from central European tutors, and his great sense of theatre - he practised origami and laboured to great effect in the garden of his Thames-side home at Goring.'

He married his childhood sweetheart Ann, who was his constant companion and support, at work and play. They produced a son and a daughter.

Captain Henry Morgan 1635-1688

The best-known story associated with Llanrumney Hall, is that which tells of Sir Henry Morgan. Colourful stories about his life as a pirate have passed down through the centuries. Henry Morgan was a member of the Morgan family who owned extensive areas of land in South East Wales. At the time of Henry's birth in 1635, his branch of the family were living at Llanrumney Hall. He was born into a comfortable lifestyle with the freedom and beautiful surroundings of Llanrumney Park. Henry was an adventurous boy and enjoyed listening to tales of sailors from tall ships which docked at Cardiff. He wanted to know what lay beyond these shores.

Leaving Cardiff with very little money in his pocket, he crossed the channel to Bristol where he worked on the docks. In the evenings he listened to shocking stories of the Brethren of the Coast, passed down by men who had sailed with Drake, Raleigh and Hawkins. This all seemed exciting to a boy full of spirit and ambition. Piracy and the Caribbean were most attractive. He soon left Bristol bound for Jamaica. Life on board ship in the mid 17th century was very hard, flogging was a common punishment and mortality amongst sailors was high. Henry's ship failed to reach its destination, for reasons unknown, but he survived and was taken to Barbados. There he was sold as a bondsman, a type of slave.

This life was not for Henry Morgan. Leading a small band of slaves he escaped, found a boat and sailed to Tortuga, stronghold of the pirates of the Brethren of the Coast. His sense of adventure and memories of previous hardships, encouraged him to join the Brotherhood of Buccaneers. During his years as a buccaneer, he progressed to become a Captain. The Brotherhood had a substantial fleet with the toughest of sailors from France, Holland, England, Wales and the Caribbean. The Governor of Jamaica, Sir Thomas Modyford, decided to utilise the strength of this group of pirates, to ensure the safety of the islands, for his own protection and the country's profit.

In 1665, Colonel Edward Morgan, uncle of Henry Morgan, joined the Governor as his Deputy. A short while later, Henry married his cousin Elizabeth, daughter of Colonel Edward Morgan. In 1666, Governor Modyford granted a licence allowing one state to make reprisals at sea on the subjects of another state. This meant that pirates were no longer buccaneers but privateers. They were given the responsibility of serving 'England's purpose in the Caribbean, against whatever country she might be at war with or felt indisposed towards.' The Cross of St. George took the place of the Jolly Roger. Henry himself preferred to be called a patriot and any treasure he

271

seized, he considered to be one of the perks of the game. Since Britain and Spain were at war, Henry and his fellow patriots were able to successfully plunder some of Spain's most prosperous colonies. Some thought he went too far and a former shipmate, in his memoirs, accused Morgan of torturing prisoners. Henry Morgan made legal history when he sued the publishers for libel. He won and was awarded damages, creating a precedent.

He was then brought back to London by Charles II after unintentionally breaking a peace treaty. Relations had broken down between the two countries once again, so Henry Morgan was pardoned, knighted and some months later, commissioned by the King to serve as Lieutenant-Governor of Jamaica. His friend, Modyford, was appointed Chief Justice of the island and in 1675 they returned to Jamaica together. Sir Henry Morgan spent time in Port Royal away from the Governor whose name was Vaughan, as the two men disliked each other. Sir Henry encouraged the privateers to act against the French whom he perceived as the new enemy. Governor Vaughan did not approve, but was unable to oppose Sir Henry as he was such a popular figure.

The islanders realised that Jamaica had benefited from Henry Morgan's activities and Lord Carlisle followed Vaughan as Governor. Though he and Henry were old friends, they did not agree on policy for the island. In 1680, Lord Carlisle eventually resigned, making way for Sir Henry Morgan to be appointed Governor. Sir Henry, now a respected figure, completely changed his attitude towards piracy. He pursued them, including the Brotherhood that he had led during his early days in Jamaica. In less than a year, he almost stamped out piracy. His governorship lasted only two years, for the British Government appointed an old enemy of Morgan, a man named Lynch. This led to Sir Henry being stripped of his offices and commands. He retreated to his estates, where he pondered on the possibility of recovering some of the treasure that had been sunk on the Spanish Main, a field in which he was an expert.

Henry had kept in contact with a friend, the Duke of Arlbemarle and in 1686 the Duke was made Governor of Jamaica. The Governor had power to organise treasure-hunting, so Sir Henry regained his position on the Council and with his friend, planned to hunt for treasure, even though he believed his life was drawing to a close. In 1678, he had been given a charm which he was told would protect him for ten years. In 1688, a Judas gum tree bled red, which, according to legend, was said to foretell the passage of a great soul to heaven. In the eyes of Jamaicans, Sir Henry Morgan was a great soul. While on his death-bed, he requested his usual glass of rum. When this was refused, he remarked that he intended to enjoy death as he had enjoyed every adventure while living. Born at Llanrumney Hall, he died in Jamaica aged 53 years and was given a State funeral at Port Royal. Captain Morgan Rum is named after him and his image and life span, 1635-1688, are detailed on the label.

When he died, Sir Henry Morgan was a rich man. He had named his favourite Jamaican estate "Llanrhymney" which he left to his wife Elizabeth, also a Morgan of Llanrumney. Another bequest was 'to my well-beloved sister, Catherine Lloyd, sixty pounds per annum for life to be paid yearly at the hands of my very honourable cousin, Mr Thomas Morgan of Tredegar.'

In his book **Princes and People of Wales**, John Mills records, 'Because of their romantic nature, Sir Henry Morgan's exploits as a pirate are remembered more than the far more important fact that he was the architect of the British Caribbean. It is also largely forgotten that he was the democrat who won for his island, the first modern constitution, conceded to a colonial parliament. Because of his courage, his skill, his foresight and his personality, Sir Henry Morgan ranks with the foremost figures, Drake and Raleigh. He was, indeed, a great man and, of course, a great Welshman.'

Edward Long did not exaggerate when, in 1774, he wrote: 'Sir Henry Morgan, whose achievements are well known, was equal to any of the most renowned warriors of historical fame, in valour, conduct and success ....'

Lilian Moreton 1904-2005

On 20th November 2004, Lilian Moreton celebrated her 100th birthday. Lilian was born in No. 1, Ty Fry Road, then known as Penmount and the adjoining cottage was called Pentwyn. Lilian was the youngest daughter of Thomas William Jenkins and Emma (nee Jones). There were four children, three girls and a boy. Ty Fry cottages were originally thatched but they were burnt down a few years before Lilian was born. On a particularly windy day the roof of the cottage caught fire and Mrs Jenkins had the presence of mind to collect valuable documents including the marriage certificate and made sure that the one daughter who was at home with her, was safe, wrapping baby Pru in a blanket and putting her in a clothes basket. Mr. Jenkins, Senior, came to the rescue, riding over to Rumney in his pony and trap which was used to ferry the family over to his farm, Pentwyni, at St. Mellons where they had to live until the cottages were rebuilt and replaced with three slate-roofed cottages. The owner of the land, Mr. Rees of Six Bells, would not sell, so the Jenkins and their neighbours had to pay rent.

Lilian went to the village school in Wentloog Road from the age of 4 years. The headmaster was Mr. James, who married a Miss Davies, who lived in the village. He was a lay preacher in the Baptist Chapel. When he left, he was succeeded by Mr Matthewson, whom everyone thought was an Irishman but in fact, he was a Scotsman. People said that he would not last long, but they were proved wrong, as he remained Headmaster of Rumney School for many years. There were only two political parties in those days; Liberal and Conservative and he liked to see the girls wearing blue ribbons in their hair at election time.

'I remember some of the teachers. There were the two Miss Morgan sisters, Lily and Ethel, who cycled to Rumney from their home in Michaelston-y-Fedw. In the winter they did not make the long journey, but lodged with Mrs. Tugwell in the village. I also remember Miss Milward, one of the Milwards, who lived at the Ball.

I left school at the age of 14 without any job to go to. I didn't want an office job. Dad said, "You can't mess about; you've got to do something". Mother knew one of the shop-walkers in David Morgan's, so that's where I learnt my trade as a dressmaker. I was taken on as an apprentice for 2/- per week and from there I progressed to become an improver and then a dressmaker. I stayed for a few years and then moved to Whitfield's in Queen Street, working as an alteration hand. This shop stood where Marks and Spencer's is today. The journey to work involved walking across the Common and then catching the tram into town from the Royal Oak; a 1d or 2d fare. I used to take sandwiches for lunch and would have a cooked meal in the evening. Sometimes I would meet girls from the village and we would walk home together, but I was not afraid when walking on my own. I can remember the disused brickworks on the Common, the Pottery and the building of the new bridge. The old bridge became unsafe and had to be replaced. My sisters went to see the opening ceremony.

Mother sent us to the Presbyterian Church in St. Mellons to Sunday School. When I was very small my legs used to ache and so my sister, Emmie, used to carry me on her shoulders when I was tired. When I was older I had to go to morning service at 10.30 a.m. The minister was the Rev. Grey Davies, a real Welshman. The chapel lacked facilities and there was no piped water. Chapel House, opposite, came in useful when there were any tea-parties as the men used to carry buckets of water over to the chapel from Church House. I mixed with the young men at the church but they were mostly the children of farmers. Then I met Len, who was a town young man. He lived in Stacey Road, Roath and worked in a warehouse in Queen Street. When he made up his mind to open a shop, so began our life's work in the retail trade. We were married in 1932 in St Augustine's Church in Rumney by the vicar, the Rev. D. J. Davies. We had two general shops, one in Riverside and another in Barry, selling papers and confectionery and at one time had 13 or 14 paperboys. We lived in large premises in Riverside but later bought a bungalow in Trelawney Crescent, Rumney.

I remember Rumney as it used to be, including the Poor houses in Brachdy Road. There was an elderly lady who occupied the end cottage and she made drinks which she sold from the house. Then there were the cottages in Beili Bach. Three of them were eventually demolished. Mr and Mrs. Hancock lived there and I believe that Mr. Hancock was the grave-digger.

The Firs was a large house at the corner of Wentloog Road and Newport Road opposite the Cross Inn. It was screened from the road by many trees with its main entrance on Newport Road and another entrance onto Wentloog Road. Miss Longcross lived there. She was a big worker in the days of the First World War and a great friend of Mr. Harris, who built the lych-gate at St. Augustine's Church. She opened her house for many events and I remember going there to a social evening for the young people of the village.

275

We played games for which she gave us prizes. We helped in the war effort and Miss Hastings would give us vegetables for the sailors and we would collect these and take them to *The Firs*. Next door to *The Firs* was the old Post Office. Mrs. Raebone was the Postmistress, but Mrs Morgan was the first Postmistress to live there.

Mr. Stark was the owner of Ty Fry Farm, when I was young and the Huxhams lived in Whitehall. (Mrs Huxham was Mr.Stark's sister.) When Mr. Stark suffered a stroke, he moved to Ty Fry House and Mr. Huxham accepted the tenancy of Ty Fry Farm.'

Lilian Moreton, a resident in White Lodge, Newport Road in her latter years, died in June 2005.

Eddie Price 1910-2001

Eddie Price was born in Abertillery, where his father had a horse and cart transport business. As an adult, he and his brothers ran a successful business from their depot near the Maerdy railway bridge and this company became one of the biggest haulage companies in the U.K. Eddie was a well-known figure in Rumney and was even better-known nationally, for his association with Tenovus, the cancer charity.

During WWII whilst loading a lorry, Eddie was seriously injured and he spent ten days unconscious in Cardiff Royal Infirmary. On regaining consciousness, he was delighted when nine friends provided him with a radio for entertainment. Realising that other patients could be helped in the same way, the friends set out to raise the funds to equip each bed in the Cardiff Royal Infirmary with a radio headset. Their gift was in appreciation for the excellent treatment Eddie had received. All nine of Eddie's businessmen friends were sitting around his bed when one of them commented "Well, there are nine of us around this bed, and it looks like this old so-and-so is going to get better, so why not call ourselves the Ten-of-us?" This was the origin of the charity Tenovus and the rest is history.

In the past sixty years Tenovus has raised money for countless charitable projects which include,

    i.   Cardiff House, a drop-in centre for ex-servicemen who fought in the Burma War.

    ii.   The Sunshine Home for Blind Babies in Southerndown.

276

iii.   A fully-equipped Spina Bifida Unit in Cardiff, the first in the world.

In 1960, Tenovus decided to focus their efforts on cancer research, later establishing the Tenovus Institute for Cancer Research at the University Hospital of Wales in Cardiff. Research and development has provided drugs such as Tamoxifen, used in the treatment of breast cancer. Some years later the Tenovus Research Centre at Southampton was built and equipped for the development of cancer drugs, such of antibody therapies and DNA vaccines. Tenovus now invests approx. £2 million each year in cancer research, patient-care, counselling and education.

Eddie Price continued to support the charity for the rest of his life and contributed to a fund-raising video only a few weeks before his death in April 2001 at the age of ninety one. He was the last survivor of the original 'ten-of-us.'

Tenovus: l-r Cecil Harris, George Brinn, Charles Rolfe, David Curitz, George T. Addis, David R. Edwards, Eddie Price, Huw Thomas, Harold Gosling and Talla Curitz.

 **Memories of Josephine Richards born 1918.**
'I was born in Splott, Cardiff and came to live in Rumney after my marriage, in December 1937, to Ewart, eldest son of Rhys Richards of Maerdy Farm. Ewart and I made our first home at Downton

Farm, Rumney and I set about learning to be a farmer's wife - something quite different from my work at Cardiff Wholesale Dairies, later City Dairies on Rumney Common. I had, in fact, met Ewart there when he came to buy extra milk for the family milk-delivery rounds. I was quite scared at Downton Farm at first, because I had never had anything to do with poultry. I was taught by Mrs. Sammy King how to pluck, clean and truss chickens. I eventually got used to the hard daily grind and realised that farming was a way of life. There were no such things as holidays and you had to enjoy the life to be able to stick it. At the Downton, I had neighbours across the lane, the Cody, Williams and Bradshaw families. There were four new houses in Downton Rise, but part of Downton Road was not then built and there were no estates.

I remember during the early part of the war when we were still at the Downton, going out into the garden and seeing a German bomber dropping bombs on Cardiff Docks. No anti-aircraft guns were firing from Maerdy Camp, for they had to get permission to fire, from the observation post at Penylan near Bassaleg. British soldiers, men and women were stationed at the Camp. They manned the gun-turrets on the sea-shore. That's how my brother-in-law met his future wife Phyllis; she was stationed down there.

Farming was a reserved occupation during war-time, so farmers were not conscripted. At the end of 1940, however, Ewart volunteered for air-crew duties in the R.A.F.V.R. He was away for five years in the R.A.F. and eventually became a Flying-Officer. In the early days he trained at Blackpool and was a wireless-operator, then an air-gunner, after taking a gunnery course at Pembrey. Then he was sent to Scotland.

Air-crews were multi-national and Ewart mixed with men of various nationalities. He flew many sorties / tours of operations from N. Ireland and there was quite a lot of sabotage from S. Ireland. Ewart became a radar-instructor and since America was preparing to go to war with Japan, he was sent to New York, then to Miami and then to the Bahamas to train American airmen. Whilst in America, he met John Leek from Downton Road, Rumney and Sid, the youngest of the Marsh boys. They went out to lunch together before the others went off to fight against Japan - because this was just before Pearl Harbour.

Whilst Ewart was away in the R.A.F., I went home to Tremorfa, with my son Bryn, born in 1939 whilst we were at Downton Farm. I worked for the Ministry of Supply, whilst another Richards' brother who did not farm, but had milk-rounds, took over Downton Farm. Downton and the Maerdy were both dairy farms, but during WWII, the Richards family had to do arable farming; barley, corn etc. for the war effort. Ewart's father Rhys carried on farming and farm-labourer Jack McCarthy, who was Irish, also stayed. They had help from a Land Army girl too.

I returned to Rumney to the Maerdy just before Ewart's demob. and we set up home at Maerdy Farm, sharing the farmhouse with Ewart's father Rhys Richards and his second wife, formerly Hettie Howells. Ewart's mother, formerly Kate Thomas, had died when he was 8 and his brother Ron was 6 years of age. Rhys had a daughter Megan from his second marriage. Hettie already had two children from before her marriage to Rhys. Her brother Ben and wife Beatie came up from West Wales, to live opposite the Rompney Castle and started a milk-round. Harcourt Howells was their son.

Maerdy Farm was a mile from the village and was originally built in the 16th century. Experts confirmed this in 1969 when the thatch was removed. They said that the ties in the wood were of that date. The land went right down to the sea-wall which was very effective against flooding. If heavy snow fell, though, we were often cut off. The farmhouse was two fields away from the sea-wall.

In 1946, the last corn was taken off the fields and we were stooking all day. The land was then put to rye-grass and silage. Ploughs were not used on moors land then; we dug it by hand with wooden spades.

My father-in-law Rhys used to wake everyone up at 4:45 in the morning and light the fire to be ready for cooking breakfasts later. The cows were milked by hand, with the ladies looking after any sick cows. Our first two cows after the war were pedigree Ayrshires. At 8:00 a.m. I cooked a breakfast of home-cured bacon and our own eggs for Ewart and our farm workers. We fattened our own pigs and then they were sent to the bacon factory and returned one half, smoked and the other half, white. At the Maerdy there was no inside toilet, only an Elsan; the toilet was in the orchard. We had no cooker either, just a range and there was no running water inside

279

the house. Water had to be brought in from outside. Our second son, John, was born in 1947 whilst we were living at the Maerdy. We had shared a kitchen with Ewart's step-mother and his father for six months in 1946 but then the house was divided and we stayed like that for 8 years. Rhys and Hettie then moved to a house opposite Downton Farm. Rhys had only lived there for two years when he collapsed and died from a dissected aorta.

We were tenant farmers at the Maerdy until 1957, but then Ewart was offered the chance to buy it. He was the sixth generation of Richards to farm there and had always wanted to own, so we bought the farm and farmed it as a dairy farm. Milk was pasteurised, nicknamed 'pulverised' and I used to make butter (8lb at a time) with Maerdy Farm milk, but we sold the milk on our milk- rounds mostly. We farmed 100 acres, having bought 70 acres with the farm and the other 30 acres when Rhys Richards died. I used to do the book-keeping, accounts and banking for our farm. There was only one teller at Lloyds Bank, top road Rumney, when we banked there. A retired police-sergeant used to sit near the counter, keeping an eye on things. I did most of my shopping in Rumney, not personally though. I used to send two lists, one to the grocer and the other to the greengrocer on a Friday and the goods were collected by the boys (our farmworkers) on the Saturday. Rumney was different then. It was a small village where everyone knew everyone else. We shopped in town for farm bits, machinery etc. at Noah Rees and Griffin in St John's Square or at John Hall in Churchill Way, Cardiff.

Our older son Bryn lived in Tremorfa with my family because the low-lying situation and climate of the Maerdy affected him badly after he had rheumatic fever, but John, our younger son, lived at the farm and as a baby was carried around Welsh-fashion in a shawl, so that I had both arms and hands free to carry on working. John went to school at Rumney and at the age of 4 used to ride his three-wheeler bike part of the way. He would leave his bike at the Scrivens' house and Annette would then take him and the others to school at Wentloog Road. Bryn never showed any interest in farming, but John loved farming from a very young age and always knew that it was the life for him. He worked on the farm with his Dad and also reared rabbits for pocket-money. He then sold the rabbits to his uncle Doug Hutchins, the butcher in Wentloog Road, who was married to Megan, Ewart's half-sister.

At the age of 16 and a half, after leaving school at Howard Gardens Cardiff, John began his studies at Usk Agricultural College. After his course finished, he farmed with his father for 4 years plus at the Maerdy. It was a case of 'like father like son.' John was the seventh generation to farm at the Maerdy. Over the years Ewart had improved the farm and had drawn up plans for new buildings. Then rules changed, every cow's milk had to be recorded and the use of the buildings changed to calf-rearing. We built a new milking-parlour and all the milk was then piped. We also bottled our own milk.

When John married our daughter-in-law Laraine, they lived in a bungalow on what used to be part of the old Army Camp. Laraine was still working for a while, so John had his breakfast and lunch at the Maerdy. Ewart did the field work, such as ploughing and hedging and John did the dairy work. John used to milk at 5:45 a.m. and then he and I did the milk-rounds, selling milk, eggs and chickens. Sometimes we killed the chickens before breakfast. After the building of the Rumney and Trowbridge estates, our milk-rounds were really big. One Christmas we sold 800 chickens on the round...all prepared by me! We had two milk-rounds but in 1972 we decided to sell off one. Fred Bird and his father often worked for us at the Maerdy as contractors on the combining in November. Apart from the milk-round, I did all the house-keeping at the Maerdy and my own baking. Cleaning was done with a brush, shovel, dustpan and mops with mats hung on the line for beating. There were no vacuum-cleaners and even Ewbank carpet-sweepers came much later at a cost of £5!

In the early 1970s, John and Laraine moved to Ty Hir Farm in Michaelston y Fedw. Ewart had always wanted to move up from the Moors. I was happy at the Maerdy, however, for the farmhouse had been modernised and more improvements were planned. For a while Ewart worked up at Ty Hir and at the Maerdy, until one day, when he was away at Ty Hir, the house was burgled and I was attacked and hurt. The villains were found and prosecuted, but the family decided that following that trauma, we would sell the Maerdy, so in 1974, Ewart and I moved up from the Moors to Michaelston y Fedw. It was a very sad day for us all when we left the Maerdy. Although farming was a hard life, I have many happy memories of Rumney from 1937 until 1974.'

Nigel Walker born 1962

Nigel lived in Rumney as a boy and attended Rumney High School where he took part enthusiastically in sports including rugby and athletics. He represented the school both in rugby and athletics on many occasions.

He first achieved world-class recognition as a high hurdler, representing Great Britain on thirty occasions. He took part in all the major events including the World Championships and the Olympic Games. He retired from athletics in 1992 to pursue a second sports career as a rugby union player with Cardiff R.F.C. In 1993, in his first season, he was capped for Wales at full international level and went on to accrue seventeen full international caps.

Prior to the introduction of full-time professional rugby, he worked as a Development Officer for the Sports Council for Wales, where his responsibilities included Sports Medicine and as a civil servant within the Welsh Office. Most recently he has worked in the media, hosting various radio and television programmes while also serving as Player Development Manager and Assistant Team Manager with the Welsh Rugby Union. His current position is Head of Sport, BBC Wales.

He also undertakes after-dinner speaking engagements at both sporting and non-sporting functions. Engagements have included talks to professional bodies, corporate entities, universities and a variety of annual dinner functions. His specialist subjects include: motivation; requirements for success; goal setting; time management; sporting issues; and other related subjects. He gained an MBA from the University of Glamorgan and Open University. Nigel still lives in Cardiff with his wife Mary and their three children.

Ernest Willows 1886 - 1926

Ernest Willows, a pioneering aviator who was associated with Tremorfa, Cardiff, flew his experimental aircraft from Pengam Airfield. Willows Avenue and Willows High School, Tremorfa are named after him. Ernest Willows lived at 8, The Green, Village Road now Wentloog Road Rumney. In 1910 he was the first man to fly across the Bristol Channel and a year later, made the first airship crossing from England to France. He set up a kite balloon factory in Westgate Street, Cardiff, after the 1914/18 War. A report in the South Wales Echo stated that on 3rd August 1926, Willows and four companions died when their balloon crashed over Bedford. He is buried in Cathays Cemetery Cardiff.

Ernest Willows preparing for take-off from East Moors, later Pengam Airport and where Tesco's Pengam now stands.

Memories of Dilys Hughes born 1920?

Dilys Hughes' family have lived in Rumney, Llanrumney and St. Mellons for generations. Dilys herself, now in her eighties, was born and brought up in St. Mellons. She remembers many village characters and personalities.

Mrs Spooner

'We children who went to St. Mellons Village school, were surprisingly fortunate in that the village sweet shop was situated on the Ton, within the playground of our village school. It was owned by a lady of vast proportions, a fount of knowledge, gossipwise, but a kindly soul. Mrs Spooner was our champion. If she ever heard parents giving their children what she considered to be an unfair wigging, her "Leave that child alone!" would result in just that. When she ran short of stock, we older ones were entrusted to journey to Tetts, the sweet wholesalers in Broadway, with her order and to carry back the boxes

283

that were not too heavy for us. We were rewarded with some samples.

The shop and only living room were combined, and it was not at all embarrassing to ask over the dining-table for a sherbert sucker or a lucky potato. To think that for a half-penny it was possible to get not only a gorgeous lump of sweet covered in cocoa, but inside a lucky charm or a lovely 'diamond' ring. Mrs Spooner's shop remained open from breakfast until bedtime. The windows were small and the dark corners gave it an air of magic. We could only guess what delights awaited us in the bottles and boxes on the two large tables and on the floor.

Two other things impress on my memory, the front hedge of periwinkle and the enormous buddleia tree reaching almost to the roof, covered in summer, with hundreds of beautiful red admiral butterflies. The sweet shop was later managed or owned in turn by Mrs Evans, Miss Ridout and Derek Ball.

Lew Rowlands was another character who lived in the detached red-brick house on the Ton. He seldom washed and always wore the same corduroys and battered hat. It was widely believed that the moon affected him, when he would become extremely bad-tempered and his eyes would flash. Perhaps we children were the authors of his lunacy, as we found it more frightening and exciting to rap on his front door when the moon was full. He would chase us, brandishing a big stick. He was a man of some wealth but a miser. When he came to pay his monthly subscription of one shilling to the Ancient Order of Foresters, (my father being the secretary of the local Court) he always grumbled that as he was never ill, he never got anything out of it. My father would ask him in, then patiently explain that surely it was much better to have good health. He would make for a comfortable arm chair by the fire and sit there ruminating. He was reputed to have fleas and my poor mother would wait in a state of apprehension until he decided to leave. She would give an involuntary shiver from head to toe and then pick up the cushion and quickly run outside to shake it. " That man is not coming in here next Club night!" she would say – but he always did.

Miss Anne (Lizzie)Davies
I think Miss Lizzie Davies was born an old lady, as she remained the same for decades. She was the church cleaner and lived as frugally as

284

the church mice, in her white, thatched cottage. If anyone deserved the fruits of the welfare state, she did. She was crippled with arthritis and was always clad in the same old skirt and jacket, literally green with age, an old pudding-basin hat with hatpins askew and buttoned boots.

In winter at Evensong, she'd light the gas in church with hooked pole and lighted taper. How we'd wish she would miss and she often did. Perhaps air would get in the pipes or she would momentarily lose her balance, steel-rimmed spectacles would fall down her nose and she'd try again. Next time, success, a loud plop as she co-ordinated gas mantle and taper and a ghastly yellow glow would fill the church. Her face would wrinkle up with pleasure and down would fall the specs again.

At St. Agnes Guild on Monday nights, young members would be given pleasant tasks of embroidery, or painting forget-me-nots on water-sets, but Lizzie would be relegated to the plain sewing group. She never complained of the monotony and stoically stitched and blinked her way along miles of plain seams. All this handicraft would be sold at the church fete, when the sun always shone.

On one thing Lizzie was adamant. She believed only in Greenwich Mean Time and never put the clock back or forward. Lizzie was the most sinless Christian I have ever met, and I'm sure must now be blessed with nimble fingers embroidering altar-cloths for Him in Heaven – a just reward.

Miss Muriel Davies 1888-1985

Miss Davies was a very well-known character in the village and throughout the county. She was born in December 1888, the fifth and youngest child of Edward and Amy Davies. Edward, so the family story goes, died as a result of an illness. At gunpoint he had brought back the local doctor to his house on a wet stormy night, to attend to Muriel, then an infant. The doctor had not wished to venture out on this awful night and Edward, already in his 72nd year, felt that intimidation was not only necessary but vital for the sake of infant Muriel's health! Muriel recovered but her poor father met his demise.

Miss Davies, Greenfield, as she was often known, had many interests, she was involved with the Suffragette Movement and was the first woman member of the St. Mellons Parish Council. She helped to introduce many amenities, amongst them the provision of piped water and sewerage systems to local homesteads.

Another interest was the Women's Institute. She was a founder member and worked tirelessly with the county and local institutes. For many years, her familiar figure could be seen pedalling her 'sit up and beg' bicycle through the lanes, to visit other institutes in the Wentloog group. She then wrote reports to be published in the local paper - the *Countryside Magazine*.

In WWII she was instrumental in getting the Women's Land Army established in the area. The welfare of the girls and their importance to local farmers, along with other interests in the War effort, were of great concern to her. She had so many other interests. She was an ardent ornithologist and encouraged local school children in a love of nature, providing prizes for competitions on Natural History. Birds were her great joy and she was awarded the M.B.E. for her work on the study of birds.

Parish Council Meeting 1950s ? Standing: Muriel Davies, Mrs. A.H.Williams, Alan Walkey. Seated: Watkin Thomas, A. H. Williams.

Unusual for her generation, she was a vegetarian and a conservationist, without allegiance to any pressure group. It says much for her adherence to this lifestyle, that she lived to be 97 years of age. When visiting her, it was appropriate to take her a small granary loaf or some grapefruit rather than flowers which she preferred to see growing.

The last years of Muriel's life were spent at 'Landscape' cottage on Old St. Mellons Hill. I remember Miss Davies recalling an early memory of grandfather telling her about the surrender of Napoleon at the Battle of Waterloo in 1815. Landscape Cottage, along with the adjoining cottages had been a part of the family estate of 'Greenfield'. Muriel and her sister Eunice had lived at Greenfield. They managed the farm together until shortly after the Great War, when Eunice eloped with a German prisoner of war. He had been confined at a local detention centre. Eunice lived in Germany, near Cologne, for the rest of her life. Her great nephew tells us that he attended her funeral in the 1970's, which was a warm and joyous celebration of her life in Germany. The entire population of the town was present.

One personal incident of 1943 stands out in my memory. The local St. John's Ambulance Brigade, of which Miss Davies was an officer, presented me with a pair of bookends as a wedding present. Miss Davies publicly chided me for getting married, saying I was too young, "a mere schoolgirl." (Dilys was 23 years of age.)

Miss Davies died on 18th April 1985 and three ministers officiated at her funeral. St. Mellons church was filled with her family, friends, and members of local organisations. Remembering her age, people were not too sad but felt that it was the end of an era. What a character!

Her great, great nephew, Alexander, grandson of the late John Davies, M.P. for Knutsford, Cheshire and Secretary of State at the Department of Trade & Industry in Edward Heath's Government, read the lesson. He was the one she would laughingly quote as having said of her previously, "I've got a great, great aunt, and she's over 100 years old!" He spoke clearly in the manner of the Davies family and endeared himself to everyone in the church, by saying that the salt had lost its "saviour!" (savour) The Rev. John Musselwhite of Weston-Super-Mare gave the main address and listed

287

among her attributes the fact that she held strong political views, but did not reserve her criticism for parties other than her own. He called her a Nonconformist, yet with a great belief in tradition. The Reverend Russell Williams, local Baptist Minister, described how he had visited her two weeks before her death. On putting his head round the door of her room he asked "How are you today, Miss Davies?" "Dying, dear boy," she replied. When he remonstrated with her saying, "Not yet, surely?" she added, "And about time too!"

I, (Dilys Hughes) was delighted to learn that during the First World War, Miss Muriel Davies and her sister, Eunice, ploughed the field on which my present home now stands in Ty To Maen Close. A fitting epitaph for Miss Muriel Davies would have been - She ploughed a straight furrow. (and certainly not by tractor) In Heaven the word must have been quickly passed around *Miss Davies, Greenfield, has arrived!* '

Reg Addis 1905-2000

Reginald Herbert Addis was born on 21st March 1905, in Llanvetherine, near Abergavenny to Herbert Edward Addis and Emmeline Addis, the eldest of seven children. The other children were Trevor, Millicent, Ivy, Gordon, Dorothy and Ronnie. The seventh child, Colin, died at the age of 4. When Reg was born his father worked as a groomsman for the church in Llanvetherine and they lived in Church Cottage. He was christened in Llanvetherine Church.

When Reg was a baby, his parents moved first to Pentyrch, then to Whitchurch in Cardiff. His Dad had a job on the road, at that time, a person would be responsible for the maintenance of a certain stretch of road and this is what his Dad did. Victor Harding, who farmed at Mynachdy in Cardiff, met Herbert Addis while he was working on the road one day and as a result of their conversation offered him a job. Herbert started working for Victor Harding at his farm in Mynachdy but soon afterwards, when the farm was taken for development, the family moved to Home Farm, Cefn Mably. At the outbreak of the First World War, Victor Harding applied to the Government for Reg's Dad to be exempt from the armed forces, as he was an experienced farmer. After a number of years, when the tenancy on the farm at Cefn Mably was given up, they moved to another of Victor Harding's farms, Pwll Coch in Druidstone Road, St. Mellons; it was here that Reg started his working life.

Reg had started school at 5 years of age and it seems he wasn't too happy during his school years because all he wanted to do was work on the farm. Vic Harding once again stepped in and applied to the Education Authorities for Reg to leave school at the age of 13, to work for him. Victor Harding's son John has records dating from the 19th century. These records show that on 23rd December 1921, Herbert Addis was paid £1-12s-0d and Reg 8/-. He was doing a man's job when he left school, ploughing etc. and with other farm-workers at that time often seven days a week. When he progressed to the man's wage £1-12s-0d, he gave his mother £1 a week for his keep.

When he was 14 years of age he was very proud to gain second place in a Ploughing Match. After Reg had been working at Pwll Coch for sixteen years, the family moved once again, this time to Wern Fawr Farm also in St. Mellons. Pwll Coch and Wern Vawr were both rented from the Tredegar Estate.

Reg didn't have time for hobbies but at 14 years of age he had started bellringing. He used to go and watch the bellringers and eventually asked if he could learn. Mr. Parrish was Captain of bellringers at that time but on his death, the honour of Captain was bestowed on Reg, aged 20, by the Rev. Connop-Price. He remained Captain until his death at age 95.

The family then moved to Marshfield, first living in *Greenfield*, and then *The Croft* which was owned by Lord Tredegar. Reg married Evelyn Pretty in 1934 and they had 4 children, Valerie, Marjorie, Verna and Gillian. At the time of his marriage Reg set up a vegetable-round in Cardiff with a horse and cart, but that didn't go too well, so he bought a milk-round from a chap called Weston in Marshfield. In 1940 the family moved to Maesycoed, St. Mellons where he carried on his milk business. At first it was very difficult as he only had about 10-15 gallons of business and just after he started, Days, who were the big Milk people at that time, started to put out milk cheaper than Reg and it nearly broke his heart. He persevered and when he sold the milk-round 25 years later, he was doing 125 gallons per day.

Reg loved to tell the story about the time he was in the

289

Home Guard in the War. He was on duty one night because they expected an invasion from the Germans. At 5.00 a.m. he got very agitated as he wanted to go on his milk round. He asked the Captain but the Captain said, "You can't go and deliver milk when the Germans are coming". During WWII Reg used to M.C. the dances which were held in the Athletic Hall in St. Mellons, as he himself enjoyed dancing. It was modern dancing, although he did especially remember the Military Two-Step. He recalls the time when there were American Service men staying in St. Mellons and a fight started between the Americans and the British soldiers. Quick thinking Reg said to the pianist, "Quick, play God save the King!" which he did and immediately everyone came to attention, thus stopping the fighting.

Due to the fact that the milk-round was such hard work his wife opened up a little cafe in the front room of their house in Maesycoed, St. Mellons in about 1950. This didn't seem to flourish, although they sold things like pop and crisps etc. so they started to get in more groceries and the shop ended up being an "open all hours" shop. Reg was able to make it his full-time living. They really had to work hard though and they opened at 7.30 a.m. until 9.00.p.m. every day except Sunday, when opening hours were 9.00 a.m. to 5.00 p.m.

Reg belonged to a Drama Group in St. Mellons and in one of the plays, he was the postman in 'The Wishing Well' which was written by Eynon Evans. They were very honoured when Eynon Evans himself went to one of the rehearsals to give them advice. These plays were performed in the Church Hall which is now demolished but used to stand near St. Mellons Church.

Parish meetings were held and Parishioners' Representatives used to be appointed by a show of hands, but if six persons stood up and said they wanted an election they would apply to Magor and St. Mellons R.D.C. for this to take place. There were nine Representatives wanted and sixteen people put up, one being Reg. He was successful and this was the start of his long Council work. The meeting took place in the Institute in St. Mellons which is the Jehovah Witness building at present. They also had a Representative on the Rural District Council and A. H. Williams, the Schoolmaster, was the Representative on that Council. Magor and St. Mellons

R.D.C. stated, however, that they should have two Representatives so Reg put up for that and won. Having been elected a Parish representative in 1946, Reg was elected to the R.D.C in 1952 and in 1965 he became Chairman, which is the equivalent of being Mayor. In 1973, he was on the Shadow Council prior to the reorganisation of local government in 1974. Magor and St. Mellons Rural District Council then became part of Newport Borough Council. He retired from the Council in 1994 aged 89 years.

St. Mellons Church was a very important part of Reg's life. He was Church Warden for many years, lay reader and eventually lay preacher. He served Communion until shortly before his death and even managed to pour the wine over the Vicar's wife who luckily had a sense of humour and forgave him. Reg spent his retirement years in Castleton. He kept very busy with his council work, with Freemason activities, gardening and his beloved Church. He was still driving at the age of 94. He died peacefully on 5th May 2000, at the age of 95 and is survived by 4 daughters, 8 grandchildren and 8 great-grandchildren.

St. Mellons Church P. C. C. 1947. Photo taken to mark the retirement of Rev. Connop L. Price.

The Bird Family

Tom and Edith Bird, parents of Fred Bird, came from very humble beginnings in Hereford to be known as one of the most popular families in the village of St. Mellons.

Tom, whose own father had been a farm-labourer, was one of fourteen children, ten of whom survived. At no time could all the family sit down to a meal together in their small cottage and his mother had to prepare a second sitting. During the First World War Tom joined the army at 15 years of age, serving in Gallipoli. Times were very hard during and after the First World War. Tom was employed in the timber haulage industry, a very demanding line of work in those days, as there was very little in the way of machinery to take the strain of long back-breaking hours that had to be worked to make a living. After his marriage to Edith, Fred was born in 1920. They were blessed with four other children, Joyce, Mary, Brenda and John.

In the Depression, as things got worse, Tom was forced to consider moving to look for work and it was in 1926 that he and his brother Arthur rode on their bicycles from Hereford to South Wales. Eventually reaching Coed-y-Gores Farm in Llanederyn, they heard that they might find work there. Dog-tired, they spent their first night at St. Mellons near contractors' huts by the side of the main Cardiff to Newport Road, which was undergoing reconstruction and being tarmacadammed. They were hired as farm labourers at Coed-y-Gores, now the Harvester's Motel and Restaurant. They milked 40 to 50 cows by hand, morning and evening, seven days a week. This was just a part of their many duties, in a long and tiring working day.

Tom and Arthur lived in a cottage near the farm. Then Arthur had an accident and could no longer work on the farm. He then met Maggie Morgan who lived in a house near Rhymney River, where a small stream which comes from Llanishen Resevoir, joins the river. This was later to become Morgan's Tea Gardens Llanedeyn and was widely used by many local people as a place where they could rest and enjoy a cup of tea and a cake. The children loved it there. Pop, crisps and chocolate bars were on sale as well as other sweets. Arthur eventually moved in with Maggie Morgan and there he remained for some considerable time.

After a few years, Tom went to work for Tom Watkins on a

farm near Llanrumney Hall. He and his family were living in one of a pair of cottages at the top of St. Mellons Hill, near the Lodge to the Llanrumney Estate. The Lodge still stands but the cottages were demolished some time ago. It was when he was working for Tom Watkins that he found an old tractor in the bushes and after much patient work set it running again. Tom became adept with tractors.

In 1936, Fred, Tom's oldest son, was sixteen and went looking for work in Llanedeyrn with his friend Jack Lever. They found jobs in a nursery and florist's, where they worked long hard hours for very little money, as general labourers. With help from the British Legion, of which Tom was a member, it was established that Fred and Jack had been underpaid and they were able to sue for the money owed to them. The result was an award of £46 each .... a great success. Fred's £46 was put towards another tractor with big iron wheels and a plough for £126. By the autumn of 1936, Tom and Fred had set up their own contracting business.

Between 1936 and 1950, Tom and Fred Bird were familiar figures on farms in Rumney, St. Mellons, Peterstone, St. Brides, Castleton, Marshfield, Coedkernew, Bassaleg and Machen. Whilst the tractor could be called upon to do some ploughing or heavy hauling, their speciality was corn thrashing. At the beginning of WWII, if there wasn't much work on the farms, Tom took extra work with Wynn's Heavy Haulage Co. a firm which was responsible for transportation of bomb cases around the country.

When the War came, corn was planted throughout the Tredegar heartland and Tom and Fred were in great demand. They had two thrashing drums and most local farmers called upon their services when the corn had been gathered into stacks or barns.

Tom rented Faendre Fach Farm, now the Heron Marsh, in St. Mellons. This was used as a base for the contract work. Tom continued to work with horses whilst Fred found some farmers difficult to convince that it was time to change to modern farming methods! They were at Faendre Fach for fourteen years. During the war Fred remembers hundreds of American soldiers who were billeted on the St. Mellons Golf Course. They were based there with their vehicles and tanks, preparing themselves for action. At this time Fred was designing his own tractor which was based around an old car with an extra gear-box welded into it. This gave the machine

293

eight forward gears which was a great advantage when working on hills and soft ground. The other important feature was the big rubber wheels which replaced the iron ones. The iron wheels had removable cleats; these had to be removed when the vehicle was taken on the road to prevent damage to the road surface. Fred now had a vehicle which could cope easily with wet and boggy conditions, enabling him to work throughout the winter. There was some difficulty however, with the supply of rubber wheels. He managed to overcome this by entering into negotiations with a representative of the American troops. By using his 'wit and charm' he secured a near endless supply of wheels! He was able to make another three machines, one each for Dai Castle, Jim Willey and Roy Sanders. Everyone was happy and no harm done!

Towards the middle of the War, Tom went back to thrashing with Fred; there was a lot to be done to aid the war effort. They worked day and night for the cause and were sent Land Army girls to assist them. This was a great responsibility as they had to be organised into an efficient unit and all their needs catered for. Tom and Fred were only too happy to take on these responsibilities!

Fred has had many jobs and pastimes during his life. To supplement his earnings, he was often employed on a casual basis, as a beater on the Llwyn-y-grant farm shoot. This was part of Squire William's estate and the operation was run by Major Cope from Quarry Hill. The Major was a very demanding employer as one might expect of a man with his extensive military background. He made sure he got every pennyworth out of his casual labourers. Fred was one of about twelve beaters and four gamekeepers who worked on the shoot. They started at 9 a.m. or earlier and worked through until 4-30 p.m. They were fed during the day with bread, cheese and farmhouse cake, all washed down with home-brewed cider, with 7/6 wages for the day; a just reward for a hard day's work. This was a better wage than he could earn doing his normal work and he would therefore drop what he was doing to work as a beater for the day.

After the war, Tom ran into difficulties with the upkeep of Faendre Fach Farm and he moved to Rumney. Fred continued on his own, doing contract ploughing and thrashing, which he built into a thriving business.

Fred met Charlotte, a nurse at the William Nicholl

Convalescent Home, in 1939. They courted for two years and were married in Newport. Charlotte went to live with Fred at Faendre Fach Farm where they had three children, Dennis, Sheila and Alan. The business was now well established. In partnership with his friend Ted Morgan, Fred started a piggery at Melrose Cottage and by 1955 they had increased the number to one thousand heavy hogs. Ted and his family lived at Melrose Cottage whilst Fred and Charlotte moved to Parkstone Avenue where they had three more children, Mike, Brian and Jennifer. In 1978, the local council made a compulsory purchase order on the piggery; the business was then wound up with the sale of the pigs and equipment.

Tom and Fred's stationary baler, baling the hay from a rick.

Lord and Lady Cope and Mr and Mrs Matthew Cope

Lord and Lady Cope and before them, Mr. and Mrs. Matthew Cope, were a big influence on St. Mellons. Mr. and Mrs. Matthew Cope came to the village in 1880. He described his wife thus, "She was so good a woman, all I can say of her on that score will be endorsed by hundreds of others. She was the good angel and lady bountiful of St. Mellons and district for nearly half a century." A lady of deep

295

religious conviction, for twenty-five years she held a bible-class in her dining-room every Sunday afternoon. When the Rev. Theophilus Rees, a widower, became Vicar at St. Mellons, she performed the religious and social duties that normally fell to a vicar's wife. She had a large room built at the back of Quarry Hill House, where meetings, lectures, dances and all sorts of social functions were held. This room became, in effect, the village institute.

Mrs Cope was a great influence on her son, William. She had very definite views on the upbringing of a child, insisting, from babyhood, on obedience, courtesy to all and respect to elders. She did not advocate the role of the 'heavy father.' She was proud of her son who, she believed had been 'steadfastly loyal to duty at school, at home and in the world.'

William Cope started his schooling in St. Mellons village school, going on to Shewbrook's School in Cardiff, then Repton and Cambridge. He gained a rugby 'blue' and played for Cardiff and the Barbarians, later gaining an International Cap for Wales. Playing cricket and tennis and boxing, he also hunted with Glamorgan, Pentyrch and Tredegar Hounds.

Practising as a barrister for nine years, he then directed his energies to the Welsh coalfields, where his father had connections. He had interests in several collieries and in the South Wales Power Distribution Company. In 1900, he married Miss Helen Shuldham. With others, he formed the Glamorgan Yeomanry and saw active service on the staff of Eastern Command in Europe, becoming a Major.

In 1918, he was elected M.P. for Llandaff and Barry, later becoming the Conservative whip for Wales, the first for many years. A very active politician, by 1923 he had voted in 343 divisions in the House, absent from only 13. He was invited to dinner at 10 Downing Street on many occasions and by the Speaker to Speaker's House at Westminster. On numerous occasions, King George V and Queen Mary invited him, his wife and daughter to State Balls and Afternoon Parties at Buckingham Palace and on 4th June 1928 to St James' Palace to celebrate the King's birthday.

He was associated with four Prime Ministers, Bonar Law, Stanley Baldwin, Neville Chamberlain who occasionally stayed at Quarry Hill and Winston Churchill. David Lloyd George was also a friend. In 1923, King George V appointed him a Lord Commissioner of His Majesty's Treasury, unpaid, so that he could remain an MP. Later he was appointed Junior Lord of the Treasury, salaried, working at 12 Downing Street, under Prime Minister Stanley Baldwin.

Garden Party at Quarry Hill. Seated: l-r: Lady Cope, Mrs Connop-Price, Mathew Cope, Rev. Connop-Price and Lord Cope.

In 1925, one year before the General Strike, William Cope was appointed Civil Commissioner for London and the Home Counties, to be responsible for Transport and Food Supplies. In 1928, he had a new appointment as Comptroller of His Majesty's Household. He frequently shot with the King at Sandringham and on retirement, the King gave him an autographed photograph, together with his Wand of Office as Comptroller. He was knighted on 28th June 1928, lost his seat in the 1929 General Election, and became, High Sheriff for the County of Glamorgan in 1932, later Deputy Lieutenant. In the 1939-1945 War years, Sir William Cope was Acting Sub-Prior of the Priory for Wales and the Order of St. John of Jerusalem. On 11th July 1945, on the recommendation of Prime Minister Winston Churchill, he was created a Baron, choosing the title, Lord Cope of St. Mellons.

His father, Matthew Cope, had died in 1933 at Quarry Hill and in the following year, Sir William modernised and enlarged the house at great expense, also improving the garden and making a bowling-green. He and his wife lived there until his death, aged 76, in 1946. He was buried in St. Mellons churchyard.

Joff Holloway 1914 - 2001

James Albert Joff Holloway was born in Barry, Glamorgan and moved to St. Mellons as a child. He attended the village school, there meeting Olive who was later to become his wife. Joff, as he was known to his family and friends, was, like his father before him, a postmaster. Joff s father, James, originally bought the land and built the post office at St. Mellons in 1926. He was postmaster for twenty years prior to his retirement in 1946, due to ill-health.

When WWII had broken out in 1939, Joff was first posted to Ilfracombe in Devon and later to Burma, where he worked in administration, dealing with military payroll. He was demobbed early in 1946, due to his father's ill-health and returned to Britain where he worked as a projectionist showing war-film footage to troops, before taking over the post-office business from his father. During the post-war era, the post-office served as a confectioner's, tobacconist's and stationer's, as well as selling newspapers. Joff ran it for twenty-nine years.

The post-office was the main focal point and centre of life in the village and villagers loved to consult Joff for advice on all sorts of matters. He always respected their confidences. Joff loved his work and threw parties for his team of postmen and postwomen who sorted the mail and delivered it on push-bikes. Men of St. Mellons village often used to congregate for a game of snooker and a chat in the games-room above the post office.

Joff and his wife Olive, who had married in 1940, worked six days a week in the post-office business, only having Sundays off. Then they would take their children, Ann and Roger, to the Forest of Dean for family picnics. The Holloway home was in the same house as the post-office, with customers flocking to the front, whilst the family lived in the kitchen and lounge at the back. In 1975, Joff

298

suffered a stroke and retired. He moved to Porthcawl with Olive, but sadly she died the following year.

Joff Holloway is remembered as a bit of a comedian who would always tell jokes and entertain people. He loved to make his friends laugh, but was always serious when it came to business.

Les Jones 1912-1971

Les Jones and his brother Hector were born in Began Road St. Mellons and were both involved in local drama and operatic groups. Les took several leading roles in the Gilbert and Sullivan productions of the Rumney Operatic Society. During WWII he served in the Royal Air Force and was stationed in Algiers for a time, where he was involved with E.N.S.A.

After the war he returned to Rumney and worked for a time as a watch and clock repairer, but he had been bitten by the 'entertainment bug' and sought a career on the stage! He was quite successful during the 1950s, appearing regularly on the popular BBC Wales radio programme, *Welsh Rarebit*. He also appeared on many other popular radio programmes of that time, including *Variety Bandbox*, *Music Hall* and the midday programme *Workers' Playtime*. With the advent of television, radio programmes lost their appeal. Les continued for many years, appearing in clubs and holiday camps around the country.

Hector's son, John **Price-Jones** exemplified the family's love of music by becoming conductor of the orchestra of the **D'Oyley** Carte Opera Company.

Llewellyn Jones lived for many years at Ty Coch Farm, St. Mellons. He was married to Mary Harris formerly of Tyn-y-parc Farm in Llanrumney. He farmed and grew vegetables, which he sold on a vegetable-round on the new estate in Rumney. They had three daughters and a son, Susan, Elizabeth, Jane and Roger. Elizabeth went to America to work, where she met her husband David. They are farming at Long Island, New York. It was David who asked Uncle Idris Jones, Llewellyn's brother, to write the family history. Idris wrote –

'Thomas Jones of Tycoch Farm, St. Mellons, the great-grandfather of your children, was born near the church at Peterstone Wentloog. His father was William Jones and he was born in 1840 on a farm in Marshfield. He married one of the Rees family of the Six Bells pub, in Peterstone, so my father Thomas Jones was brought up in the Six Bells as one of the family, as the pub was about 50 yards from his home.

The family only spoke Welsh, so until he went to school, he never spoke English. The school was only 30 yards further on, so his early life centred around the Six Bells Pub. His father, William Jones, was foreman of a gang who maintained the sea walls. They also maintained the reens which drained the low land and carried the water from the high ground, which was considerable in winter, so preventing flooding of farming lands. The water was channelled through gouts in the sea-bank. These prevented sea water coming in and let clean water run freely out to sea when the tide went out. The levels i.e. the farming land, are an average of 16ft below high tide level, so the gouts had to be taken care of. The gang comprised about sixteen men in regular work.

My father did not work regularly in the gang, though he knew all about it. He had fishing nets out at low tide and was more interested in fishing. Fish were taken into Cardiff in a high-wheeled gig (light two-wheeled one horse-carriage). A good cob (a sturdy short-legged horse) could go fast with it, because it was not heavy or cumbersome. He also collected cheese, which all farms made in summer, from the farms to take to Caerphilly cheese fair. The cheese was sold to the coal miners, as miners did not like to take meat underground. So my father did not farm as a young man, but enjoyed life, shooting and fishing on the foreshore.

About 1870, the G.W.R. (Great Western Railway) decided to lay another two railway lines for coal-carrying rolling stock. The work was put out to contractors, in sections, for the twelve miles between Cardiff and Newport. The contractors found they had money to spare and not liking banks wherein to deposit their money, they bought farms and anything for sale, but had no time to farm. This was the case with George and Francis Stubbs who had bought a good farm called Sluice Farm in Peterstone. They suggested to William Jones that if he cast (cleaned) all the ditches (reens) on the farm for twelve months, he could have the farm for twelve months free of rent. So William Jones accepted, with a good gang, who knew the work. Now William Jones had a farm and a grown family, but my father, William's son, did not join in with them. I believe he had other things on his mind, for in 1898 he got married and went to Tycoch farm, St. Mellons. For a few years he helped his father, harvesting in summer. His father helped him at Tycoch with hay-making. It did not last long, however, for his brothers offended him and my father did not go to Sluice Farm again.

In 1920 William Jones died at Sluice Farm and the farm was split into two and sold. That was the end of Jones Sluice Farm. Glanrow, brother of my father Thomas Jones, went to Canada and we heard no more of him.

Now I shall endeavour to pay tribute to my own father. After 1900, he was married with one daughter, (Jenny) with a farm of his own. (Tycoch) He was a tenant of Tredegar Estate, in the parish of St. Mellons. His neighbour, another farmer, boasting to be a first-class ploughman, brought his team and ploughed up a 4 acre field near the house. This was a man we knew as Dai the Vaendre and this put my father on the road to market gardening. He proved to be a first-class producer of vegetables selling potatoes and cabbage to green-grocers in Cardiff. He was already well-known because he had sold fish and cheese to the shops from Peterstone. On his way back from Cardiff he would bring horse-manure on his trolley from Solly Andrews, who kept a lot of horses for work in Cardiff. The manure was applied to the ground as a fertilizer to grow his potatoes and cabbages.

He sold hay, which he had to cut and truss and take on the trolley into Cardiff to the undertakers, who kept about six horses and were the best buyers of good hay. One of my brother's first horses was given to him by the undertaker. It was a Belgian gelding which he wished to retire but did not want to put down. It proved to be a good worker on the farm and in harness.

Once we got the trolley (wagon) over St. Mellons Hill, it was downhill all the way to Cardiff. A trace-horse was often needed to get over the steep part half-way up the hill, then the trace-horse could go home. Sometimes we provided trace-horses for neighbouring farms. I would earn 2/6 or half a crown, which was a lot of money for me at that time.

So my father had to work hard, but not having stock to look after on Sunday, he did not work on that day. It was his rest day, so all the family went to the Calvinistic Methodist Chapel, (later Presbyterian) which was very close. They had many friends there. When it came to haymaking in summer, friends joined in and made light work of it. They did it for nothing as my father did not have money to spare.

My mother did a lot of outside work, picking peas and beans and helping generally in the garden. We lived off whatever was going on the farm. She was a good cook and was well used to catering for a large family at Whitecross Farm St. Brides, as her mother died comparatively young and she had kept house before she got married. She was well-schooled in making the best of things.

After Jenny, Wilf was born in 1902, Reg in 1905 and in 1907, I was born. Mother s family were disgusted by her having a large family on such scant income, but Jenny and Wilf were conscripted into work for everybody s benefit. Then to cap it all, when I was born my father got scarlet fever. I don't think he was very ill himself, but he was sent to Chepstow Isolation Hospital so that his children would not get it. He named me Idris by letter home, from a book he was reading. This was April 4th 1907 at Easter, when Spring work on the 4 acre ploughed field really should have started. The men members of the Chapel, who were packers on the G.W.R. and others who were excellent gardeners anyway, took over Ty Coch and organized and did all the necessary work so that when my father came home a few weeks later, all the work was done in the ploughed field. It had been cultivated and planted up to date, thanks to members of the St. Mellons Chapel.

Reg, Wilf, Idris and Llewellyn Jones

On April 16th 1910, my brother Llewellyn was born. Now the first 10 years of the 1900s had given my father enough trouble, but he was getting used to it. Wilf, my oldest brother, was a big lad at school and they nicknamed him Peter because he was impetuous and would fight anyone who crossed him. He did more work at home, missed school a lot and after 12 years of age did not go any more. Reg worked hard at school and went on to Cardiff College.

The year 1914 brought war with Germany, but my father being a farmer, did not have to go. This was fortunate for us because we did not run the risk of receiving a dreaded telegram. Towards the end of the War, mother was making potato bread every day, mostly boiled potatoes and a bit of flour, but it was better than the shop brown bread.

After the War, we were glad we were living on a farm, compared with the poverty and privation of others.'

Connie Nurse nee Gerrish 1913-1994

Connie Gerrish loved St. Mellons. Her whole life was centered around it. She was a village girl in the true sense of the word, having lived in Bethania Row, the real heart of the village. The Presbyterian Chapel played a very important part in her young life. In those days there were Eistedfoddau, Anniversaries and so many varied activities, including the 'Band of Hope.' She was later to become secretary of that Chapel.

After attending the Village School, she went on to further education at Bloggs' College in Cardiff. She then became secretary to Tom Salisbury, owner of the 'Salisbury' leather shops in Cardiff. The business became so successful that the head office moved to London and Connie went too. She found it impossible however, to settle away from her beloved St. Mellons and joined the offices of Marks & Spencer with the understanding that she would eventually return to the Cardiff branch. Connie's wartime years were spent working at M & S in Cardiff, living in St. Mellons, doing various voluntary works. During this time, she became involved with the W. I. her mother being a founder member. This was to lead to a life-long love and commitment to the W. I., first as secretary and later as a well-beloved President. The clock and plaque on the wall of the Village Hall are proof of her popularity. She was also an active member in the Pensioners' Luncheon and Social Club, known as the Thursday Club. She served with the W.R.V.S. for 15 years earning a Long

Service Medal award.

In 1943 she married Fred Nurse and two daughters Marilyn and Margaret were born to them. Fred developed an acute form of rheumatoid arthritis early in their marriage, resulting in a lot of hardship. Connie was always cheerful despite Fred's illness and managed to lead a full and active life. She worked in the Sea View Stores and later looked after the village school-children at lunchtime and in the playground. This was a job she really loved, meeting most of the children and adults in the village.

W.I. committee meeting. Standing: l-r: Connie Nurse, Nancy Leeburn, Eluned Hale, Myfanwy Williams, Janet Davies, Olive Rees. Seated: Shirley Mortimer, Joan Meazey , Connie Adams.

In 1992, just a week after returning home from a wonderful holiday in Hong Kong, Connie suffered a massive stroke from which she never recovered. She spent the last fifteen months of her life in Castleton Nursing Home supported by family and friends.

The singing of Jerusalem, the W.I. anthem, on the day of Connie's funeral will never be forgotten and was an acknowledgement of the love, affection and esteem felt by all who knew her.

William Packer c 1897 - 1986

Little is known of William Packer's early life, but it is rumoured that he was descended from a Manchester mill-owning family. An intelligent man, who considered the beauty of the countryside far more important than material possessions, he was said to be the black sheep of the family'. A First World War veteran, Bill came to Cardiff to recover from his war-wounds in a military hospital. The area suited him and he never returned to his native Manchester.

He was a gentle, witty and charming man, always ready to lend a helping hand, asking for no more reward than the hand of friendship. He was quite content to do labouring, grave-digging and work as a night-watchman on local building-sites. He sometimes drank too much and neglected himself, but he was a remarkable and interesting man, loving nature's offerings in their beautiful simplicity. Known affectionately to his friends as 'Scrumpo', he was able to appreciate the splendour of a bird in flight or the beauty of the arrival of Spring.

Bill's intention was to spend his retirement peacefully in his stone hut near the banks of the River Rhymney. His tiny stone cabin had been bequeathed to him by the squire of Llanrumney in appreciation of his forty years service as a gardener and odd-job man. Bill's little house, tucked away behind the houses in Ball Road, was a former stone pigsty converted into a one-room dwelling, eight feet by twelve feet, with a tiled roof. Bill had put in a fireplace, installed storm lamps and painted the name Mill Cottage on his garden gate. The little cabin was kept spotlessly clean and whitewashed.

His retirement was blighted when his life became tormented by some young people from the local housing estate. They stole flowers and vegetables from his kitchen garden, ripped down his hedge and vandalised his tool shed. The little cabin became the centre for vicious attacks by mindless young people. When Bill reached the age of 74, his little Llanrumney home was gutted by fire when vandals broke in and set it alight.

Bill enjoyed a pint of cider and often visited Llanrumney Hall – the Inn that used to be the home of the Squire he had served as second gardener. It was on his return home one night that he found his home ransacked and his possessions burnt. Bill was broken-hearted. Llanrumney also had many kind-hearted residents however, who helped to bring new heart to old Bill. Some of his neighbours rebuilt and restored the little house and the Llanrumney Hall Friends in Need Association helped him with the garden.

Unhappily poor Bill never really recovered and he died a pauper. His many friends were not prepared to see him rest in a pauper's grave and as a tribute to this special man, Bill's body was allowed to rest overnight in Llanrumney Hall, where, for many years, he had tended the gardens with such loving care. The Reverend Gower Rees, vicar of St. Mellons, conducted the funeral service at the Hall, then Bill's body was taken to Thornhill Crematoriam and his ashes were later scattered over his well-tended garden. Bill was a very private man who would have greatly appreciated the final tribute made by friends at his funeral.

Christopher Potter 1946-1988

Christopher Potter, the eldest of three children of Mac and Edna Potter of Began Road, St. Mellons spent most of his childhood in the area having enrolled at St. Mellons School in 1954, when his father left the Royal Air Force. Kip, as he was known to all, was a prolific story-teller and Hywel Richards, the headmaster and Reg. Phillips, Kip's teacher, were soon aware of all the happenings at home. Everything was revealed in Kip's compositions.

He was an avid reader from the age of four and this encouraged and gave him his love of writing. At the age of 11 years, he went to Bassaleg Grammar School where English was his favourite subject. In an essay on crocuses, he wrote that they were 'pushing their green periscopes through the dark brown soil', a wonderful metaphor for a first-year pupil. In no way was Kip a model student. Never becoming a prefect, he did, however, join every good cause, including C.N.D. He was often seen on television on a march, or standing in a campaign lorry in a First World War uniform. Kip was full of surprises.

In 1964, his teacher entered two of his essays in two national competitions. In both of these he won first prize. The prize for 'Television & Arts' was a cheque and tea with the late Lord Kenneth

Clark, who was at that time a big hit on television with his 'Civilisation' series.

First prize for the other competition, run by Brooke Bond Tea, was a trip to India accompanied by his English teacher. This was an incredible experience. Everything was first class, all expenses paid, including pocket money. A garland presented to Kip by the then High Commissioner of India, holds pride of place in the family heirlooms.

After India he went to King's College, London, where he first read Mediaeval English. He spent much of his time working on the college magazine and realised that he preferred journalism. The University offered to change his course, but Kip wanted to work 'in the field.'

Michael Buerk, his wife-to-be Christine, Sue Lawley, Kip's girl-friend at the time, Kip Potter.

He joined the Western Mail & Echo in Cardiff, where he served his apprenticeship with such people as Sue Lawley and Michael Buerk. Loving his time there, he met many famous people including Elizabeth Taylor and Richard Burton. In 1966, Kip was at the Aberfan disaster for four days and this affected him more than anything he did before or after.

When the Sun newspaper commenced publication, he was 'head-hunted.' Kip became a Parliamentary Political Correspondent, was a member of the Lobby, travelled extensively all over the world with Mrs Thatcher, Lord Whitelaw, Jim Callaghan, Neil Kinnock and eventually became Chairman of the Press Gallery in the House of Commons. Everyone knew him and he seemed to know everyone.

Tragically he died in September 1988 at the age of 42 years. Not only did many of his colleagues and Members of Parliament attend his funeral in St. Mellons, but in December 1988, a Memorial Service was held for him in St. Margaret's Westminster. The church was packed and the Speaker of the House of Commons, in all his regalia, began the service. It was not only the well-known who attended; two rows of seats were filled by uniformed nurses who had cared for him in St. Thomas's hospital, just across the river from the Houses of Parliament. Kip made a lasting impression on all who met him.

View from St. Mellons Church Tower. In the background to the left, is Machen Mountain and to the right Twm Barlwm. In the foreground are allotments and houses in Eurwg Crescent.

SOURCES / BIBLIOGRAPHY

A History of Monmouthshire Vol. 5 The Hundred of Newport.
Sir Joseph Alfred Bradney. Edited by Madelaine Gray
The Pleasant Land of Gwent Fred Hando
Monmouthshire Sketchbook Fred Hando
Princes and People of Wales John Mills
The City of Cardiff, Some Aspects of its History
Project by pupils of Cardiff High School for Boys 1958
St. Mellons and Rumney Countryside Magazine 1921-1936.
Editor Harold Combes.
The Women of Botany Bay Portia Robinson
Domesday Book
Rambles around Rumney with Camera and Sketch-Book William Booth
The Story of St. Mellons Alison Bielski 1985
The Gwent Village Book Gwent Federation of W. I.s 1994
An Historical Tour in Monmouthshire Archdeacon William Coxe
The King's England – Monmouthshire Editor Arthur Mee
Who's Who in Wales First Edition 1920 Editor Arthur Mee
Welsh Royalists J Rowlands
The Custumal of Rumney Manor. A.C. Reeves
A History of Police in England & Wales 900 to 1960
T.H. Critchley
The Wentloog Level: a Romano-British saltmarsh reclamation in S. E. Wales
J.R.L. Allen and M.G. Fullford
Gwent Levels: The Evolution of a Landscape Stephen Rippon
The Oxford Companion to Local and Family History
Editor David Hey
Rumney Castle, a Ringwork and Manorial Centre in South Wales K.W.B.
Lightfoot
Sunlight Soap Year Book 1897
The History of St. Mellons Baptist Church 1794-1984
Russell Williams
A History of Religion in St. Mellons-Chapel Life Reg Jones
Architectural Antiquities in Monmouthshire No. 5 St.Mellons E.A.Freeman
William Thomas Diaries
Records of Ancient Local History J. Barry Davies
Extracts from Rumney Parish Records Dr. D. Elwyn Williams
Notebooks of A.H.Williams Headmaster of St.Mellons Mixed School 1904-1936
**Momouthshire Merlin & South Wales Advertiser, South Wales Echo,
Western Mail, Cardiff Times, South Wales Argus, Daily Express.
Rumney Parish Church Records
St. Mellons Parish Church Records**

ACKNOWLEDGEMENTS

Special thanks to:- Fred Bird, Melba Crabtree, Dilys Hughes, Vera Makin and Jean Watkins, part of the original group of ten. Sincere thanks to Terry Evans for the cover design, Ian Malcolm for map illustrations and Vivian Parr for his artistic contributions.

We gratefully acknowledge help given by the following individuals and institutions.

Jill Adams, Neville Atherton, Fred Baker, Olive Ball, Muriel Beck, Graham & Jeanette Best, Lyn Blacklock, Ann Holloway Blake, Malcolm & Vera Booth, Anne Brassington, David Buck, Elsie Burchell, Evan Chapman and the Department of Archaeology and Numismatics at the National Museum and Galleries of Wales, Cardiff, Mary Clarke, Bryan & Susan Clatworthy, Dawn Clease, Dean Jackson-Johns, Caldicot and Wentloog Levels Drainage Board, Carmel Davies, Stephanie Davis, Peggy Flook, Robert Giles, Rosemary Gonzales Margaret Gower-Rees, Colin Green, John & Marilyn Harding, Frances & Margaret Hobbs, Debbie Howells, Ellis Howells, Eddie Humphries, Rosemary Humphries, Trudi Inseal, Noel Ivins, Mary Jackson, Bill James, Rosemary James, Ursula John, David Jones, (Vaindre Farm) Roger Jones, Rev. David Kellen, St. Mellons Parish Church, David & Pauline Kimber, Tricia Lewis, Isabella McManners, Frank Maggs, Jane Marrin, Verna Jones-Mathias, Carolyn Moore, David & Jennnet Mundy, John Neal, Dr David Neville, St. John's College, Jean North, Old St. Mellons Community Council, Old St. Mellons Village Association, Philip Parker, Edna Potter, Lionel Pretty, Dillwyn Prosser, Thora Rae, Vivienne Ratcliffe David Rees, Elfed Rees, Graham Rees, Peggy Rowsell, Doreen Shepstone, Patrick Simpson, Jennifer Spackman, Susan Stroud, Pauline Sydenham, Gordon Tanner, Jimmy Taylor, Elaine Tetlow, Iris Thomas, Philip Thomas, Irene Thomas, Mary Nicholls, Neil Walton, David Williams, Freda Williams, Rev. Russell Williams, Hazel Williamson.

Thank you all for your contributions. If they do not appear in the book, they will certainly be on display at the Cardiff Centenary & Jubilee Exhibition in August 2005 and thereafter in the archives of Rumney and District Local History Society. We respectfully apologise for any errors or omissions.